HIGH LATITUDE,
NORTH ATLANTIC

For James A. Houston.

Son of the North and friend and teacher,

your love of northern lands and peoples

has inspired me for forty years.

HIGH LATITUDE, NORTH ATLANTIC

30,000 Miles Through Cold Seas and History

JOHN R. BOCKSTOCE

MYSTIC SEAPORT®
THE MUSEUM OF AMERICA AND THE SEA™

Mystic Seaport
75 Greenmanville Ave., P.O. Box 6000
Mystic, CT 06355-0990

First edition

Project development by The History Bank, Woodinville, Washington
Editorial management by Christine A. Laing
Design and production by David J. Boe
Project management for Mystic Seaport by Andrew W. German
Printed in Canada by Bolder Graphics, Edmonton and Calgary, Alberta
ISBN 0-939510-82-0

FRONT COVER: Belvedere *approaching Cape Makkovik, Labrador,* 1996
BACK COVER: *John R. Bockstoce.* CHRISTOPHER CUNNINGHAM

All photographs by John R. Bockstoce unless otherwise credited

Other Books by John R. Bockstoce

Eskimos of Northwest Alaska in the Early Nineteenth Century (1977)

Steam Whaling in the Western Arctic (1977)

The Archaeology of Cape Nome, Alaska (1979)

(editor) *The Voyage of the Schooner Polar Bear: Whaling and Trading in the North Pacific and Arctic, 1913–1914,* by Bernhard Kilian (1983)

(with William Gilkerson) *American Whalers in the Western Arctic* (1983)

Whales, Ice and Men. The History of Commercial Whaling in the Western Arctic (1986, 1995)

(editor) *The Journal of Rochfort Maguire, 1852–54. Two Years at Point Barrow, Alaska Aboard H.M.S.* Plover *in the Search for Sir John Franklin* (1988)

Arctic Passages: A Unique Small-Boat Voyage in the Great Northern Waterway (1991, 1992)

Arctic Discoveries. Images from Voyages of Four Decades in the North (2000)

Other Mystic Seaport Titles of Related Interest

America and the Sea: A Maritime History, by Benjamin W. Labaree, William M. Fowler, Jr., Edward W. Sloan, John B. Hattendorf, Jeffrey J. Safford, and Andrew W. German (1998), 694 pages, 360 illustrations, ISBN 0-913372-81-1 (cloth) $65.00

Mystic Seaport Watercraft, by Maynard Bray, Benjamin A.G. Fuller, and Peter T. Vermilya, 3rd edition (2001), 420 pages, 721 illustrations, ISBN 0-913372-94-3 (cloth) $39.95

For Oil and Buggy Whips: Whaling Captain of New London County, Connecticut, by Barnard L. Colby (1990), 224 pages, 80 illustrations, ISBN 0-913372-54-4 (paper) $17.95

Building a Greenland Kayak, by Mark Starr (2002), 120 pages, 130 illustrations, ISBN 0-913372-96-X (paper) $24.95

CONTENTS

*F*ISHERMEN, EXPLORERS, AND SAILORS share a kinship of the sea, a bond across the centuries that links a medieval Norse voyager with today's yacht sailor. I know that bond, and I experience it whenever I'm on the water, whether racing or just playing the breeze with my sails.

John Bockstoce and I share that kinship of the sea, too. For us, there is no finer experience in life than combining the elements, the boat, and the crew and being so immersed in the sailing that nothing else matters in the world—except sailing across the finish line first, of course!

John has won over and over again in his contests with the sea, the weather, and the calendar on dozens of voyages of discovery. His race spans centuries as well as miles, and he experiences and writes of engineering marvels that aren't from twenty-first-century nautical geniuses, but instead are the handiwork of those early Norse mariners who discovered northern American waters long before Columbus was born, let alone planning a voyage.

I've always enjoyed a good read—especially stories of adventure (preferably on the water) and of successful sailing wherever it takes place. I've come to expect that from John Bockstoce, even though he doesn't seem to fit what most readers might imagine when describing a sailor or adventurer. As a historian, he sails in the past, and he sails where technology is sparse. His résumé includes a doctorate in archaeology from Oxford, a stint as a museum curator, and forty years of high-latitude exploration in open boats as well as ocean-going vessels.

John has the credentials of a historian and archaeologist, but he hardly writes like either. On these pages John has become an artist with words, painting vivid pictures of the extremes of nature amid the islands and icebergs of the Far North. With telling detail he depicts what the mariners who preceded him saw and did in those

stark waters. John writes eloquently of the complex interplay of human history and nature in these high latitudes. You feel as if you're aboard *Belvedere* and experiencing John's passion for the North, from the challenge of the open sea to the welcome of tiny coastal communities perched on the edge of the wilderness.

In the many hours John and I have shared, I've been reminded of the kinship that sailors always feel, whether at the helm of *Stars & Stripes, Belvedere,* or any other boat. John's found a way to tell a story, with his words and his photos, that is honest adventure, riveting history, and great voyaging. *High Latitude, North Atlantic* will sweep you away, whether you're a sailor or have only dreamed of being one.

Great stuff.

Dennis Conner
Four-time winner of the America's Cup

In 1988, on our way to completing the first eastbound yacht traverse of the Northwest Passage, we were stopped by pack ice in James Ross Strait.

Bellot Strait, Gateway to the Eastern Arctic

ZENITH POINT is the northernmost piece of land in continental North America. A chunk of ancient brown rock that juts into the roiling waters of Bellot Strait in Arctic Canada, it reaches just beyond the seventy-second parallel of latitude, putting it within 1,200 miles of the North Pole. Sixteen hundred miles to the west of Zenith Point, by water, lies the next most northerly point of land, Point Barrow, Alaska, a low, eroding sandspit that is only a little more than forty miles farther from the Pole. Between Zenith Point and Point Barrow are the inner waters of the Northwest Passage, the water route between the Atlantic and Pacific Oceans across the top of the New World.

Even today, 500 years after Europeans began searching for a northwest passage to the Orient, and a century since Roald Amundsen completed the first traverse, these waters are seldom visited. Only a handful of vessels—a few tugs and barges, the odd icebreaker, ice-strengthened tanker or adventure-travel ship, and, very rarely, a small

John Bockstoce's voyages in the Northwest Passage, 1972–1988

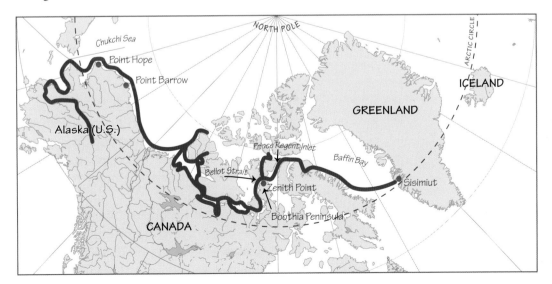

cruising yacht—are found there, among the ice floes, during the two-month navigation season between the ice cover's break-up and the Passage's return to freeze-up.

I have spent twenty seasons in those waters, studying the history of the fur trade and the whaling industry in the western Arctic. In 1969, when I began my research, I understood that merely burrowing away in libraries and archives would yield only a pallid record of what I considered to be a vibrant, energetic, and self-reliant age, populated with heroes. I knew that I would have to work in those waters, see the land, and feel the wind in my face to achieve an understanding of what it was like to have been there in those days: I would have to go back and forth in those sinuous waterways and poke into every corner where people had been, searching for historical sites, graves, ship-wrecks, and the living participants of those long-gone industries. I was fortunate that these activities were part of the responsibilities of my job as curator of Arctic collections at the New Bedford Whaling Museum in Massachusetts.

I would have to go back and forth in those sinuous waterways and poke into every corner where people had been.

In the 1970s I began by working close to shore in a thirty-two-foot Eskimo umiak that I had rebuilt. Its hull was a wooden lattice frame, covered with walrus hides, and it was shaped something like a Banks dory. Most importantly, because it was tied together, not bolted or screw-fastened, it was very flexible and supple, giving it great resiliency against the punishment of our repeated launchings and landings, and frequent encounters with floating ice-pans. In all, I covered about 6,000 miles in that boat.[1]

As my research progressed, however, I found that I needed to work farther offshore, to visit distant places that I had been unable to reach in my umiak. So, in 1982, I bought my present boat, *Belvedere*, a sturdy sixty-foot, steel-hulled, long-distance motor-sailer. I traveled another 14,000 miles in her for that Far North project, and, although I was occasionally frightened by the power of the North, I enjoyed every mile.[2]

During my two decades in the Northwest Passage the ice, fog, and gales constantly challenged me. But the reward was seeing a wonderful, pristine beauty and feeling that I was almost a participant in an age that was now remembered and celebrated by only myself and a few others. It was this close presence of history and, as I traveled through those waters, a growing understanding of the challenges those early whalers and traders had overcome that made the whole adventure so vivid and worthwhile.

The North has been in my blood since 1962. As soon as I had graduated from high school I began a summer job as a volunteer laborer for the Grenfell Medical Mission in Newfoundland and Labrador. I remember my first impressions on arriving in Flowers

Cove, Newfoundland, on the Strait of Belle Isle. As I later wrote, "It was incredibly exciting to gaze across the strait at the Labrador coast, low and blue in the morning haze. With the voyages of the first European discoverers fresh in my mind, it seemed a heroic place. I wasn't very far north, but it felt like a frontier, and I was as happy as if I had been standing at the northern tip of Greenland. That day in July 1962 the North reached out and grabbed me, and to this day, I am glad to say, it has never released its grip."[3]

A few years later I discovered another part of my fascination with the North. I was then a green graduate student in Arctic archaeology, and I recall looking from Point Hope, Alaska, across the ice on the Chukchi Sea to "Cape Lisburne, low on the horizon, fifty miles to the northeast. I found myself desperately wanting to visit it. But I also began to realize that each time I might reach one of these capes that had barely been discernible in the distance, there would be another, far away beyond it, and another beyond that, and another."[4] That was a pretty fair assessment of my thinking then and now.

After finishing my work in the western Arctic in 1988, I made the easy decision to continue eastward and visit new Arctic locations. On August 15, after several frustrating days waiting to work through the milling pack ice that blocked *Belvedere*'s way northward into Larsen Sound, I at last negotiated the drifting floes and headed toward the western entrance of Bellot Strait.

At once the richness of the far North Atlantic reached out to us. We saw schools of Beluga whales, milky white against the dark water, while gray fulmars swooped and soared around us, skimming the water with their syncopated wing beats. There were even a few polar bears that stood out from the gloomy backdrop of the cliffs. This chorus of activity sang out in vivid contrast to the comparatively barren waters behind us, which lack the benefit of the Atlantic's infusion of nutrients and mixing of water masses.

Bellot Strait is narrow and deep. A twenty-mile fjord-like slash that separates Somerset Island from the Boothia Peninsula, this east-west alley is only half a mile wide at its narrowest and is flanked by cliffs that rise to more than 1,000 feet in places. Most importantly, it is the gateway to the eastern Arctic. Here the waters of the western Arctic meet those of the east, and thus, 8,000 miles from the southern tip of South America, it is the first meeting of the oceans north of Tierra del Fuego. The result is a dangerous tidal current that can run as fast as nine miles per hour. When this millrace boils around its principal hazard, Magpie Rock, the rips and eddies are frightening to see, even from an aircraft. If the strait is ice-free, the passage can be made without trouble between the tides, near slack water; but if ice is present, it can be very dangerous indeed, because the current shoots

'I also began to realize that each time I might reach one of these capes …there would be another, far away beyond it, and another beyond that, and another.'

the floes like bowling balls. Even large steel ships, including one icebreaker, have had difficulty there.

Aboard *Belvedere*, that day in 1988, I had carefully worked out the timing of the tides, and we reached the strait near slack water, as planned. An ebb tide then carried us swiftly to Prince Regent Inlet and into the waters of the eastern Arctic. For me, however, that twenty-mile leg was another important milestone as well: It marked the beginning of my third decade of northern voyages.

As *Belvedere* worked her way into Baffin Bay, toward Greenland, I began to comprehend how different the area was from what I had experienced for twenty years in the western Arctic. Instead of relatively shallow waters, hemmed around by pack ice and a sandy continental shore, there were big seas, rolling across thousands of miles. The waters were brimming with life—to say nothing of the heaving, bruised sea ice and icebergs that were driven by powerful weather systems and ocean currents. Moreover, the jagged coasts were mostly unforgiving hard rock cliffs and ledges, not the soft beaches and shoals of the western Arctic that I had only recently left. I felt both menace and challenge. It was thrilling.

But equally I felt an intense curiosity, a curiosity about what had gone on before in those great waters. I was fascinated by the rich and complicated human history of the Atlantic Arctic. In two millennia, and more, it had witnessed the expansions and contractions of native peoples, both European and American, and in the last thousand years, the tortuous encounters between Native Americans and the Europeans who were moving westward across the seas: the Norse, the Basques, the English, the Portuguese, the French, the Irish and others, who came as explorers, hunters, traders, loggers, adventurers, miners, missionaries, fishermen, soldiers, and sailors.

At once it struck me that my life, for the foreseeable future, would be absorbed with studying the cold waters of the North Atlantic, pursuing the thesis that contact between the Old World and the New, in high latitudes, has been regular since about A.D. 1000. As with my previous voyages, I hoped to record and share these journeys through my journals, photographs, and historical research.

With new seas and new challenges before me, my fascination with the Arctic was as strong as ever.

When Belvedere *reached the western entrance of Bellot Strait in Canada on August 25, 1988, she was at the threshold of the eastern Arctic.*

CHAPTER ONE

Transatlantic to Scotland (1991)

I BROUGHT *BELVEDERE* DOWN the west coast of Greenland and home to New England in 1989. There I began a thorough refit to repair the wear and tear from her six continuous years in the Arctic. But while this work was underway, I had something else on my mind. Although I knew that the North Atlantic would certainly keep me busy for a long time, I had a more immediate project.

Having completed a traverse of the Northwest Passage, suddenly—and temporarily, I am glad to say—I was struck with the notion to undertake an expedition in that other great northern waterway, the *Northeast* Passage, across the top of Asia. The project had a nice symmetry to it, but I wasn't naïve enough to assume that this voyage could be accomplished merely by setting out with a good boat and crew and a proper set of charts. So, I pushed ahead with the preliminary work for a voyage in the Northeast Passage, but just in case it didn't pan out, I did parallel planning for a series of voyages in the northern North Atlantic. In fact, a voyage to Spitsbergen and then home along the Viking route seemed as interesting and almost as challenging. As things turned out, I was glad that I had the back-up plan ready to go.

During the winter of 1989–90, while the Soviet Union was lurching along in its final months, I flew to Moscow, hoping to gain permission for a voyage in their Northeast Passage. On reaching what I had been told was the appropriate controlling directorate (it may not have been), I entered a crumbling Stalin-era concrete building that smelled of cabbage soup and toilet cleaner. I walked up a couple of floors (the elevator was broken) and down dim corridors where only every third or fourth light socket had a bulb. Shortly before reaching the head-man's office, I noticed that the cabbage-and-disinfectant odor had been overtaken by a smell that reminded me of burning horse manure.

I turned the corner into a shaft of light glowing through a blue fog of sub-export-grade circassian tobacco smoke. Letting out a weak cough, I introduced myself to the scowling secretary, who was in the process of lighting one cardboard-tipped cigarette from the butt of another. She grudgingly rose, clomped over to another door, and with a wave of her hand ushered me in to the big guy himself: an approximately 280-pound bull-necked, warty, squinting commissar. Apart from reminding me very much of an alpha-male walrus, his baggy, blood-shot eyes, jowls, and ectoplasmic girth gave me a strong clue that "perestroika" and such westernisms as "lean cuisine" and "white wine spritzer" hadn't yet trickled down to his level.

But I needn't have worried. Once the secretary left us, I made my pitch in a pidgin of English and halting Russian. Amazingly enough, it turned out that such a voyage might indeed be possible, though I took a not-very-subtle hint and offered the possibility of a small "honorarium" in U.S. greenbacks for the extra "vigilance" that he and

Beginning the 2,000-mile transatlantic leg of our voyage, Belvedere *leaves St. John's, Newfoundland, on July 3, 1991.*

HERB DAVIS

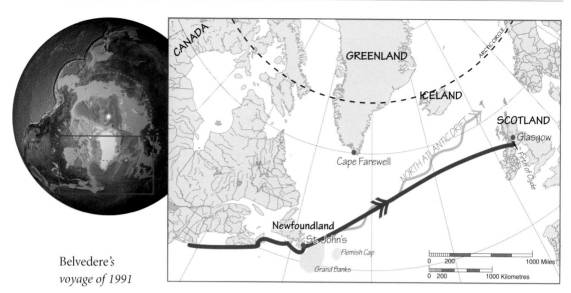

Belvedere's
voyage of 1991

his staff would have to devote on my behalf. It all went so smoothly that I began to wonder whether I had been sent to the wrong directorate. (In fact, I later learned that this might well have been the case.) I returned home under the pleasant delusion that I had made some real progress.

My plan was to take *Belvedere* across the Atlantic and position her in a convenient area for jumping off for the Barents Sea and Soviet waters. For a number of reasons the Firth of Clyde, near Glasgow, Scotland, seemed a good choice, especially because, in the event the Soviet option fell through, I could just as easily head to Spitsbergen from Scotland and, later, back across the Atlantic via the northern route.

So, in June 1991, with *Belvedere* refitted for another series of Arctic voyages, I set off with six sailor-friends for Europe. Our route took us from Massachusetts to Nova Scotia in one hop, then via the French island of Saint Pierre to St. John's, Newfoundland. Most of that run was amid icebergs, in dense fog, and much of it, at night. In St. John's we prepared for the crossing by taking on fuel and fresh provisions, putting plywood covers over some of the windows and Plexiglas over others for protection against any heavy boarding seas. Of course we lashed down everything securely.

Here I should add that I had spent the previous two winters reading up on the Atlantic crossing and talking with as many mariners as possible who had done it. The decision came down to choosing one of two routes: either a long crossing of more than 3,000 miles departing directly from Massachusetts; or one by which I would nearly halve the open-sea time by going coastal as far as Newfoundland. I have always found that days upon days of gray seas get pretty boring and, when gales strike, sometimes frightening. Thus the Newfoundland route seemed the more attractive alternative, though it meant having to cope with icebergs and fog.

Once I had decided on the northern track, a study of the pilot charts (monthly compilations about the state of wind, waves, currents, fog, and ice) showed that a departure from St. John's in early July gave the best chance of finding less than gale-force following winds. Furthermore, the problems that icebergs and fog present in crossing the Grand Banks seemed acceptable, because there would also be a fairly good chance of having northwesterly winds. Being off the land, and hence relatively dry, they would give us good visibility among the bergs—unlike the southwesterlies that pick up moisture over the warm waters of the Gulf Stream, which turns into fog over the chilly Labrador Current east of Newfoundland.

A visit to the ice-forecasting office in the Canadian Coast Guard headquarters in St. John's was reassuring. The analyst on duty there told me: "The Labrador Current is carrying the icebergs down along the east Newfoundland coast in pulses, as it usually does. There are two groups nearby, one is about to ground on Flemish Cap, the southernmost corner of the Banks, and the next group is north of us by fifty to a hundred miles. Bergs only travel about ten, or, at most, twenty miles a day around here. It looks as if you'll be able to run right between the two concentrations."

Next came the weather forecast. I drove out to Environment Canada's meteorological office at the airport and again was greeted by helpfulness and good news: It turned out that a big, northwesterly flow of air would arrive in forty-eight hours and, even better, they were confident that it would last for several days.

We left St. John's on July 3, 1991 and reached Troon, Ayrshire, in western Scotland ten and a half days and 2,000 miles later. We crossed through the icebergs and over the Banks with good visibility, and once past them, the Gulf Stream (there called the North Atlantic Drift) pushed us along toward Europe. Only one gale caught us, and when it did we were just a hundred miles west of Malin Head at the northern tip of Ireland. But by then we could smell the barn and didn't mind rocking and rolling along at eleven knots, helped by a strong tidal current flooding toward the Irish Sea.

When we reached Troon we were all so accustomed to the boat's motion that walking in a straight line on dry land was difficult and made us nauseous. After we had recovered from the raucous arrival party, most of the crew left for some European sightseeing. Then my wife, Romayne, who used to participate in my umiak voyages but doesn't enjoy ocean passages at all, and my fifteen-year-old son, Johnny, who would have liked to have crossed with us, arrived for a short family cruise, visiting friends and in-laws in the beautiful Western Isles of Scotland. I then hauled out *Belvedere* for the winter at a boatyard on the Gareloch, near Glasgow.

Only one gale caught us, and when it did we were just a hundred miles west of Malin Head at the northern tip of Ireland.

I flew home on August 19, 1991—the same day that Hurricane Bob put a hundred boats ashore in my home harbor in Massachusetts, and the same day that Boris Yeltsin foiled the first coup attempt in Moscow, essentially collapsing the Soviet Union. The wreckage in the harbor was an apt metaphor for my Soviet plans.

I returned to Moscow that winter, to the same grungy building, but instead of the old heavyweight behind the desk, I found a po-maded smoothie filing his nails in a shiny suit that might have passed for an Armani somewhere east of the Urals. Worse, this guy was smoking Marlboros.

I figured I was sunk, and sure enough, the price of the "honorarium" had gone through the roof—well into six figures in U.S. currency. This guy had certainly learned a lot about capitalism, and fast. It made me positively nostalgic for the old sausage-fingered Bolshevik—and I never did learn whether I had even gotten to the proper office.

Belvedere *heads into the Atlantic, bound for Scotland*

HERB DAVIS

Belvedere *to Spitsbergen*

The Western Isles, Shetland, Norway, Svalbard, and Orkney (1992)

URING THE WINTER of 1991–92 not only did Russia's problems worsen, but also information leaked out about the Soviet Union's scandalous handling of its nuclear wastes. There were reports that thousands of tons of radioactive material had been dumped into the shallow waters of the Barents and Kara Seas and their tributaries, waters through which I would have to travel on a traverse of the Northeast Passage.[1]

That finished it for me. I discarded any remaining thoughts of voyaging in Russian Arctic waters. Remembering the powerful fascination I had felt in 1988 when I exited Bellot Strait and entered the Atlantic's waters, it was an easy decision to return to those plans. I turned my attention first to Spitsbergen, far north of Norway, in the Atlantic's most easterly group of Arctic islands. I also decided that along the way I would travel the Norwegian coast; thus I hoped to get a feeling for the beginnings of the European expansions throughout the Arctic and, later, to follow them westward across the Atlantic.

As I mentioned earlier, I had left *Belvedere* for the winter in a boatyard on the Gareloch in the Firth of Clyde, the multipronged waterway that connects Glasgow to the Atlantic. It was just as easy to begin a voyage from there to Spitsbergen, as it would have been to Russia; in fact, the first thousand miles or so would be identical. So we set off aboard *Belvedere* at the end of June 1992, bound for the High Arctic.

My companions onboard all had plenty of blue-water sailing experience. Andy Rowe and Willy Fox, for instance, both from coastal Maine, had crossed the Atlantic with me the year before. Joining them for the first leg of the trip were Jem and Maur Tetley, friends from Cornwall, England, who had made many double-handed trips to the Azores, as well as an Atlantic crossing. Andy and Willy had grown up

PHOTO, OPPOSITE PAGE

Belvedere *in Bergen, Norway*

KIM HART

in boats, and the Tetleys, ever affable and unflappable, had long since stopped counting their ocean miles.

We ran down the Firth of Clyde, past its many small villages, and caught an ebb tide that flung us round the Mull of Kintyre, the massive rock bulwark at the tip of the peninsula that encloses the Clyde waterways. Then, turning north, we moved on amid the soft, green beauty of Scotland's Western Isles, in and out of narrow channels, among gentle islands studded with ancient castles. After a couple of days' running, we emerged from the protection of the Isle of Skye into The Minch, the wide sound that separates mainland Scotland from the Outer Hebrides.

From there the passage north is very exposed, and, because strong winds were forecast, we ducked between palisade-like cliffs, amid clouds of seabirds, into the safety of Loch Laxford's red granite hills. In Loch Laxford we were close to Cape Wrath, the northwesternmost point of mainland Britain. Cape Wrath was important in the early history of the British Isles. It lies on an old Norse raiding and trading route and was the point where the Norsemen turned their ships' prows south, toward the Hebrides and Ireland. In fact, "Wrath" derives from

Belvedere's Route of 1992

hvarf in Old Norse, a "turning point," and truly enough, the cape's sheer, red, 360-foot cliffs make it a dramatic right-angle turn.

Here too we turned, though at less than a right angle, and headed northeast into the North Atlantic, toward the southern tip of Shetland. To the west we passed Stack Skerry,[2] a lonely rock that looked like a ship under full sail, and then Skerry Bank, long and low, with a lighthouse on the end. To the east Orkney lay in the distance, highlighted by another stack, the Old Man of Hoy, a 450-foot rock pillar set off by green-topped 1,000-foot cliffs.

I suddenly felt the North approaching: We had entered the ancient domain of the Norsemen, and as we crossed rich fishing banks, northern fauna appeared. Dolphins played around *Belvedere*, and puffins, gannets, and guillemots milled nearby, feeding on small fish. Piratical skuas, powerfully built and aggressive raptors, harassed the smaller birds, forcing them to drop their catches, so that they could steal them in midair.

Our good weather held, and less than twenty-four hours after leaving Cape Wrath, the cliffs of Sumburgh Head, at the southern tip of Shetland, rose boldly from the sea. Reaching the capital, Lerwick, we docked at the town's gray stone quay, to take on supplies, knowing that we would return for a longer visit at the end of the summer. Even so, the town had a palpably different feel than those of the Western Isles, and the green, treeless hills seemed more northern Norwegian than Scottish. Shetland lies only 110 miles from Scotland, but its traditions are mostly Norse. The original Celtic inhabitants were colonized in the ninth century by the Norse, who called these islands *Hjaltland* (*Shelfland*). Scotland annexed the islands in 1472.

Late that night a hearty post-pub-closing Shetlander, full of wassail, wandered by the boat somewhat unsteadily and doffed his hat, a plastic "Viking helmet," complete with plastic horns. "Burp! Top o' the mornin' to ya." We assumed he had some Celtic blood as well.

Off the next morning, we headed east, driven by sails and engine, over the gray North Sea toward Norway. Halfway across, near midnight, we passed through oil and gas fields ablaze with the sodium-vapor lights of seven or eight production rigs, each of which had a supply boat standing by. These, as well as a passing cruise ship and the rigs' many anchor buoys, kept everyone in the pilothouse on their toes.

By 7:00 A.M. a heavy northerly swell had leveled out, and with it, the wind, leaving us to furl the sails and motor along over glassy seas toward Marstein Light at the entrance to the fjords that lead to Bergen, Norway. As we headed up Korsfiorden we were struck by how different the farms were from those we'd seen elsewhere. Tidy and well spaced, with red roofs, each had the national flag flying from a pole.

By noon we had cleared customs in the ancient Hanseatic League city of Bergen. The port was alive with small boats and ferries scurrying here and there. Gazing at the buildings ringing the inner harbor, Jem

Belvedere's Route in Scotland, 1992

said, "I wonder why one side of the harbor looks so damned modern, while the other seems to have been built in the Middle Ages?" A Norwegian friend, who had come aboard for a visit, looked up as he fed his friendly elkhound a large dried fish, and replied laconically, "During the German occupation, the Norwegian resistance blew up an ammunition ship on that side of the harbor." I could see that *a lot* of one side was very new. Jem's comment: "It must have made a bit of noise and disturbed the commandant's nap."

We worked through multitudes of small rock skerries, while the bottom rose and fell like a roller coaster.

At Bergen we did a quick crew change. Jem and Maur Tetley left us to return to Cornwall. We were sad to see them go, for we knew we would miss their constant good humor, their sea sense, and Maur's truly delicious cooking. Joining us, however, were three old *Belvedere* hands: Bonnie Hahn, a retired high school teacher from Nome, Alaska, who had been aboard on most of the voyages since 1983; my old friend Terry Vose from Boston, a dealer in American paintings and shipmate on my Greenland-to-New England voyage of 1989; and Carl Emil Petersen, a fit, white-haired Norwegian explorer, wartime partisan, concentration camp survivor, adventurer, and national hero, who had sailed with us in 1987 in the Northwest Passage. Among his many accomplishments, Carl Emil is a seasoned Arctic sailor, having achieved the first circumnavigation of the Svalbard archipelago in his beloved wooden ketch, *Rundø*, built in 1925.[3]

We were off Bergen's quay on July 10, 1992, northbound. Once underway, we worked through multitudes of small rock skerries, while the bottom, as seen on our depth sounder, rose and fell like a roller coaster every quarter mile or so. "You must be careful," Carl Emil cautioned, "but you'll make it." And we did, finally getting into deep fjords where we often could not find the bottom at 600 feet.

This coast also is famous in the early history of North Atlantic navigation. The Norse voyagers, who possibly navigated by "latitude sailing,"—that is, by keeping the sun or the North Star at a constant height above the horizon, thus ensuring that they would travel either due east or due west—knew they could sail directly to Greenland from here with fair seasonal winds. Iceland's *Landnámabók (Book of Settlements)*, compiled in the thirteenth century, gives the following directions for reaching Greenland from Norway: "From Hernar in Norway one must sail a direct course west to Hvarf [Kap Farvel, Cape Farewell] in Greenland, in which case one sails north of Shetland so that one sights land in clear weather only, then south of the Faroes so that the sea looks halfway up the mountainsides, then south of Iceland so that one gets sight of birds and whales from there."[4] Today, these sailing directions from "Hernar" would carry a boat close to the sixty-first parallel of latitude, all the way to Greenland.

Piloting was tricky amid the thousands of rocks and islands on the Norwegian coast. Andy Rowe (left) picks out the marks, while Willy Fox takes the helm. I was keeping track of our position on the chart.

～

Hernø ("Hernar") is very close to Stadlandet, and our first objective was to round the great cape at Stadlandet, the westernmost point of Norway. Here we had to go "outside" into the Norwegian Sea because there is no fjord system behind it. "This can be a really bouncy place," Carl Emil pointed out, adding that he had doubled Stadlandet many times. "It has strong tidal currents, and the waves reflect off that rock face so that you can get hit by two wave trains at the same time." Once again he was right, and we did some rocking and rolling before getting away from there.

Once past Stadlandet, we shaped a course directly for the Lofoten Islands, 450 miles ahead, and right away we began to learn why the Norwegians are such good pilots. For 1,500 miles the Norwegian coast is a morass of millions and millions of rocks and shoals. There is very little sand or silt; it is mostly granite and basalt. Fortunately, every inch is both well charted and closely marked. There aren't many buoys in those waters, but there are thousands of small lights, as well as monuments and spindles (iron marks fixed with directional arrows indicating the safe side to pass) protruding above the water.

Carl Emil had brought aboard more than 200 Norwegian charts for the 1,200 miles between Bergen and Tromsø—and we needed every one of them. We constantly tried to stand offshore to avoid the rocks inshore, but the winds were always on our nose, forcing us to take the inside route. At times progress was so complicated, moving amongst those masses of rocks, islets, and ledges, that we needed three of us in the pilothouse: one to steer, one to keep track of our exact position on the chart, and one with binoculars, searching for the next mark.

Right away we began to learn why the Norwegians are such good pilots.

Each day, after twelve to fifteen hours of this, we were exhausted, especially after watching the depth sounder ricochet between "off soundings" and fifteen feet, over and over again. I don't know how many times in those days one of us—usually the one on the helm—would let out a "Holy Shit!" as we watched the bottom rocketing up toward us on the depth sounder's display. Usually, when the light grew faint, making it difficult to pick out the marks ahead, we found a little harbor to anchor in and get some sleep until morning.

But the payoff for enduring this was the magnificent scenery. My camera was going all the time, and I went through rolls of film,

'It's an old tradition in Norway for all mariners to throw it down in one gulp just as they pass the Circle.'

Crossing the Arctic Circle on the way to the Lofoten Islands

capturing the bold, gray granite cliffs crowned with green tundra and scrub spruce. The cliffs were traced here and there by wispy trails of delicate waterfalls gently drifting down the faces of the bare rock. Between the cliffs and at the heads of the fjords, wherever there was a bit of arable land, were tidy, well-kept farms. Their minuscule size, compared with the grandeur of the landscape, reminded me that, in the seventh and eighth centuries, while the population of Norway grew dramatically, most of the usable land had already been taken. That left only the sea and overseas colonization to relieve the pressure.

On July 14, on our way toward the Lofoten Islands, we crossed the Arctic Circle at sunset. Its orange glow beautifully backlit a small island, on which stood a monument marking exactly 66°33' N latitude. To celebrate, Carl Emil brought out a bottle of special high-octane Norwegian *aquavit* and offered it to us in large shot glasses. "It's an old tradition in Norway for all mariners to throw it down in one gulp just as they pass the Circle," he said. We all, save Bonnie, obliged him—and that clear liquid turned out to be so strong that our throats seemed attacked by a flamethrower. Carl Emil immediately asked, "How'd you like it?" Willy Fox, a rugby player by avocation, and hence no stranger to strong drink, looked up with watering eyes, gasping hoarsely, "God, that's smooth!"

~

Leaving the protection of the inside route at the Circle, we went back out into the Norwegian Sea and hobby-horsed along, punching our way into a twenty-five-knot headwind and accompanying sea. As we crawled toward the shelter of the Lofoten Islands, their mountaintops jutted up from the ocean like a row of shark's teeth. But once we got under their lee, the sea settled down, and the islands were truly dramatic in their raw massiveness.

These are also the waters of legend, for it is here, at the southern end of the Lofotens, that the Maelstrom has claimed the lives of many mariners who have had the temerity to challenge its waters during the strong period of the tidal cycles. At times the current runs at nearly fourteen miles per hour. When there is a large difference in the height of the Norwegian Sea and the waters inside the Lofotens, the tidal current, ebbing from inside the islands, rushes westward in dozens of streams that can quickly become vortex-like eddies.

In 1555 Olaus Magnus, a Swedish ecclesiastic, wrote of these waters in his *Historia de Gentibus Septentrionalibus*: "I refer to Röst

The Maelstrom—here depicted by Olaus Magnus in Historia de Gentibus Septentrionalibus, *Rome, 1555—has challenged and claimed the lives of many mariners over the centuries.*

The John Carter Brown Library at Brown University

Entering the narrow and steep palisades of Trollfjorden, Norway

and Lofoten, between which there is in the sea such a great chasm, or whirlpool, that, when mariners approach it carelessly, their helmsman is deprived of his strength and resourcefulness and they are swallowed up in an instant by the sudden swirl of water."[5] The Old Norse word for the Maelstrom is *havsveg* (hole in the ocean). Because the *havsveg* appeared to be a bottomless hole, with water pouring in, it spawned the legend used to such literary effect by Jules Verne, Herman Melville, and Edgar Allan Poe.[6]

Traveling among those islands proved to be unpleasant. Just as we entered the reefs and shoals, dark rainsqualls shut the visibility right down. Three of us were in the pilothouse as usual, picking out the marks as best we could. Then, in the gut between Store Mølle and Ostvågø, the channel narrowed to only thirty or forty yards, with a charted minimum of only ten feet. *Belvedere* draws only six feet, but nevertheless our tension rose considerably as the depth sounder suddenly registered twelve feet. After another "Holy Shit!" Carl Emil said, "Keep right on boys. It looks a lot worse than it is. I did it last year without any trouble." He was correct again.

Almost immediately we turned left into the tiny rock cleft called Trollfjorden. We entered between vertical granite walls 500 to 1,000 feet high, but less than 100 yards apart. The eerie, towering rock faces glistened with rain, while white skeins of waterfalls cascaded over them. At the base of the cliffs, and in their lower crevices, were lime-green deciduous trees, thick coverings of moss, and a riot of lupines; at the tops, snowfields lay just below the lowering, drifting clouds. Surveying the place with his art dealer's eye, Terry Vose piped up, "I know why they call it Troll Fjord. I can just about see those little buggers out there in the weeds. This reminds me of one of Albert Pinkham Ryder's spooky scenes." We secured to a tiny wharf that was firmly anchored to the rock face, and then all turned in. It had been a long day. No trolls boarded *Belvedere* to demand a forfeit that night.

Thirty-six hours later, after another complicated run amid countless islands, we reached Tromsø. Lying at 69°39' N, it is not far south of the latitude of Point Barrow, Alaska. With 51,000 inhabitants, it is the northernmost city in the world, and it possesses the northernmost university and brewery as well. Like all of Norway, Tromsø is clean, efficient, well run, and orderly—and like the rest of Norway, vastly expensive, a fact that was driven home to us when Bonnie came racing back to the boat, freaking out, "It cost nearly 400 dollars to do forty-five pounds of laundry!"

'It cost nearly 400 dollars to do forty-five pounds of laundry!'

Seafood, on the other hand, was very cheap and very fresh. Tromsø is an old fishing, sealing, hunting, trapping, and whaling center, and its fleets once covered the seas between East Greenland and Novaya Zemlya.[7] As we secured to Tromsø's quay, a small sign caught my attention. It was a hand-lettered notice taped to the window of the fish market right across from *Belvedere*. It read: *Beklager vi har ikke hval kjott* ("Today we have no whale meat").

A day or two earlier, when a fishing boat with a forty-millimeter harpoon cannon on the bow passed us on the way north, it seemed so exotic to me that I realized I had become accustomed to the United States' ban on whale products. Norway, after making serious efforts to cooperate with the International Whaling Commission's attempted ban on all commercial whaling, had, in 1993, decided to

A whale catcher, with a harpoon gun mounted on the bow, passes us near Rorvik, Norway.

reinstate its policy allowing minke whale hunting. The Norwegians argue that the whales they harvest are used only for food and that their small coastal hunting and fishing communities require whale meat for subsistence and for the maintenance of their traditional lifeways.

In 1998 the Norwegians established a self-imposed annual quota of 671 whales. They caught 625 that year; in 1999, a season of very unfavorable weather, only 589 were taken, out of a quota of 753. The minke whale population of the northeast and central North Atlantic is estimated at approximately 184,000. A whale in 1998 was worth about $6,000, or, for the 36 licensed whaling boats, a total catch of about $4 million.[8] In the year 2000 the price had fallen steeply: the price of blubber was one U.S. cent per kilogram "due to the lack of a market in Norway for this commodity."[9] In the year 2001 Norway returned to the practice of exporting whale meat and blubber for the first time since the mid-1980s. Japan was expected to be the main market.[10]

To our surprise we also found that there was an outdoor flea market in Tromsø's central square, where people sold fish and fresh vegetables and crafts. There were even a few Lapps in native costume selling tanned reindeer skins and antler artifacts. But by far the largest group was Russians selling the usual Soviet-style knickknacks, matryoshka nesting dolls, enamel pins, postcards, and other cheap stuff.

Carl Emil told me that, historically, in the "Pomor Trade" there had been much interaction between Russians and Norwegians along the Pomor coast between northern Norway and the White Sea. Later, during the chaos in the Soviet Union from 1918 to 1940, a number of Russians emigrated to northern Norway. When the Cold War ended, Norway allowed these Russian traders to sell their wares in Tromsø, where large numbers of cruise ship tourists come to see the midnight sun. The traders, mostly young men and women, traveled from Murmansk by boat and usually spent three or four days there before returning with what might amount to a month's earnings in Russia.[11] Norwegian authorities have since ended this trade because of illegal traffic in alcohol, tobacco, and some drugs.[12]

Tromsø is also the traditional jumping-off place for the Svalbard archipelago, the island group halfway between Norway and the North Pole. That passage, on the cusp of the Norwegian, Greenland, and Barents Seas, is nothing to sneeze at, and, of course, there are no harbors of refuge along the way. I watched the weather carefully and, with the help of the friendly staff of the meteorological office in Tromsø, concluded that the conditions would be relatively benign for

The winds were so light that we had to motor most of the way ... accompanied by seals, white-beaked dolphins, puffins, guillemots, fulmars, kittiwakes, and skuas.

several days. I'm glad to say that our analysis was on the money. The winds were so light that we had to motor most of the way, some of the time accompanied by seals, white-beaked dolphins, puffins, guillemots, fulmars, kittiwakes, and skuas feeding on the fish in the waters below.

On the evening of July 20 we began to parallel the southwest coast of the island of Spitsbergen, the largest of the Svalbard archipelago. From the vantage of several miles offshore the land reminded me of the Diomede Islands in Bering Strait: steep, dark gray cliff sides, slashed with vertical streaks of snow and capped with wisps of stratus clouds. What set them apart from the Diomedes were the great rivers of ice flowing between the 3,000-foot peaks. Winding down toward the shore, some of them were streaked with sinuous black medial moraines that perfectly mimicked every turn in their tortuous descent to the sea.

The Arctic's profound silence was broken only by the occasional deep, dull KERWHUUMP of a glacier calving into the bay.

About 4:00 A.M. on July 21 we anchored in Hornsund, the southernmost of the large fjords on the west coast of Spitsbergen. The land was torn and jagged and magnificent; the sun was low on the horizon; and the sky was the purest robin's-egg blue I'd ever seen. The Arctic's profound silence was broken only by the occasional deep, dull KERWHUUMP of a glacier calving into the bay a half mile from *Belvedere*.

"Isn't it good to be back in the Arctic?" declared Carl Emil. "You bet it is," I replied. "This is the best," Terry added, as we stood on the foredeck, drinking in the marvelous scene and taking photographs.

It was indeed. Here, at 77°N, the land was almost devoid of vegetation. In fact, a 1942 U.S. War Department report on Svalbard states the following: "Agriculture. There is no agricultural development.... Forestry. There is none. There are no trees except a few midget birch, height two inches."[13] The only reason I could think that the land was free of ice at all was the warming effect of the Gulf Stream (there called the North Atlantic Drift). Those sun-warmed surface waters finally give up their last bit of heat, having become heavy and saline, before descending to the abyssal depths of the Arctic Ocean. This inflow of heavy water in turn helps to produce the flow of cold deep Atlantic water, which spills out over a low sill in the Arctic Ocean's rim and pours south, between Iceland and Scotland, past the Faroe Islands. This flow "constitutes a submarine river ten miles wide and more than six feet deep, with a flow twice that of all the world's freshwater rivers combined."[14]

The warmth of the North Atlantic Drift also accounts for the fact that the coast of Norway is ice-free in winter and the sea ice boundary is usually not very far south of the Svalbard archipelago. In fact, the ocean has such an ameliorating effect that it skews the

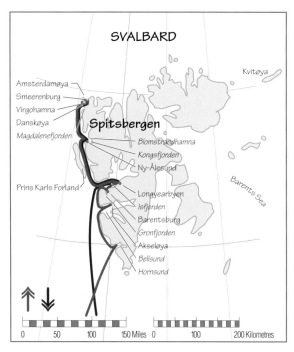

SVALBARD

Kvitøya

Amsterdamøya
Smeerenburg
Virgohamna
Danskøya
Magdalenefjorden

Spitsbergen

Blomstrandhamna
Kongsfjorden
Ny-Ålesund

Prins Karls Forland

Barents Sea

Longyearbyen
Isfjorden
Barentsburg
Gronfjorden
Akseløya
Bellsund
Hornsund

0   50   100   150 Miles 0   100   200 Kilometres

Belvedere's Route in Svalbard, 1992

Hudson was probably using Barentsz's map and, like him, also sought a northern passage to the Orient.

timing of the seasons: in northern Norway August, not July, is the warmest month, and February, not January, is the coldest.[15]

The name Svalbard (*Cold Coast*) first appears in the *Icelandic Annals* of 1194. It appears again in the *Landnámabók*, the history of Iceland that was written in 1200s, where it is stated that Svalbard lies four days' voyage north of there. While there is little doubt that Norse traders reached Russia in the ninth century,[16] it is unlikely that there was a Stone-Age settlement of Svalbard,[17] and it is a matter of debate whether this Icelandic "Svalbard" actually refers to the archipelago that, until recently, was commonly and inclusively called "Spitsbergen,"[18] or, possibly, to East Greenland or even to Jan Mayen Island.[19] Nevertheless, the island of Spitsbergen was discovered (or, if the *Annals* actually refer to this island group, rediscovered) in 1596. In that year Willem Barentsz, a Dutch mariner and explorer on his third voyage in search of a northern passage to the Orient, found his way blocked by ice at 80°10′N in the Greenland Sea. Turning south, he spotted the northwest corner of the island. He named the land Spitsbergen because of its jagged peaks.

Barentsz then turned east at the southern tip of the island and, equally impressively, made his way nearly 1,000 miles east and rounded the northern end of Novaya Zemlya, the sickle-shaped island group that divides the Barents and Kara Seas. There he was trapped by the ice and forced to spend a winter of privation and suffering in a driftwood shelter. Barentsz died in the spring, but his crew made their way to the mainland in boats and eventually returned to Holland, where Barentsz's journal was soon published.[20]

Spitsbergen's waters then lay unvisited for a decade—until Henry Hudson rediscovered the island in 1607, and on his return south became the first to see Jan Mayen Island, naming it "Hudsons Tutches."[21] Hudson was probably using Barentsz's map and, like him, also sought a northern passage to the Orient. Most importantly, Hudson reported great numbers of Greenland (bowhead) whales on the west coast of Spitsbergen.[22]

In 1610 Hudson was followed by Jonas Poole, an experienced Arctic mariner and walrus hunter, who confirmed Hudson's

Carl Emil Petersen in Hornsund, Spitsbergen, with Belvedere *in the background*

sightings. The following year England's Muscovy Company sent two ships with Basque harpooners (who had learned their skills in the Bay of Biscay and on the coast of Labrador) to hunt the whales. Two years later, in 1612, the company outfitted another whaling expedition. On arrival they found, to their dismay, that the news had leaked out: Dutch and Spanish whalers were already cruising there.

After several years of contest and conflict, with armed ships accompanying the fleets, the whalemen arranged a *modus vivendi*. They agreed essentially to partition Spitsbergen: the Dutch, with the strongest fleet, took the best whaling area, at the northwest corner of the island, with the Danes nearby; the English claimed the southwest coast. The whalers of other nations had to fend for themselves.[23] The Dutch also set up shore stations on Jan Mayen Island.[24]

At first, the whalemen captured the bowheads near the coast. This allowed them to practice shore whaling, wherein a catcher ship or boat towed the whale to a station at the water's edge. There the men stripped the carcass of its thick blubber and rendered it into oil in tryworks (large cauldrons set over fire pits). But shore whaling didn't last long. As the seventeenth century wore on, the hunters took so many whales that the inshore waters were soon empty. The fleets then resorted to pelagic whaling, out in the Greenland Sea. There the whalemen had the more difficult task of stripping the carcasses alongside the ship. Later, with the Greenland whale population in steep decline, the ships cruised among the ice floes for their quarry, and before long they "fished out" the entire Greenland Sea. By the end of the seventeenth century the ships were forced to hunt in Davis Strait, west of Greenland.[25]

For the next 200 years Spitsbergen was the province of over-wintering hunters and trappers, primarily from Russia and Norway. Then, in the early years of the twentieth century, several companies began mining the island's rich coal seams.[26] But essentially the entire Svalbard archipelago (24,000 square miles, two-thirds of which is covered by glaciers) remained a *terra nullius*, a "no man's land." In 1920, however, as part of the Versailles Peace Settlement, the Allies and other states recognized Norwegian sovereignty over Svalbard, but retained rights of access for industrial, mining, and commercial operations there—on a basis of full equality with Norway.[27] To date, forty nations have signed the treaty, which also prohibits warlike activities in the archipelago.

Accordingly, when *Belvedere* anchored in Hornsund, our first item of business was to go ashore to report our presence to the Norwegian authorities. These "authorities" turned out to be only one friendly and casual semiretired policeman who lived alone in a small hut as the representative of the *Sysselmann* (governor) of the archipelago. He was there to keep an eye on the occasional campers who visit the national park, which comprises all of southern Spitsbergen. The formalities were simple: After filling out a form, I was given a numbered card and told to hand it in when we left Svalbard. Other than that, his only order was to remind us that it is a

The site of a seventeenth-century English shore whaling station in Hornsund, Spitsbergen

requirement to carry a heavy-gauge firearm when ashore—because in Svalbard polar bears are everywhere and dangerous.

This is going to be an interesting visit, I thought to myself as I loaded three 12-gauge slugs into my pump shotgun, followed by two blank, black-powder rounds. If challenged by a bear, I would use the two blank rounds to try to scare it off; but if in mortal danger, I would use the slugs to attempt to save the lives of my friends and myself. I am glad to say that I needed to do neither.

After a good sleep and a quick hello at the small Polish Arctic research station nearby, we motored south across the fjord to the mouth of a small river, where four archaeologists from Tromsø were excavating the remains of a seventeenth-century English shore-whaling station. The site was on an eroding glacial outwash plain, and was littered here and there with large whale bones.

All that remained of the station were the outlines of a small one-room house built of timber and stone, and the tryworks, which could be identified by a pile of bricks. An early-twentieth-century Russian expedition had built its privy near the site; the diggers were now using it as a place to get out of the chilly wind while they worked on their field notes.

The team lived in tents, and the perimeter of the tents was ringed with a trip wire, a sort of booby trap. It was rigged to set off what looked like M-80 firecrackers if a bear should blunder into the wire. On top of the spot where the Russian expedition's hut had stood was a one-room trapper's cabin, built about 1930. The archaeologists

A trapper's camp in Bellsund, Norway. The tripod keeps meat out of the reach of polar bears.

It is a requirement to carry a heavy-gauge firearm when ashore.

were using it for a dining hall. It looked very cozy and efficient, with one small window that provided a dramatic view out over the fjord, which was surrounded by jagged, snow-streaked peaks.

In the morning we moved up the coast to the next fjord, Bellsund, and spent the night at the foot of a glacier in a lovely little bay called Fridtjovhamna. Part of the fjord system there is nearly blocked by Akseløya, a narrow, four-mile-long revetment of vertically warped, striated rock that nearly spans the mouth of the fjord and gives good protection to its inner waters. Our anchorage was behind a glacial moraine that had been sculpted by the waves into a small, protecting hook.

Onshore was a trapper's camp, complete with a large, high, tripod cache on steel legs, as well as a spotlessly clean cabin and storehouse in first-class repair. On the table in the cabin was a note from the trapper, saying that he had gone to the south end of Akseløya for the summer. It was signed "Hiawatha." Hiawatha was clearly a very capable person, and an intelligent one. We all admired his cache, which during the winter presumably held seal and bear meat (judging from the grease marks on the stones below) away from any marauding polar bears. We also admired his choice of this sublime place.

The next day we ran north into Isfjorden and then, round the corner, into a tributary embayment, Grønfjorden, the site of Barentsburg, the town where the Soviet— now Russian—company Trust Arktikugol has been operating a coal mine since 1932. The Soviet Union was the only signatory to the Svalbard Treaty to take advantage of its right to maintain settlements in the archipelago. As several Norwegians pointed out to me, the Soviets had tried to exploit any possible legal gray areas in the treaty to expand their "land rights" by "alternately challenging or demanding participation in certain Norwegian activities." In 1944, for instance, the Soviets demanded joint administration of the entire island group and the direct cession of Bjornøya (Bear Island), lying between Svalbard and Norway, to the Soviet Union, claiming that their right of egress to the Atlantic was threatened.[28] Norway held fast.

I can't remember why we decided to stop at Barentsburg, but almost from the moment we had secured to the crumbling, coal dust-covered pier, I knew we'd made a mistake. The shifty-looking manager immediately jumped aboard, wearing a leather raincoat and flashing his steel teeth. Right away he hit me up for some steep "dockage fees." While collecting these in hard currency ("Any hard currency will do—it doesn't matter....") he told us that the mine was having trouble selling its coal and consequently that pretty much everything else was for sale. I looked up at the grim rows of Stalin-era concrete buildings clinging to the steep cliff side and wondered

I can't remember why we decided to stop at Barentsburg, but from the moment we had secured to the crumbling, coal dust-covered pier, I knew we'd made a mistake.

Belvedere *at a Russian coal company's dock in Barentsburg*

why anyone would want to buy anything here; but, as if to prove his point, someone showed up at the dockside and offered to sell me an almost-new KGB uniform. For a moment I thought it might make a great Halloween costume for my son, Johnny, but then I began to consider how I might talk that one through U.S. Customs.

On the other hand, I wish I'd put a bid in on the incredibly ugly granite head of Lenin that cast its grim gaze over the main square. We needed a good mooring weight there, and if twenty bucks would have sealed the deal, that and thirty fathoms of chain rove through the Great Man's septum might at least have given me a secure night's sleep.

In any case, once I had been fleeced of the "dockage fee" for a couple of hours' stay, the guy with the steel teeth announced with a sinister stare that we *shouldn't miss* (his emphasis) the guided tour of the town (for another fee). It would, he said, be far more rewarding for us than simply wandering around in ignorance. He added that the tour would "open doors." I was pretty sure that I didn't want *any* doors opened in that creepy place, but I paid up for that one too. I wanted to get out of there as soon as possible, and I most sincerely hoped that it wasn't a soup-to-nuts, cover-everything-tour that I'd just signed up for. Unfortunately it was.

Our guide turned out to be a sweet Ukrainian girl in her early twenties who was itching to get out of Barentsburg but hadn't yet worked off her labor contract. Despite her genuine efforts to make it seem interesting and attractive, the place was unspeakably dreary.

The only vegetables that this town of 1,300 received were from some well-tended greenhouses.

Dodging wheezing, 1960-ish military lorries, we hiked up the face of the cliff on a zigzagging concrete road that seemed paved with ground-up coal, as were the soccer fields. We wondered if anyone in Barentsburg had ever called the People's Fire Department with the report: "The road's on fire! We're worried that it might light up the soccer fields too!"

As we moved past smelly, cracked sewer pipes spewing into the bay, we encountered an even stronger smell—a barnyard. As we walked past a hen house, our guide told us that the only vegetables that this town of 1,300 (900 men, 300 women, 100 kids) received were from some well-tended greenhouses, the side of one of which remained punched in from the force of the winter storms.

In Barentsburg the children's milk came from the world's northernmost dairy, which housed a dozen healthy, docile cows, several playful calves, and one large, dangerous-looking bull, all of which survived on imported fodder. Also in the menagerie were a couple of scruffy barn cats. We assumed that they, too, must have been the northernmost barn cats in the world and wondered if they were there to catch the northernmost barn mice.

Another stop took us to the museum. It was clearly intended as a political statement confirming the Soviet Union's party line that Russian trappers had preceded all others to the archipelago, a claim that is not accepted by most historians. The collection also included a natural history section consisting of badly stuffed models of reindeer and birds, among other things, but the *tour de force* was a shark, the skin of which had been sewn around a log and which had curiously human-looking glass eyes pointing in different directions.

The town's inhabitants, trudging among the dormitory-like buildings that were arranged in unrelieved precision along the central street, all looked as if they would far rather be somewhere else. We went away feeling depressed and sorry for all those people who had been robbed of their youth and energy in the service of such a hideous and unproductive system.

As we made our way back to *Belvedere,* I spotted a rusty steel hammer-and-sickle emblem on a heap of rubbish near the dock. It was an insignia that had recently been cut from the stack of one of the small, equally rusty and beaten-up harbor tugs that creaked and groaned against one another at the pier. The tugs were now flying the white, blue, and red flag of Russia, and that hammer-and-sickle ensemble is now fastened to one of *Belvedere*'s bulkheads, right above the trash bin.

The museum…was clearly intended as a political statement confirming the Soviet Union's party line that Russian trappers had preceded all others.

~

A day later we reached Longyearbyen, the capital of Svalbard, so that Terry Vose could catch a plane for home. Although we were still in Isfjorden, the contrast to Barentsburg was dramatic. Longyearbyen was founded in 1906 by the American coal-mining pioneer John Munro Longyear and his partner, Frederick Ayer of Boston. Their Arctic Coal Company operated the mines until 1916, when they sold their operation to the Store Norske Spitsbergen Kulkompani A/S of Oslo, which is still in business and employs 60 percent of the Norwegian population of the island. The town is clean and orderly, the buildings ascending a glacially scoured valley. The remains of an old aerial bucket line tramway, which at one time had moved coal from the mines to the docks, runs through the valley.

The remains of an old aerial bucket line tramway, which at one time had moved coal from the mines to the docks, runs through the valley.

There is also an impressive historical museum in Longyearbyen containing exhibits that address, among other topics, Svalbard's role in the Second World War. After Germany invaded Norway in 1940, the Allies became concerned both about the possibility of Spitsbergen's abundant coal supplies falling under Axis control and about the potential for Spitsbergen, and Bear and Jan Mayen Islands, being used as bases for broadcasting weather information in the brutal convoy battles that took place when the Allies' ships carried supplies to the northern Russian ports of Murmansk and Archangel.

In August and September 1941, a joint expeditionary force comprising Canadian, British, and Norwegian troops evacuated the Norwegian and Russian civilians and destroyed the mines and fuel supplies at Barentsburg and Longyearbyen, among other sites. Quickly, however, the Germans established a small garrison at Longyearbyen and set up meteorological stations there, as well as at other sites in Svalbard.

In riposte a small force, primarily Norwegian, landed at Barentsburg in 1942. Although German aircraft attacked Barentsburg,[29] soon after, the Germans evacuated Longyearbyen. The next year, however, they sent the battleship *Tirpitz* and battle cruiser *Scharnhorst* and nine destroyers to fire on and destroy Barentsburg, Longyearbyen, and one other mining town. Although the Germans took some British and Norwegian prisoners, the majority of the garrison escaped into the mountains. The Germans bombed and destroyed more mines the following year and established other clandestine weather stations there as well.[30] The coal in Mine 2b, on the scree slope up the valley from Longyearbyen, burned from 1944 until the 1960s.

On the dock in Ny-Ålesund, Norway, Andy Rowe prepares to make a call at the "world's northernmost phone booth."

This iron man was the first person to traverse the Northwest Passage ... to reach the South Pole ... and in all probability first reached the North Pole by air.

On the evening of July 26 we reached Ny-Ålesund in Kongsfjorden (King's Bay), having run up the coast on a dreary day, inside the protection of the narrow and mountainous island, Prins Karls Forland. At 78°50′N, Ny-Ålesund proclaims itself "the northernmost town in the world." Founded by the King's Bay Kull Company A/S, and named after its hometown in Ålesund, Norway, the company operated the world's northernmost coal mine there until 1962, when the mine was closed after a disastrous explosion. Now the settlement is used primarily for scientific research.

Under gray skies we secured *Belvedere* to an evil-looking pier, full of rusty I-beams, and, once we had climbed onto the pier, we discovered that what we had assumed to be a privy was, in fact, the world's northernmost telephone booth. On its wall, right above the working pay phone, Willy Fox wrote his mother's phone number in Maine, adding, "For a good time call Robin." Later, in fact, she did get one call from a tipsy Scottish tourist.

King's Bay is famous in Arctic history. It was from here in 1926 that Richard E. Byrd and Floyd Bennett took off in a Ford trimotor airplane and claimed to be the first to fly over the North Pole, a claim that has been disputed with considerable justification—occasionally acrimoniously—ever since.[31] Nevertheless, a few days later the great Norwegian explorer Roald Amundsen, with Lincoln Ellsworth and Umberto Nobile, indisputably flew the dirigible *Norge* across the Arctic Ocean, via the Pole, before crash-landing at Teller, Alaska, near Bering Strait.[32]

In the dusk of midnight (here the sun remains above the horizon from mid-April to late August) Bonnie, Carl Emil, and I walked through the tiny, orderly town. At the outskirts, rising above the thin tundra cover, stood the *Norge's* rusty mooring tower and, nearby, a monument to Amundsen. His portrait bust was large, stoic, and imposing—perfectly befitting this iron man who was the first person to traverse the Northwest Passage, the first person to reach the South Pole, and the leader of the team that in all probability first reached the North Pole by air while completing the first aerial crossing of the Arctic Ocean.

A small herd of reindeer grazed quietly nearby, while snow buntings fluttered about them. To Bonnie and me, who were used to the proportions of the Alaskan caribou (which are wild reindeer), with their larger size and longer legs and muzzles, these small, rotund Spitsbergen reindeer seemed quite curious. "They look like cute, hairy pigs," Bonnie said. In shape they reminded me of the Peary caribou of northern Greenland and Canada's High Arctic islands. We wondered whether many centuries ago a herd might have migrated the 300 miles across the sea ice to Greenland and then onward, to North America. And if the reindeer had made that crossing, we wondered whether human beings might have followed them....

The next day found us farther north, at 79°30′, in Magdalenefjorden, near the northwest corner of Spitsbergen. I knew that Magdalene Fjord is famous for its beauty, but I was unprepared, and for once my usually frenetic pace of photography slowed to a crawl. The fjord is ringed with severe granite ridges, from which several glaciers descend to the bay, and during our visit they calved many pieces of deep blue ice. The fjord's steep gray slopes were highlighted in the ravines by streaks of green tundra and by snowfields tinted light pink from a curious algae growing on them. A lovely sand beach enclosed the bay, and fifty yards away, sunning itself on an ice floe, was a huge bearded seal.

In 1818 Lieutenant Frederick William Beechey of Britain's Royal Navy was in the same spot, and his words are evocative: "There was a stillness which bordered on the sublime—a stillness which was interrupted only by the bursting of an iceberg, or the report of some fragment of rock loosened from its hold. These sounds, indeed, which came booming over the placid surface of the bay, could hardly be considered interruptions to the general silence, for, speedily dying away in the distance, they left behind a stillness even more profound than before."[33]

As at Hornsund, onshore was another policeman's hut, and the incumbent, like the man in Hornsund, was friendly, relaxed, and semiretired. We spent a pleasant evening with him aboard *Belvedere*, and Bonnie, as she has done every summer, opened her "barbershop" for a crew haircut, an offer that the jolly policeman gladly accepted.

After reminding us to carry firearms always because of bears, he asked me, "How many visitors do you think have been here this summer?"

I answered, "A couple of dozen, at best?"

"No."

"A hundred?"

"No."

"A thousand?"

"No. As of July 27 we have had already 25,000, almost all of them aboard cruise ships."

"Then I guess *Belvedere*'s crew won't skew your figures much," said Bonnie.

The policeman then showed us a three-page, single-spaced document. It was the summer's list of, I would imagine, about seventy-five scheduled visits by cruise ships.

'There was a stillness which bordered on the sublime.'

Amid the beauty of Magdalenefjorden

CARL EMIL PETERSEN

≈

Our next stop was even farther on, at 79°44′N, less than 700 miles from the North Pole and almost equidistant from Point Barrow, Alaska, and Paris. Here we anchored off Amsterdamøya (Amsterdam Island), the site of Smeerenburg ("Blubbertown"), which was probably the largest of the Dutch shore stations. In the first part of the seventeenth century as many as eight Dutch companies had tryworks close to the water's edge at Smeerenberg, as well as houses, sheds, tents, and other structures.[34]

Set on a northeast-facing sandy beach and backed by a small lagoon, a more desolate place to live and work is hard to imagine. Glaciers and dark gray, snow-streaked mountains ringed the bay in majestic, cold grandeur, and the shore was littered with a jumble of drift logs from the rivers of western Siberia. The ground near shore was composed entirely of rounded granite boulders, some of them covered with thin moss. I saw very little vegetation, yet there must have been enough to support the five reindeer and one calf that grazed nearby. The lagoon was alive with geese and goslings, and masses of little auks dove away from us in the salt water.

Only a mile to the southwest, on Danskøya (Dane's Island), the ocean's litter of driftwood on Amsterdamøya was echoed by mankind's industrial litter. There, at Virgohamna (Virgo Harbor), the earliest chapters of nineteenth- and twentieth-century polar flight were written not far from the site of a sixteenth-century Danish whaling operation. Making our way ashore over the cobbles, we encountered heaps of century-old man-made rubbish, the detritus of two men's quixotic attempts to reach the North Pole by air.

In 1897 the Swedish engineer Salomon August Andrée set off in a hydrogen-filled balloon, hoping to drift over the Pole. At the eastern end of the flat shingle, backed by steep, dark cliffs, were the twisted remains of his prefabricated balloon shed, while at the western end was an even greater mess, the site of Walter Wellman's motorized airship expeditions in the first years of the 1900s.

Neither man achieved his goal. Andrée's balloon drifted off into the vastness of the Arctic, and, with the exception of a couple of routine reports sent by the passenger pigeons that he released, nothing was heard from him again. His fate was discovered by accident in 1930 when the crew of a Norwegian Arctic expedition landed at Kvitøya (White Island), the northeasternmost land in the Svalbard archipelago. Kvitøya is almost entirely covered by ice, but on the only exposed bit of land, a scrap of beach on its western end, the men found the remains of the expedition, with, amazingly enough, its diaries and photographic materials. The eerie images and words revealed that the expedition had lasted only three days before crashing on the ice. The men marched to Kvitøya, where they hoped to await discovery by searchers. It is thought they may have died from trichinosis, having eaten undercooked polar bear meat, or possibly, from carbon monoxide poisoning from the camp stove in their tent.[35]

The site of the Dutch whaling village, Smeerenburg ("Blubbertown"), on Amsterdamøya, is less than 700 miles from the North Pole. Here, at 79°44′N, Andy Rowe weaves through drift logs from the rivers of western Siberia.

Not far away at Virgohamna were the remains of Walter Wellman's camp. Wellman, a reporter for the *Chicago Record-Herald*, became fascinated with the possibilities of dirigibles after participating in expeditions to northeast Svalbard (1894) and to the Franz Josef archipelago east of there (1898–99). During the second expedition he had twice failed to reach the Pole by sledge; consequently the aerial option was highly seductive. He proved to be a better fund-raiser than aeronaut.

Wellman's expedition, aboard the ship *Virgo*, reached Virgohamna from Tromsø in 1906. The men immediately began blasting the rocks away to create a level area for the hangar that would stand 190 feet

long, 82 feet wide, and 85 feet high. There were also outbuildings and a dormitory. The crew lugged ashore 125 tons of sulfuric acid and 75 tons of iron filings that, when combined, would produce the highly explosive hydrogen gas to lift the airship. But Wellman's organization of the project was so haphazard that the men were unable even to inflate the dirigible that season, and they scrambled against the approach of winter simply to complete the hangar.

He returned in 1907, and after a summer of delays, caused in part by poor weather, late in the season he brought the rudderless airship *America* out of the hangar. She was then towed out of the harbor to begin a voyage that would traverse only about fifteen miles and would last just about three hours. The craft, lacking a rudder, was uncontrollable. Wellman, to save his own life and the lives of the crew, ordered a crash landing on a glacier. He had achieved only one record: the first motor-driven voyage by an airship in the Arctic.

It was clear that we were going to need to find a good harbor for the blow that was coming.

Back again in 1909, now with improved apparatus, Wellman covered about forty miles before part of his new steering gear fell off. Only through chance did a Norwegian ship rescue them. On his return he learned that both Frederick Cook and Robert E. Peary separately had claimed to have reached the Pole by dogsled. It was not until 1926 that a lighter-than-air ship did reach the North Pole, when, as noted, Amundsen, Ellsworth, and Nobile took the *Norge* from Kongsfiorden to Alaska.[36]

As we walked among the camps at Virgohamna we were amazed at the sheer volume of junk there. We could pick out Andrée's camp, but knew that Wellman's men had scavenged much of the wood to make a floor for their hangar. It wasn't hard to spot the great collapsed hangar ribs and the mass of broken timbers around them. There were also about fifty 100-gallon gasoline drums that carried the fuel for Wellman's airship. We wondered about the potentially highly explosive mix of hot engine fumes and hydrogen gas as we walked carefully amid tons of scrap iron filings and jagged shards from the two-inch-thick walls of the porcelain carboys that held the sulfuric acid. Eyeing the broken porcelain and iron scrap, there were so many sharp edges and puncture points that Willy Fox blurted out, "We all should get tetanus shots right away."

∽

A ship's report that the pack ice lay just north of Amsterdamøya told us that we would not be able to make any further northern progress. That, and a falling barometer, with darkening skies, hastened our departure for the south. It was clear that we were going to need to find a good harbor for the blow that was coming. Almost as soon as we emerged from the cover of Danskøya, the wind came up strong from the south, as much as forty knots, making *Belvedere* buck hard in the rising sea. After a couple of hours of this we decided that, instead of heading for a harbor behind Prins Karls Forland and beating our teeth out on the way, we would duck into Blomstrandhamna (Blomstrand's Harbor), across from Ny-Ålesund.

Grateful to be in calm water again, we anchored across the harbor from a calving glacier. I took the dinghy to the foot of a row of bird cliffs covered with large patches of the urea-selective orange lichen that thrives below birds' nests. While kittiwakes, guillemots, and gulls wheeled above me, I walked over the moraines that lined the water's edge. These wild, disorganized heaps of glacial rubble were utterly without any vegetation, looking so fresh and unsorted that it seemed a bulldozer might have heaped them up only yesterday. In fact, as I learned a few hours later, they *were* very new. A pair of Norwegian geologists stopped by *Belvedere* in their dinghy and told us that this glacier, Blomstrandbreen, had been stable since approximately the seventeenth century, but inexplicably had started to recede only last year. That night we listened to great, dull booms as gigantic pieces of ice collapsed from the glacier's face into the harbor.

> *This heart-shaped island became a slaughterhouse as successive waves of hunters systematically exterminated the great populations of whales and walruses there.*

On August 2, 120 miles south of the southern tip of Spitsbergen and about a third of the way to Norway, Bjornøya's (Bear Island's) solitary profile rose from the horizon ahead. Bear Island entered modern literature via Alistair MacLean's thriller of the same name about murder on "the loneliest, most desolate island in the world," but its history runs much deeper, having been discovered in 1596 by Willem Barentsz. He wrote:

> The 12th of June in the morning wee saw a white beare, which we rowed after with our boate, thinking to cast a roape about her necke; but when we were near her, shee was so great that we durst not doe it, but rowed back to our shippe to fetch more men and our armes, and so made to her againe with muskets, hargubushes, halbertes, and hatchets. . . . And so being well furnished of men and weapons, wee . . . fought her while four glasses were run out [two hours], for our weapons could do her little hurt; . . . and at last wee cut her head in sunder with an axe, wherewith she dyed; and . . . wee fleaed her, and found her skinne to be twelve foote long: which done, wee eate some of her flesh; but wee brookt it not well. This island wee called the Beare Island.[37]

In 1603 Stephen Bennet, an English mariner, rediscovered the island, named it Cherie Island after Sir Francis Cherie, one of his sponsors, and noted the huge walrus herds there. England's Muscovy

Company immediately sent out ships to hunt these creatures, and, as Frederick William Beechey reported, "We are told that these adventurers were so successful in their occupation, that not less than nine hundred, or a thousand animals were captured in the short space of seven hours, by the crew of a single vessel."[38]

From then on, this heart-shaped island, about twelve miles long and ten miles wide, became a slaughterhouse as successive waves of hunters systematically exterminated the great populations of whales and walruses there. Bear Island is almost completely rimmed by vertical cliffs, some more than a thousand feet high, but as we sailed along its east side, at one place—Kvalrossbukta (Walrus Bay)—with a gentler slope, we saw piles of bleaching bones where there had been, presumably, a walrus rookery and hunters had been at work.

Apart from a small Norwegian meteorological station on the north coast, Bear Island is uninhabited. In the twentieth century some desultory coal mining was attempted there, but what makes its name ring in recent history is its geographical position (74°30′N) between Norway and Svalbard. During the Second World War it became a stationary bulwark in the midst of the convoy routes to Russia. Its location made it an important piece of real estate in the lethal cat-and-mouse game between, on the one hand, the Allied fleets heading for Murmansk and the White Sea to keep the Eastern Front alive and, on the other, the Luftwaffe, and the Kriegsmarine's surface ships and submarine wolf packs that sought to strangle it.

The contest was to the death, and the cost was appalling. On the Allied side 214 vessels were lost or damaged, 22 of them warships. Thousands of men lost their lives, winter and summer, in those frigid seas, as they dodged about in storms, freezing spray, murk, and pack ice, often using Bear Island as a blocking post. The cost to the Germans was five surface ships,[39] including one battleship, a large number of aircraft, thirty-two U-boats, and probably as many men as the Allies lost.[40]

As we sailed over those places I thought about how many brave souls, of many nations, lay below *Belvedere*'s keel and how heroic their actions had been. I was humbled by their sacrifice. To my knowledge there is no cenotaph on Bear Island to commemorate the bravery of those sailors.

Thousands of men lost their lives in those frigid seas, as they dodged about in storms, freezing spray, murk, and pack ice.

⁓

The north side of Bear Island is of low, flat limestone with small cliffs onshore, but as we ran down its east side, fighting a more than two-knot current, the brownish-gray cliffs rose and we passed Miseryfjellet (Stephen Bennet's Mount Misery). Its three peaks, one of them more than 1,700 feet high, and its name, formed a dreary backdrop to the rising palisade at the water's edge. We then rounded up into Sørhamna (South Harbor) on the southeastern point of the island. Although it is only about a half-mile long and three-quarters of a mile wide, and even though it is exposed to the south, Sørhamna is the only thing approaching a harbor anywhere on the island.

We were amazed to find that Sørhamna is entirely surrounded by warped and folded limestone cliffs up to 300 feet high, offering no access to the island. With the exception of two tiny beaches washed by a heavy swell, there was no place to land. But the cliffs were teeming with sea birds. As we approached the harbor, fulmars soared and glided around *Belvedere*, and when we entered that amazing amphitheater the air was thick with the ammonia odor of urea and with birds calling and wheeling around us. There were masses of gulls and guillemots roosting on little clumps of bright green vegetation in every cranny on the cliffs, which were themselves white with bird droppings, while on the surface of the clear, almost Bahamian-blue water, fulmars bobbed patiently and alertly.

What is worrisome is that the Komsomolets carried not only a nuclear reactor...but also plutonium-tipped torpedoes.

After a short rest we pushed on to the southern tip of the island. There the cliffs rise more than 1,300 feet. At their base huge limestone needles jut up from the water in jagged majesty amid thousands of milling birds. The largest of the stacks, Stappen, rises to 600 feet. At Stappen we also found two strong ocean currents converging, one from the northeast and one, it seemed, from the southeast. The result was a nasty cross-chop that quickly had *Belvedere* rolling thirty-five degrees to either side as we slogged along with crashes of pots and pans rising up from the galley.

Bonnie also "brookt it not well" and looked particularly queasy. When an especially loud crash rang out, someone asked, "What can that be?" "It's just the knives falling off the magnetic rack. I've heard it many times before," she answered in a thin voice, as she sat in the pilothouse inhaling the full blast of the forty-three-degree sea air roaring in from the open door. I thought, What a good sport! How many times in the last ten years has she been on *Belvedere*, feeling just as ill?

South of Bear Island we passed over yet another sad place: the grave of the Soviet Mike-class nuclear submarine *Komsomolets*, the 6,400-ton prototype for a new class of deep-diving attack subs. With an estimated submerged speed of thirty-eight knots (judging from her hull shape and presumed propulsion system) it is assumed that this boat was designed to challenge the U.S. Navy's *Los Angeles*-class submarines.[41]

The *Komsomolets* was abandoned during a disastrous fire on April 7, 1989. She sank in 6,000 feet of water, taking forty-two men with her. What is worrisome is the fact that the *Komsomolets* carried not only a nuclear reactor containing Cesium 137, but also plutonium-tipped torpedoes. Recent examinations of the wreck by remotely operated submersibles have revealed that the impact of the hull hitting the seabed has opened the outer torpedo-tube doors and cracked the inner doors. According to scientists, both Russian and American, it is only a matter of time before the radioactive materials begin to leak—in an area where there are three-knot currents running along the ocean floor.[42]

Just as we were congratulating ourselves on how well we were taking it, the jib ripped in half.

∼

Nearing the Norwegian coast, we were glad to pick out the big headlands of the Torsvåg approaches that lead to Tromsø, for we weren't sorry to be leaving the Barents Sea, which is famous for its changeable weather and big winds. To be fair, however, we had had a remarkably easy trip down from Svalbard, enjoying light airs and fairly flat seas. Everyone was grateful for that.

After dropping off Carl Emil Petersen, who was, if I remember correctly, about to fly to Mongolia to join an expedition, we kept on down the coast, making long daily runs amid magnificent scenery. On August 8 we anticipated a short run to the town of Bodø, but it was not to be. Shortly after leaving our anchorage in the tiny fishing village of Rotnesvåg on a gray, murky day, the wind came up to about twenty knots out of the southwest, right on our nose, then rose to thirty as we punched along into it. Once we left the shelter of the islands, the seas came up too, but we kept on, making only about five knots over the bottom, and pitching as much as thirty degrees forward. We were getting close to Bodø, but by the time we reached the high, massive island of Landegode, the wind was up to thirty-five knots, with dark rain squalls coming through every half hour or so.

Just as one of the squalls overtook us at the north end of Landegode, it gusted to fifty knots, blowing sheets of spray across the boat and rolling us down thirty-eight degrees to port. Then, with jet-black skies all around us—highlighted by brilliant white wave crests—and just as we were congratulating ourselves on how well we were taking it, the jib ripped in half with a huge BOOM and started flogging wildly. We wound it up without too much trouble but of course lost its steadying force. With the wind gusting now to forty-seven knots we were happy to reach the protection of Bodø's harbor an hour later. Once we were secure we found that the jib had wound itself so tightly around the forestay that we couldn't lower it. "Lay aloft, Willy Fox," said Andy cheerfully, and Willy, who, as usual, was ever agreeable, climbed into the bosun's chair to be winched up to the masthead to secure the flogging remnants temporarily. We hauled it down at the dock in Bodø, replaced it with an old spare, and had it repaired in Scotland during the winter.

I was ashore in Bodø, buying supplies, when it struck me how "modern" the town looked: it seemed to be all glass, aluminum, and recent architecture. When I asked the harbormaster about this, he reminded me that Bodø had been heavily bombed by the Luftwaffe in the early days of the World War II and later had endured a brutal German occupation. It struck me that the Cold War wasn't far away either: As we motored out of the harbor, we passed a military airfield. It was to have been the destination of Francis Gary Powers when, in 1960, he took off from Peshawar, Pakistan, in his U-2 reconnaissance aircraft to over-fly the Soviet Union at 90,000 feet. A surface-to-air missile shot him down over Sverdlovsk (now known by its former name, Yekaterinburg, where the Russian Royal Family was murdered), and the incident allowed Chairman Nikita Krushchev to cancel a summit meeting with President Dwight Eisenhower, giving the Soviets a huge propaganda coup.

We were glad to be underway again, and, having been in such seemingly barren places in Svalbard, as we went south, we delighted in the sight of the land progressively becoming greener as the air grew warmer. First there were only little patches of moss and grass in the bottoms of sheltered valleys, but the "green line" gradually rose higher and higher on the flanks of the hills, occasionally with a few sheep grazing on them. Next bushes and small trees appeared, and then, as we motored in to Åfjorden, to anchor in the mirror-calm of the small land-locked harbor at Selnes, suddenly we were overwhelmed by the wonderful scent of growing things: conifers, juniper, bay, and cut hay. Four small, tidy farms surrounded us, and ashore, the banks were covered in a colorful riot of raspberry and blueberry bushes, ferns, willows, birch, Queen Anne's lace, and wildflowers.

A brief stop in the fjord city of Trondheim allowed a visit to its magnificent gothic cathedral—the northernmost in Europe, and made entirely of soapstone—on the site of an earlier church where King Olaf had brought Christianity to the Norse about A.D. 1000. Then we dodged on down the coast in a series of long day runs that often ended, to our dismay, finding floating salmon pens in harbors where we had planned to stop. Their mooring cables made it impossible for us to anchor; so, heavy with fatigue, we would have to push on to another.

We dodged on down the coast in a series of long day runs that often ended, to our dismay, finding floating salmon pens in harbors where we had planned to stop.

Atlantic salmon farming has expanded rapidly in the last few decades. It began in Norway in the 1960s, and its initial success soon stimulated operations in the United States, Canada, the United Kingdom, the Faroes, and Chile. By 1997 the world production of farmed salmon was worth two billion dollars. Today more 660,000 tons of farmed salmon are produced annually. But, as with many promising initiatives, salmon cultivation first seemed to hold out the promise of being a great revenue producer and a perfect answer to the limited quantity of wild Atlantic salmon, but as the industry grew, it created unforeseen problems.

Salmon are fed fishmeal (pellets made from "sprats, anchovies, sand eels, and pilchards"), much of it imported from South America, and about 2.8 pounds of meal are required to produce one pound of farmed salmon.[43] The salmon feces have polluted coastal waters, and the high density of the penned salmon have caused outbreaks of salmon diseases and parasites such as sea lice, which in turn have required the use of antibiotics and pesticides. Equally worrisome is the problem of escaped farmed salmon, which may lead to the genetic degradation of the wild salmon populations.[44] "When storms or seals damage the salmon pens," Alan Cowell writes, "tens of thousands of the farmed salmon escape, they head upriver, challenging the wild fish for partners and space."[45] Today, the market for this delicious, oily fish is considered to be saturated.

We stopped briefly in Bergen to put Bonnie on a plane for home and set off across the North Sea toward Shetland, following in the heroic wake of the "Shetland Bus." This was the route of small Norwegian fishing vessels that, defying German orders during the Second World War and at great danger to themselves, regularly ferried agents and escapees to and from Shetland. With gales forecast in the North Sea we passed through the Odin gas field at about 4:00 A.M. on August 26 and by mid-day had almost reached Lerwick, Shetland, when it began to blow a murky thirty knots out of the southeast. On our way into the harbor, with visibility less than a quarter of a mile, suddenly a gagging, rotten, dead-fish odor enveloped us.

"Ugh," said Andy Rowe, wrinkling up his nose in mock horror while he shot a sideways glance that suggested he thought Willy had been at the beans again. "Wasn't me," said Willy sweetly. Just then the mists parted a bit to reveal a fleet of ancient ships at anchor. Drawing nearer, we passed among a dozen rusty, beaten-up Russian fish factory ships, all trailing oily slicks astern. The ships were there to buy and process the Shetlanders' herring catch, and they were discharging the smelly gurry waste overboard.

We waited out the gale secured to Lerwick's quay, and, to

On our way into the harbor, with visibility less than a quarter of a mile, suddenly a gagging, rotten, dead-fish odor enveloped us.

pass the time, we rented a car to see the island. Driving south past emerald-green fields dotted with grazing sheep, we stopped near the tiny St. Ninian's Isle and walked across a narrow sand isthmus to view the ruins of its ancient one-room stone church. The isle was named after an Irish missionary: Shetlanders embraced Christianity in the seventh and eighth centuries, just before they were overrun by the Norse expansion into the Atlantic lands. The hoard of silver plate and coins discovered beneath the church may have been evidence of a hurried burial during a Norse raid.[46]

With a fairly good weather forecast in hand —despite a very low barometer—we were off Lerwick's quay at 6:00 A.M. on August 29. The run south from Shetland was easy, marred only by a strong tidal current that at times slowed us to four knots, although with the jib and mainsail up we were moving at more than eight knots through the water. As we passed east of Orkney, I saw beautiful, well-tended farms, and masses of sheep in the fields. I recalled that in Lerwick someone had said to me, "Here in Shetland we're fishermen with small farms; in Orkney they're farmers with small fish boats."

After a long day's run we decided to stop for the night in the harbor at Whitehall on the Orcadian island of Stronsay. The town was very quiet, and the quay was fronted by a row of dour gray stone houses that had a slightly menacing countenance. Rising at 9:00 A.M.

'Here in Shetland we're fishermen with small farms; in Orkney they're farmers with small fish boats.'

The gale in Wick, Scotland

the next day, we looked forward to a two-hour run to Kirkwall, the capital of Orkney, to see the famous Cathedral of St. Magnus, built in 1137 in honor of the Norse earl of Orkney who had been murdered twenty years prior. But when we turned on the radio to get the weather forecast, we were surprised to learn that strong gales would be arriving all across the North Sea in twenty-four hours. I remember hearing a report on the conditions southeast of Iceland. It went something like, "force ten and gusty." Force ten wind means storm strength of about 60 miles per hour. I wondered why the "gusty" mattered.

For our route, the closest strongly protected harbor was Wick, at the northeast corner of Scotland. We shoved off at once for a bouncy run past the racing tides of Pentland Firth, separating Orkney from Scotland. Late in the afternoon we motored into Wick's inner harbor, past three sets of massive, twenty-foot-high stone breakwaters. Securing to the quay with eight lines and all the chafing gear we could rig, we awaited the gale.

The entry in my journal for August 30, 1992 begins, "Thank God for Wick Harbour!" The morning dawned gray and lowering, with a twenty-knot breeze from the southeast. Then the barometer began to drop steeply, and by noon the wind was at forty knots. By 2:00 P.M. it was gusting to fifty-five. The North Sea's waves washed easily over the top of the twenty-foot-high barriers and drenched *Belvedere* with sheet after sheet of water that flew seventy-five feet beyond the seawall and left the boat coated with sand and mashed-up seaweed. When it was over, it looked as if someone had thrown a huge garden salad at the boat.

"John," said Willy, eyeing the mess, "if only you were a little more sensitive and open to the idea of accepting natural foods into your primitive, meat-centered diet, you could probably make it through the winter on this junk—and the sand would provide good roughage."

The rest of *Belvedere*'s 5,000-mile summer was uneventful.

Home Along the Viking Route:

The Hebrides, Faroes, Iceland, and Newfoundland *(1993)*

*T*HE FOLLOWING YEAR, 1993, having completed our voyage to Spitsbergen, I planned to learn about the Norse expansions westward across the Atlantic. It was time to go home, and the "Viking route" beckoned.

The crew that summer included Andy Rowe again and Sam Davenport, a cheerful young law student who replaced Willy Fox, his college roommate. Also aboard on the first part of the voyage were my old friends Jem and Maur Tetley, who had sailed to Norway with us in 1992. They arrived on June 26, and everyone eagerly awaited Maur's excellent cooking. My wife Romayne and son Johnny were also there to see us off. The three of us had just spent a week in Scotland, visiting some of Romayne's cousins, and as soon as we were to depart, Johnny was to fly to Alaska for a summer's job in the salmon fishery.

We dropped down the Firth of Clyde, headed not for the Mull of Kintyre this time, but rather for the Crinan Canal at the north end of the Kintyre Peninsula. This nine-mile cut, with fifteen locks, was opened in 1801. At that time, before railways, there were only a few military roads in the region. It was said that the canal would "not only enable the inhabitants to avoid entirely the very dangerous passage around the Mull of Kintyre, but by affording a ready market for all the productions of the Western Isles, it will invite the people to pursue a variety of kinds of industry, to which they have hitherto been strangers. Above all, it will enable them to supply themselves with salt and coals...."[1] Thus the Crinan Canal, though never a successful speculation for its investors, brought the west coast of Scotland and its outer islands into commercial contact with Glasgow and the Clyde. In 1854, for instance, it carried 33,000 passengers, more than 27,000 sheep, and 2,000 cattle.

As we approached the entrance of the canal in the little town of Ardrishaig, it barely seemed as if there would be enough room for

Belvedere to pass between the lock's walls, but fit we did, and quickly began working through the heavy lock gates. The Crinan is a do-it-yourself canal. We put three of the crew ashore to handle *Belvedere*'s mooring lines, then to crank open the sluice doors and, once the lock had filled and lifted *Belvedere*, to push the heavy counterbalance arms, opening the lock's thick wooden gates. Meanwhile I stood on the bow with a boat hook, keeping us away from the rough stone lock walls and securing the mooring lines. Jem was at the stern, doing the same, and Maur tended the fenders that hung along both rails.

The drill went like this: Andy would steer us into the lock, the crew would close the gates, crank down the sluice doors, and secure the lines ashore, then run ahead to the next gates and open the sluice doors. Once the lock had filled, raising *Belvedere*, the others closed

The Gareloch, on the Firth of Clyde in western Scotland, was Belvedere's *winter home from 1991 to 1993.*

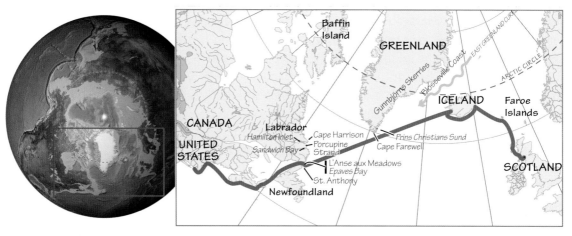

Belvedere's Route
of 1993

the sluice doors, opened the gates, and *Belvedere* would proceed. It was hard work, but it saved us a lot of time that would otherwise have been involved in a long and bouncy slog round the Mull of Kintyre.

At the top of the canal, sixty-four feet above sea level, we entered the summit reach, Cairnbaan, (*white cairn* in Gaelic), a reference to a Bronze Age burial mound nearby. This stretch of the canal receives its water from eight reservoirs in the neighboring hills, and in turn this water fills the locks.[2]

Our descent was spectacular, and of course we operated the locks in reverse, cranking open the sluice doors to lower *Belvedere* and fill the lock ahead of us, swinging the gates open, entering, closing the gates behind us, opening the forward sluice gates to lower *Belvedere*, and so on. We stopped for the night in the canal in a quiet basin surrounded by masses of wildflowers: iris, marguerite, vetch, cow parsley, wild strawberry, Queen Anne's lace, campion, heather, thyme, and ferns. In the peaceful stillness of the evening we enjoyed a lovely view to the northwest, to the ancient Duntrune Castle, one of the oldest inhabited houses in Scotland, and farther, over the Sound of Jura.

The next day, in a near calm, we motored north, along the east coast of the Isle of Jura. At Jura's northern end we passed the Gulf of Corryvreckan, the gut between Jura and Scarba Islands. Looking west, whorls and breakers interrupted the skyline between the islands' bluff headlands. Suddenly the north-flowing tidal current swept us up and carried us along at ten-and-a-half knots over the ground, while whirlpools buffeted *Belvedere* this way and that.

Mariners have always had a healthy respect for the Corryvreckan (*Coirebhreacain* in Gaelic), "the cauldron of Brechan," where legend has it that Prince Brecan, the son of Norway's king, was drowned.[3] And they fear it with good reason, for there can be a huge difference in the height of the waters on the east and west coasts of Scarba and

Jura. This disparity spawns a vicious current that can run as fast as ten miles per hour through the narrows, but it is the seabed that occasionally makes the Corryvreckan very dangerous.[4] My friend Maldwin Drummond, historian and sailor, describes it well: "The sea in the gulf is seldom quiet…. The entrance of the gulf is deep, from 60 to 120 fathoms, and there is little to impede progress. Suddenly the bottom rises to within 15 fathoms of the surface, for a great rock ledge, the Cailleach, or 'the Hag,' near the centre, extends southward from the Scarba shore and interrupts the watery gallop. The torrent has to slide over this obstacle and tumble down the other side, leaving whirlpools and overfalls which can be seen in the quietest of weather."[5] Of course, when a strong wind opposes the tidal current, the milling waters can be terrifying: It "becomes a seething maelstrom of broken whitewater and whirlpools whose roar can be heard miles away. It has claimed many vessels down the centuries, and who shall live and who shall drown is said to be determined by the Cailleach, the witch who controls the race."[6]

Soon we were clear of the Corryvreckan, but not of the strong tidal rips. We carried on north, amid the small islands of the Inner Hebrides, into the Firth of Lorne, with ever more spectacular scenery. We passed Duart Castle, the massive thirteenth-century fortress guarding the entrance to the narrow passage between the Isle of Mull and the mainland. It in turn led us to the cliffs of Ardnamurchan, the westernmost headland of mainland Britain, which, because of its exposure to the west and its strong tidal currents, can be as difficult to

'Who shall live and who shall drown is said to be determined by the Cailleach, the witch who controls the race.'

Pausing in the Crinan Canal—and saving ourselves a bouncy ride round the Mull of Kintyre

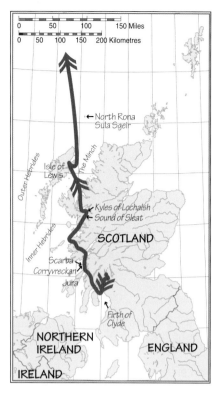

Belvedere's Route in
Scotland, 1993

round as the cape at Stadlandet, Norway's
westernmost promontory. Fortunately the weather was
settled that day. Pushing onward, we motored up the
Sound of Sleat and through the Kyles (narrows) of
Lochalsh, separating the Isle of Skye from the
mainland. Skye's ancient, warped massif, the 3,000-
foot Cuillin Hills, rose in the distant haze above a
brilliant green foreshore.

At once, the familiar gannets, puffins, guillemots,
razorbills, gulls, and terns were all around us. They
seemed a friendly mass, announcing our return to
the cold northern seas. And with each mile of our
northing we pushed farther into waters that a
thousand years ago were under the suzerainty of the
Norsemen. Departing the Kyles, we entered, first,
Inner Sound, and then The Minch. Between twenty-
five and forty-five miles wide, it too is known for its
rapid tidal currents. As one sailor put it, the Minch
"can be a restless bit of sea."[7] Restless or not, it was a
conduit through which the Norsemen traveled on
their way to plunder and to conquer—and later to
settle—in the British Isles.

**'Even the sheeps is
lonely here.'**

In the last decade of the eighth century, Norse raiders swept out
of Scandinavia and down from Shetland and Orkney, which they
had already taken over, to the islands west of mainland Britain. The
Celtic inhabitants, who had been converted to Christianity in the
sixth century by the great Irish monk, St. Columba (*Columcile*, in
Gaelic), were overwhelmed. By the mid-ninth century the Norse had
settled widely in the Hebrides[8] and used their new homesteads as
bases for further raids.

They held the region, which they called *Sudreyjar* (Southern
Islands), until 1266, when the Scottish chieftains gained control of
what *they* called the Western Isles. During the 400 years of Norse
sovereignty a fusion of Norse and Celtic culture developed, and the
result was a cultural florescence that is evident to this day. In fact,
after we had run up The Minch to the town of Stornoway on the Isle
of Lewis, though the town had a northern feel, it wasn't surprising
to hear a couple of customers speaking Gaelic in the post office.

Stornoway, a seaport, fishing port, and market town on the Isle
of Lewis, is the largest town in the Outer Hebrides and has been
called "the metropolis of the Western Isles." Still, as we ran north, we
sensed that the population was thinning out fast. That evening, while

we watched an enormously fat and docile gray seal swimming slowly around the harbor and puffling gently, a man offered me this observation from the quay: "Even the sheeps is lonely here."

Our next stop was to be in the Faroe Islands, 200 miles away, and roughly halfway between Scotland and Iceland. With good weather forecast we left Stornoway the next day, the first of July, at 6:00 A.M. Almost at once we picked up a strong southeasterly breeze that drove us along splendidly, with a good assist from the tidal current. But, as we drew abreast of the Butt of Lewis, the northernmost point of the Isle of Lewis, and of the Outer Hebrides, we found a large swell setting in from the Atlantic. It gave *Belvedere* a lively rolling-and-pitching motion, resulting in a few crashes in the galley and sending several of the crew to their berths.

A few hours later we passed between the tiny and desolate islands of North Rona and Sula Sgeir. These tall specks of storm-swept rock are surely, along with the Flannan Islands and St. Kilda to the southwest, the most remote parts of Britain, and all are home to large colonies of sea birds.[9] Mankind, too, has lived here: until the nineteenth century all were inhabited, or regularly visited. In fact, today, hunters from the Ness of Lewis, the northern tip, travel to Sula Sgeir, as they have for six centuries, to harvest *gugas* (young gannets) and salt them for the winter's food.[10]

The wind finally veered west, giving us a fast run north and pushing us along all night. In the early morning we found fog, but at 8:00 A.M. it lifted suddenly and the cliffs and seabirds of Suðuroy, the southernmost of the Faroes, emerged out of the mist. At noon on July 2 we secured to the quay at the town of Tvøroyri in Trongisvágsfjørður.

I liked the Faroes at once. They are a group of eighteen volcanic basalt islands, comprising only 540 square miles. Rising austerely and dramatically from the ocean, the islands slope from west to east: On the west, layer-cake cliffs, green topped and alive with clouds of birds, open to deeply indented harbors on the east. These islands lie exposed to the sea from all sides, yet their boisterous weather is moderated by the steady warmth of the North Atlantic Drift, which also carries a fertile broth that manifests itself in the incredible richness of life in their surrounding seas.

Isolation is a fair description of these wonderful islands. They are about 200 miles northwest of Shetland, while nearly 300 miles to *their* northwest lies Iceland. In the Faroes, with an estimated

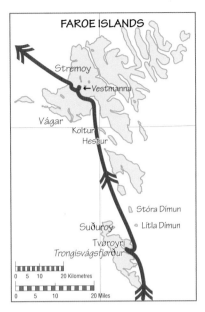

Belvedere's *Route in the Faroe Islands, 1993*

Hunters travel to Sula Sgeir, as they have for six centuries, to harvest gugas (young gannets) and salt them for the winter's food.

population of less than 50,000—smaller than Tromsø, Norway—there is plenty of isolation.

And isolation may well have been what attracted mankind to settle here in the first place. Ascetic Irish monks, eremetical pilgrims, may have been the first human beings to visit these isles. "Life for the Irish sea-pilgrims was not only migratory," remarks Geoffrey Ashe, "but sometimes more migratory than they planned."[11] These anchorites, *peregrinari pro Christo* (wanderers for Christ), are known to have traveled widely in hide-covered open boats, *curraghs*, seeking the solitude of uninhabited islands for a life of prayer and contemplation. It is likely that they lived in severe isolation on all of the outermost skerries of Ireland and the Hebrides.

Isolation may well have been what attracted mankind to settle here in the first place.

It is possible, too, that these islands may have been visited in the mid-sixth century by Brenaind (St. Brendan), the Abbot of Clonfert, during his famous, semifabulous seven-year voyage in search of the *paradisum terrestre*. This is recorded in the *Life of Saint Brendan* and in the Irish *immrama* (heroic sea narrative), the *Navigatio Sancti Brendani Abbatis*, but St. Brendan's narrative may well have been conflated with other Irish monks' voyages that took place a century or two later.[12] Nevertheless, the anchorites probably brought sheep with them to these islands; the *Navigatio* mentions an Isle of Sheep, a description that seems to fit the Faroes, and in fact the word "Faroe" means "sheep islands" in Old Norse.[13]

And in A.D. 825 Dicuil, the learned Irish monk and geographer, who was a resident in the Frankish court during the reign of Charlemagne and after, described the islands in his monumental work, *De Mensura Orbis Terrae (On Measuring the Earth)*: "There are many other islands in the ocean to the north of Britain which can be reached from the northernmost British Isles in two days' and two nights' direct sailing.... On these islands hermits, who have sailed from our Scotia [Ireland] have lived for roughly a hundred years." He added, "Now, because of Norse pirates, they are empty of anchorites, but full of innumerable sheep and a great many different kinds of seafowl."[14] Recently, pollen analysis has confirmed that oats were grown during a seventh-century, pre-Norse occupation of the islands.[15]

The Norse, who instead grew barley, arrived soon after A.D. 800. The *Færeyingasaga*, a compilation of extracts from other sagas, states that Grimur Kamban was the first Norse settler, and the historian Gwyn Jones believes that he probably arrived via Ireland or the Hebrides. It is said that he and others may have fled there from Norway, escaping the tyranny of King Harold Fairhair, but population pressure in Norway may also have been an important factor in their decision to emigrate. The Faroese converted to Christianity around A.D. 1000 and came under the rule of Norway about 1035. Later, the Kingdom of Denmark absorbed them, where they remain today as an autonomous, self-governing region of the Kingdom. The Faroese rely primarily on fishing and sheep-raising for their livelihood.

We found Tvøroryi to be a friendly place; a very tidy community, with neat houses topped by red, green, and black corrugated metal roofs and dominated by the central church. But the theme of isolation was also evident in the grocery store. "Greens are like gold dust here," Maur muttered, "and the miserable cauliflowers are exorbitant!"

What had my attention, however, was the next day's planned run to the island of Streymoy. The Faroes are famous (or, more precisely, *infamous*) for the very strong tidal currents that sweep among the islands. The sailing directions say, for instance, that "there are numerous severe and very severe races which should be treated with great respect in all but the calmest weather. They pose the greatest problem for an approach in bad visibility."[16]

The theme of isolation was also evident in the grocery store. 'Greens are like gold dust here.'

Because our route would indeed lead us among the islands, in Tvøroryi I bought a copy of *Streymkort fyri Føroyar, Tidal Current around The Faroe Islands,* a booklet that shows in graphic and frightening detail the relative strength and dangers of the currents for each hour of the tidal cycle. As if this weren't gut-wrenching enough, there is a page (in English) entitled "A happening east of Sandoy":

> In the middle of the twenties it happened that a steamship under way to Iceland touched at Tórshavn for a little repair. Leaving Tórshavn the captain decided that his ship was too large to turn starboard over at the south end of Streymoy, so he would go east of Sandoy, and well clear there, he would turn starboard over . . . The weather was fine, a little breeze from southeast, but the southeast going current was in very bad spirit, and before the captain thought about it, they were in a very critical situation. In the afternoon the steamship again arrived at Tórshavn, but this time without funnel and boats. The ship was about 4,000 tons deadweight. The engine amidship, as the custom of the time was.[17]

Obviously, with that sort of warning we wanted to make very sure of our departure time before heading to Streymoy. Accordingly, Andy, Jem, and I independently worked out the time of the moon's meridian passage and checked it against the British Admiralty Pilot book. Then, with this in hand, I visited the Tvøroryi harbormaster. He confirmed our calculations, suggesting that we should leave the harbor at 1:00 P.M.

We got it wrong and so did he.

Avoiding a hardy water-skier, we motored out of Trongisvágsfjørður and headed northwest in a near calm, over flat seas and through the passage between Suðuroy and the 1,350-foot rock stack, Lítla Dímun. As we admired the stunning scenery of sheer cliffs topped with brilliant green slopes, suddenly we found ourselves swept along on the tide, carried at twelve knots over the ground, although our speed through the water was actually only about five.

Just then the helmsman spotted a fishing buoy. He wanted to check the strength of the tidal stream by observing its turbulent "tail." None of us was aware of how fast that current was running. Right away we were carried down over the float, and its line immediately hung up on our rudderpost, and then our propeller fouled it and wound it right up.

Belvedere was sucked into a whirlpool and thrown this way and that by steep ten- to twelve-foot seas.

Suddenly we were in a very dangerous situation. That warp, being quickly wound around the propeller and constricting onto the shaft, could easily have stopped the engine cold, just as we were being swept into the most dangerous part of the tidal rip. I knew that the line-cutting "spurs" that I had installed on *Belvedere's* propeller shaft in 1990 for just such an event would make quick work of that polypropylene line, but none of us wanted to cut a fisherman's warp, so Sam Davenport and I raced to the stern with a boat hook, fished the line up on both port and starboard rails, quickly tied the warp back together, and threw it overboard just as a thousand bits of finely masticated plastic line hit the surface.

Less than a minute later, thinking all was now well, and congratulating myself on saving a fisherman's gear, I looked up in horror at the horizon ahead. It was all rough waves and frightening standing overfalls. At once we were swept right into it. With Andy fighting the wheel, steering at a *right angle* to our drift and gunning the engine to get away, *Belvedere* was sucked into a whirlpool and thrown this way and that by steep ten- to twelve-foot seas that sloshed across the deck. The waves rolled us forty-six degrees to starboard and thirty-six to port, throwing everything around below decks and spewing flour across the galley. We motored out of it with the engine at maximum revolutions. I took the wheel while the crew set a steadying sail. To achieve our course over the ground, I had to steer thirty-five degrees to the right—and by that time we were already out of the worst part!

But the crew stood up to it well and kept cool heads during the fracas. Everyone pitched in and exercised a lot of initiative and common sense. "Golly, that was fun. Why don't we try it again?" Sam Davenport deadpanned as we picked up the litter in the galley. "Phew!" and "Wow!" were about all the rest of us could say, but I could tell that our "shake down" period was now complete, and we would all work confidently together.

As Lítla Dímun and its larger companion, Stóra Dímun, quickly sank astern, the current flushed us along with diminishing strength, past Skúvoy and Sandoy, then past Hestur and Koltur (horse and colt), whose summit, Kolturshamar, rose 1,568 feet into the mist. The islands were bluff and lime-green, with sheep grazing high on the slopes and even a tiny farm clinging to the edge of a precipice. Then we moved between Vágar and Streymoy and entered the snug protection of Vestmanna harbor, where we fit neatly between a fishing boat, which the crew kindly moved for us, and a couple of large, rusty, laid-up deep-sea trawlers.

Lítla Dímun, Faroe Islands, where Belvedere *was caught in the frightening tidal race*

Vestmanna is designated a "winter harbor," and it is easy to understand why—it is bulletproof. Completely enclosed among high cliffs, it is an ideal place to wait for a favorable patch of weather for crossing to eastern Iceland. Watching the fishermen move about in their double-ended lapstrake boats with high stems and sternposts, we could easily understand their descent from their Norse ancestors of a thousand years ago. And seeing the flocks of sheep grazing on the steep cliff faces and on the green tops, we felt the close connection the Faroese have with the Old Norse way of life.

But the sight of those trawlers was sad—sad to see good ships rusting away, but sadder still to understand the reason: The North Atlantic is being fished out by increasingly large vessels and sophisticated technology. In fact, all throughout the 1990s, from Norway to Great Britain, Iceland, Greenland, Labrador, Newfoundland, Nova Scotia, and New England—wherever we have sailed—the story has been the same: mankind is sweeping up the richness of the oceans and leaving lifeless, sterile seas behind.

In the Faroes, for instance, the fishing fleets worked mainly in foreign waters until the 1970s. But with the advent of the general extension of fishing territories (the "200-mile limit") by most nations, and because of the Law of the Sea Convention of 1983, national fishing fleets have generally kept within their own waters, putting great pressure on home fishing grounds. Regrettably, this problem was made worse by various nations' subsidies to the fleets in one form or another (such as cheap fuel, tax relief, or price supports, for instance), and the result has been a decline in catches everywhere. One darling of fisheries management was, as we have seen, salmon farming, but the price of salmon collapsed because of over-production after all the North Atlantic fishing nations jumped into the renewable form of fishing.

In the last decade, however, several countries have put in place more far-sighted and intelligent fisheries policies that include area closures, limited entry to the fishery, size limits, regulated fishing seasons, and boat-and-license buy-back programs—but at the cost of considerable personal pain for the fishermen. Perhaps the new policies are working, because herring and cod catches in the Faroes have increased.[18]

The Faroese also face another international fisheries problem: opposition to their traditional annual hunt for long-finned pilot whales. Several political groups want them to abandon their annual harvest of these small whales, but the Faroese consider these protests to be a thoroughly unwelcome and illegal intrusion by outsiders into their domestic affairs and ancient lifeways.

The Faroese hunt for pilot whales, the *grind*, has gone on for a thousand years, since the Norse colonization of the islands. The islands are divided into seven whaling districts, each with a whaling foreman who is responsible for organizing the whale drives. When the whalemen spot a school of these pilot whales, they put out in small boats and herd the whales into a shallow bay, where the whales are killed and butchered. The whaling effort involves virtually everyone in the community, and the meat and blubber are divided equally among the inhabitants of the district according to a complex, traditional sharing system that is unique to each whaling district. To this day the hunt is important for the annual meat supply, but it also has strong cultural meaning for the Faroese, who regard the *grind* as

Mankind is sweeping up the richness of the oceans and leaving lifeless, sterile seas behind.

a central element in maintaining their unique culture.[19]

Recently, Sea Shepherd International, the International Fund for Animal Welfare,[20] and other animal rights groups have tried to force the Faroese to end the *grind* because, they say, it is both needlessly cruel and it reduces an endangered species. The Faroese contend that the *grind* is deeply rooted in their history. They state, truthfully, that it is a traditional, communal, and noncommercial hunt. They also state, correctly, that the whales are not endangered, pointing to the fact that the Scientific Committee of the International Whaling Commission estimates that there are 778,000 pilot whales in the northeast Atlantic; hence their small catch is not a factor in the health of the pilot whale population. Records dating back to 1584 reveal an average catch of 850 whales per year. The Faroese have recently taken strong action to ensure that the whales are dispatched as quickly and painlessly as possible.[21]

While we waited in Vestmanna to cross the nearly 300 miles to Iceland, I scanned the weather charts with increasing unease, because the conditions definitely looked unsettled. Unable to make up my mind about when to leave, each day I walked a mile and a half through drizzle and low clouds to the only public telephone in town. Feeding a fistful of ten kroner coins into the slot, I called Bob Rice in Massachusetts. Bob is a man whom I deeply respect. He is a highly knowledgeable meteorologist who was at that time working at a

The harbor of Vestmanna in the Faroe Islands. We waited here for a weather window that would allow us to cross to Iceland.

private weather service. "John, the high pressure system that usually is centered on the Azores is flanked by a low over Iceland," Bob said, adding, "and this is followed by another low that came out of Hudson Bay and stalled as it neared Iceland. The weather won't be great. Get some sleep."[22]

After several daily calls, masses of ten kroner coins, and little change in the weather pattern, at last, his advice was, "You'll have to make the best of a bad situation and leave the Faroes by noon GMT on Tuesday, July 6. That way, you'll have about forty hours of relatively benign, but unsettled, weather between the passage of two low-pressure systems. Then those systems will organize, producing strong gales by 6:00 P.M. on Thursday. Otherwise," he added, "you might find yourselves bottled up in the Faroes for a couple of weeks."

In the middle of the fjord, a violent tidal rip tore along, filling the water with whitecaps.

At *Belvedere*'s usual speed, about seven knots, a forty-hour weather window would only allow us to get to the nearest port-of-entry in Iceland—Seyðisfjörður—a fishing harbor at the eastern end of the island, so Seyðisfjörður it had to be. With something of a pit in my stomach I talked it over with the crew, but we all agreed to give it a try. A light northwesterly was blowing as we motored out of the harbor and turned west into the fjord separating Streymoy from Vágar. Clinging to the north shore to gain the advantage of a tidal eddy there, we made our way toward the North Atlantic. Here the cliffs rose majestically, straight from the sea. On the islands sheep and lambs stood impassively, punctuating the green fields on the steep slopes, while, in the middle of the fjord, a violent tidal rip tore along, filling the water with whitecaps.

At first we made only about four knots and rolled quite a bit, but as we pressed out into the gloom, the cliffs disappeared in the mist behind us, and the foul current vanished, while a nine-foot swell and thirty knots of wind took its place. We bounced around for about twelve hours on that gray and evil-looking sea under low, murky clouds. But then the wind backed a bit, allowing us to set not only a double-reefed mainsail, but also the jib and staysail.

Almost exactly forty hours from Vestmanna the looming, snow-topped mountains of Seyðisfjörður, Iceland, came out of the mist. We passed the fjord's heads, Skalnes and Boganes, then rounded up to take in the sails, and on deck, the wet, chilly forty-degree wind seemed to cut right through us. As we motored up the magnificent fjord, a ten-mile glacial gash rimmed by mesa-like mountains, we were struck by the fact that, although the slope of the green cliffs lining the fjord was gentler than in the Faroes, the snow-topped mountains were much higher.

Once past Brimnes Light, the British Admiralty sailing directions advised keeping a lookout for a dangerous wreck, which I later discovered was *El Grillo*. A Panamanian-flagged British tanker, she was on Admiralty service as a fleet oiler when she was heavily damaged by German bombs and quickly scuttled on February 10, 1944.[23] We failed to find her, but only after we reached the customs dock at the head of the fjord did we learn that the wreck is in forty fathoms (240 feet) of water and is only dangerous to a trawler with gear down.

In sheeting rain we crossed the harbor and secured to the dock to which the police had directed us. Almost at once the wind began to build, while paradoxically so did the barometer, to 1,020 millibars. The next day, July 8, I again phoned Bob Rice in Massachusetts to thank him for his advice on the passage to Iceland and to ask his opinion about our future movements. When I told him about the high barometer, he replied, "That's not a good sign. It means that a high is moving in close to the low that's tracking in from Greenland. You'll definitely have some strong winds. *Stay put!*"

Sure enough, the wind continued to build until it was a steady forty knots in the harbor. Twenty-four hours later it was gusting to fifty-four knots. We were on the windward side of a nice smooth-sided wooden dock but were banging against it pretty hard. There was no place we could move to in the harbor, and we already had all our fenders down, but we came up with the idea of setting an anchor at ninety degrees from the bow to relieve some of the strain. Three of the crew wrestled their way into thermal deck suits and set a seventy-five-pound anchor from the dinghy, about 100 yards out. It worked pretty well, and as soon we took strain on the line with the windlass, we rode out the next two days of the gale quite easily.

During the gale, spume flew across the harbor, and our walks ashore were conducted in full rain gear; sometimes we were bent nearly double. Nevertheless, we were impressed by the greenery on the slopes—mosses and wildflowers—and by the number of waterfalls that cascaded in wispy strands from the cliff tops. Even more impressive, when the gusts of wind hit them, they blew the skeins of water vertically, right back up the cliff faces. We had never before seen a *rising* waterfall.

The gale blew itself out in the early hours of July 12, and we were off from the dock in Seyðisfjörður at 6:00 A.M. As we ran out of the fjord we were amazed to find that the snow line, which had hitherto been near the tops of the mountains, now was only a few hundred feet above sea level, giving the whole place a decidedly wintry look.

Another call to Bob Rice had revealed that we could probably count on a forty-eight-hour period of settled weather once the gale had blown through. This was good news, for it would allow us to try for Keflavik in southwestern Iceland. Once at sea, however, there

'A high is moving in close to the low that's tracking in from Greenland. Stay put!'

wouldn't be many choices of harbors. In case things took a turn for the worse we would probably just have to keep on going. In fact, in the 150 miles between Höfn, in southeastern Iceland, and Vestmannæyjar (the Vestmanna Islands), off the south coast, there are no harbors at all—and from there to Keflavik there would be nothing suitable for *Belvedere.*

Outside Seyðisfjörður's heads, a strong swell set in from the northeast, but soon it was on our stern as we turned to starboard and proceeded down the coast. Later the swell died down and the sun broke through the clouds, the first sun we had seen in two weeks. The wind cooperated too, and we began to surge along with all sails drawing nicely.

Moving along the handsome, rugged coast of southeastern Iceland, we passed the outlying islands of Papey and Papos. *Papar* (priests) is the name the early Norse gave to the Irish anchorites who, as in the Faroes, had preceded them here; thus Papey and Papos are places where holy men must have lived. In fact, Papey's silhouette is remarkably similar to the holy island of Iona in western Scotland, where St. Columba is said to have brought Christianity to Scotland from Ireland, founding a monastery there.[24]

On the rugged south coast of Iceland

In fact, "Vestmanna," ("Westmen," or Irishmen) is a Norse place name found in both the Faroes and Iceland, as I have mentioned. But beyond these place names there is no physical evidence of an Irish presence, with the exception of some curious incised crosses that are found on the walls of caves, especially in the Vestmanna Islands.

These appear to be similar in style and proportion to incised crosses that are found on Iona. This cross form is thought to have disappeared by the early ninth century—that is, before the arrival of the Norse in Iceland.[25]

But Europeans may have known of Iceland even before the *Papar* arrived. Pythias of Massilia (Marseille), a Greek cosmographer of the third century B.C., wrote of a northern land called Thule, which lay six days' sail north of the British Isles, and one day farther lay a congealed sea. He also stated that at the summer solstice there was little night; nevertheless, his fragmentary writings are only found in secondhand sources at best, and they include some information that would disqualify Iceland.[26]

On the other hand, it is quite possible that the Romans had some knowledge of the seas west of Britain and of Iceland. Tantalizingly enough, in 1930 fishermen found a fragment of Roman pottery in a trawler's net on Porcupine Bank, 140 miles west of Ireland.[27] And three Roman copper coins, dating from the reigns of Aurelian, Probus, and Diocletian (A.D. 270 to 305), were discovered among Norse ruins in Bragdhavellir in southeast Iceland.[28] Referring to the coins, the Icelandic scholar Magnus Magnusson notes, "This time-span covers the period when the Roman navy in Britain was at its height under the command of Carausius. It is not unreasonable to wonder whether the coins were left by sailors on a long-range patrol boat."[29]

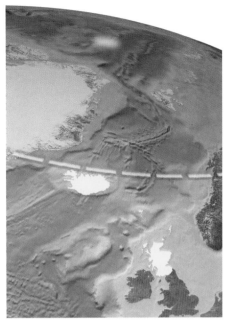

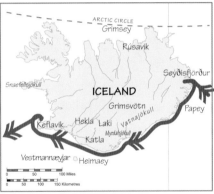

Belvedere's Route in Iceland, 1993

Interestingly enough, Mausaeus Carausius had put together a fleet for the Romans to help suppress Saxon pirates in the North Sea and English Channel; but instead, he then sided with the pirates and set up an independent state in Britain.[30] It seems to me that a storm-driven, shipwrecked boat is equally likely to be the origin of the coins. As one can easily imagine, a pre-Roman and Roman knowledge of Iceland is a matter of much conjecture and debate, but it should also be remembered that the coins were found on the coasts of Iceland that lay closest to Britain.

There is little doubt, however, that Irish monks lived in Iceland before the Norse. The monk Dicuil, who, in A.D. 825 wrote of the Faroes, also wrote of Iceland:

> It is now thirty years since clerics, who had lived on the island from the first of February to the first of August, told me that not only at the summer solstice but in the days round about it the

sun setting in the evening hides itself as though behind a small hill in such a way that there was no darkness in that very small space of time and a man can do whatever he wished as though the sun were still there, even remove lice from his shirt, and, if one stood on a mountain top, the sun perhaps would still be visible to him.[31]

The northern point of Iceland, the island of Grimsey, lies on the Arctic Circle; hence Dicuil's report has considerable veracity.

Compelling information is also found in the *Immrama* of the Irish saints. The most famous of these is the account of Saint Brendan's voyages. Whether it was written in St. Brendan's time or several centuries later is not important: the fact is that the narrative reports a mountain spewing fire and smoke.

Indeed, aboard *Belvedere* we passed along the black lava sand beaches west of Höfn and later spotted the island of Heimaey in the

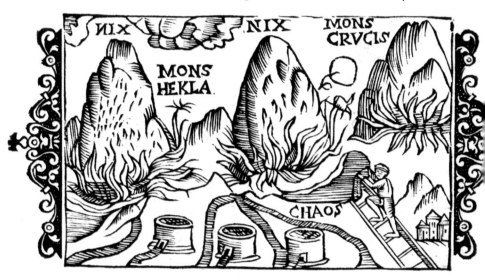

Iceland's volcanoes— from Olaus Magnus, Historia de Gentibus Septentrionalibus, *Rome, 1555*

Vestmanna Islands. Its volcano last erupted in 1973 and the lava nearly buried its town. Farther away, and to the southwest, lay Surtsey, one of the earth's newest islands, which had risen from the sea in a spectacular eruption ten years earlier.

I could well see the truth in the *Navigatio Sancti Brendani Abbatis*. Iceland, of course, sits atop the Mid-Atlantic ridge—indeed was created by it—because pieces of the earth's crust, the North American Plate and the Eurasian Plate, separate under the Atlantic and allow magma to well up from the center of the earth. Iceland has been described as, "a cyclopean fistful of volcanic slag thrust up out of the North Atlantic."[32] There is truth in this, for in Iceland there are about 200 volcanoes, 30 of which have erupted in the last 1,200 years. Hekla is Iceland's most notorious volcano, known in the Middle Ages as the realm of the damned.

But on June 8, 1783, the Laki fissure erupted. "This was the most violent, extensive and prolonged volcanic episode which has occurred in the northern hemisphere during the modern era," according to the geographers John Grattan and Mark Brayshay. The eruption lasted from June to the following February, destroying much of Iceland's pastures, and killing three-quarters of the sheep and horses, half of the cattle, and probably a quarter of the human population—or about 10,000 people. Its tephra and gasses showered western Europe, killing vegetation and bringing about the "greatest decrease in surface air temperature caused by a volcanic eruption in recent history."[33]

And the Laki eruption's effects did not end there. Its "sulphurous gasses…combined with water in the upper atmosphere to form crystals of acid that reflected solar radiation back into space," and girdled the earth, giving Japan "the summer that never came," and reaching even northern Alaska. William A. Oquilluk, an Eskimo from Bering Strait, recorded his people's folktale: "Just as the Eskimos were getting ready to collect the meat and fish and berries during the critical but brief hunting season [*sic*]. But just as summer began to dawn, the north wind came, bringing weather so bitter that the hunting season ended before it could begin. Of all the villagers in that region only about ten survived." Two who did make it through to the next summer survived by eating the hide covering of a sealskin boat. Dendrochronological analyses (tree-ring dating studies) have confirmed the existence of the terrible summer of 1783 in northern Alaska.[34]

But as we passed Vatnajökull, the third largest icecap in the world, which completely covers the Grímsvötn volcano, I had no idea how dangerous these Icelandic volcanoes could be. Three years after our voyage, in 1996, a fissure between Grímsvötn and the nearby Bardarbunga volcano opened and erupted for two weeks. Its gasses and red-hot magma melted the overlying glacier, creating a *jökulhlaup*, a roaring sub-glacial river that raced thirty miles under the ice to its margin, carrying thirty-foot-high blocks of ice as far as three miles beyond. For a short time it spewed out water at a rate of 1.6 million cubic feet per second, equal to the flow of the second largest river on earth, the Congo.[35]

Then on July 17 and 18, 1999, the Katla volcano, beneath the Myrdalsjökull icecap, blew up, creating a depression nearly a mile wide and more than 150 feet deep. The *jökulhlaup* surged out, tearing down power lines and flushing blocks of ice more than four miles out to sea. At its peak the volume of flow was twice as great as the Nile's.[36]

Not long after we passed Vatnajökull, in Rekyavík I heard an Icelandic woman say, "We come from a place where you might not be here in a week. It makes you very humble."

'This was the most violent, extensive and prolonged volcanic episode which has occurred in the northern hemisphere.'

∼

Knowledge of Iceland must have been abroad in the Norse world of the ninth century because of the activities of the Irish holy men. According to the *Íslendingabók (Book of the Icelanders)* and Iceland's *Landnámabók (Book of Settlements)*, when the first settlers arrived on the island, the monks left quickly, never to return. In any case, the first Norse visitors may have arrived after about A.D. 870, and Ari the Wise, who wrote the *Íslendingabók*, mentions that the Norse found Irish religious articles (croziers, books, and bells) when they arrived. One account of the first settlements reports that a group led by Naddodd, sailing from Norway to the Faroes, missed those islands and fetched up in Iceland. Another report states that Gardar Svavarsson, a Swede, followed him and built a house on the northern coast at Húsavík. A few Norwegian immigrants may have gone to Iceland to escape King Harold Fairhair's tyranny, but most probably went there because they saw opportunities: their motive was settlement, not raiding or trading.

Some of the Norse probably emigrated from Ireland too, from whence, after about A.D. 865, the Irish, rising up, began to expel them.[37] And while the leaders of the immigration were certainly Scandinavian, there was also a large Irish element among them— Celts who were taken there as slaves or wives. In fact, the blood groups of today's Icelandic and Irish populations are remarkably similar, and somewhat distinct from those of the Norwegians.[38] Some Y-chromosome DNA studies suggest that 20 to 25 percent of the early Icelandic population may have been Celtic.[39]

And there is much Irish influence in Icelandic poetry and sagas. In fact, it has been said that the Icelandic passion for creating and recording poetical historical sagas grew, not from their Norse background, but rather from their Celtic ancestral traditions, which originated from Irish wives and slaves.[40] In fact, in the tenth and eleventh centuries Iceland was the cultural center of Scandinavia, possibly due in part to its Celtic influences.

By about A.D. 930 the island was fully settled. The leaders immigrated to Iceland for several reasons. Because of a population surge in Norway, by about A.D. 800 free arable land there was scarce. The historian Gwyn Jones puts it succinctly, "A number of needs, pressures and desires had come together at the right time: political compulsions and economic dissatisfactions, personal ambitions, and our human desire for the good things of life."[41] To reach the new lands the Norse obviously needed seaworthy sailing boats, and the *knörr* had come of age. A beamy cargo ship with plenty of freeboard that allowed it to carry people, goods, and livestock, the knörr was seaworthy and spacious.

The blood groups of today's Icelandic and Irish populations are remarkably similar, and somewhat distinct from those of the Norwegians.

Of equal importance was the Norse worldview, which comprised an inner sea ringed by land;[42] hence, to them, there *must* have been land available to the west. The Norse expansion took place from about A.D. 800 to 1300, a span of time when temperatures lengthened the growing season and reduced the amount of sea ice in the northern hemisphere. And lastly, political strife in Norway may have driven them to leave—rather than to become subjects of King Harold Fairhair, who partially consolidated Norway under his brutal rule.[43] "To be sure, this caused sorrowing and pain among the chieftans he displaced, and his methods were certainly not gentle," cautions the historian Kirsten Seaver, "but neither he nor [his son] Eirík Bloodaxe was unusually brutal in an age notable for physical violence."[44]

These thoughts were on my mind as we worked our way westward along the southern coast of Iceland toward the safety of Keflavik's harbor.

We rounded the high concrete breakwater in Keflavík's bulwark-protected harbor, near the southwesternmost point of Iceland, at 4:00 A.M. on July 14. Once we were secure to the quay, we began a flurry of preparations (changing engine oil, buying fuel and provisions, doing laundry, taking on fresh water) for what I had planned to be the next leg of our voyage—a hop of more than 600 miles to southern Greenland.

But Greenland, in fact, is a lot closer to Iceland than that: it is less than 300 miles from Iceland's northwestern peninsula to the Ammassalik region of East Greenland, and closer still to Greenland's Blosseville coast. On the Blosseville coast the highest mountain rises to more than 12,000 feet, and the glaciers behind are visible for a great distance at sea. About A.D. 860 or 870, Gunnbjörn Ulf-Kråkuson (Ulf the Crow's son) may have been the first European to see Greenland. A storm drove him far to the west of Iceland, where he saw a group of islands. For many centuries they were called Gunnbjarnarsker (Gunnbjörn's Skerries). In 978, with good land in short supply in Iceland too, Hrólfr Thorbjarnarson and Snaebjörn Holmsteinsson led a group to Gunnbjörn's Skerries and attempted to settle there, on what was a severely inhospitable coast.[45] As the Norse scholars Magnus Magnusson and Hermann Pálsson put it, "Trouble broke out among the members of the expedition, culminating in murder, after which the survivors returned to Iceland to face a savage vengeance."[46]

And, most significantly for the history of North America, it was the knowledge of Gunnbjörn's Skerries that drew Eiríkr rauði Thorvaldsson to Greenland. "Eirík the Red, a red-headed, red-bearded, and on occasion red-handed man,"[47] who "seems to have had a nose for trouble," was expelled from Norway with his father,

Thorvaldr Asvaldsson, because of "some killings" and blood feuds. He reached northwest Iceland in the latter part of the tenth century, but there his violence and manslaughter continued, and about A.D. 981 or 982 he was sentenced by the regional assembly to "lesser outlawry"[48] and banished for three years.[49] "If a lesser outlaw ... failed to leave the country within three years, he became a full outlaw," writes the historian Jesse Byock. "A full outlaw was denied all assistance in Iceland; he was not to be harboured by anyone, nor could he be helped to leave the country. In effect, this punishment was tantamount to a death sentence, for [an outlaw] could be killed with impunity."[50]

As *Eiríks Saga Rauða (Eirík the Red's Saga)* relates, with Norway closed to him, he chose to explore the only place available: the land Gunnbjörn had seen. Eirík sailed west and spent three years investigating the fjords of West Greenland, and when he returned to Iceland about A.D. 984 he made arrangements to found a colony in Greenland.

As a recent article in *The Economist* titled "A Thousand Years of Con-Tricks" described it: "The millennium began with a brilliant feat of creative marketing. A Northman known as Erik the Red had discovered an Atlantic island almost completely covered by snow and ice. Hand on heart, like any estate agent, he described it as a desirable residence ... including fertile farmland and a mild climate. A con it was. Numbers of people were beguiled into going there to set up a colony. It did not last. Erik's fertile prose did. You will find the island in any atlas, named as he named it: Greenland."[51]

That is unfair and inaccurate. Eirík's immigration took place during a time when the northern hemisphere's climate was warmer than at present.[52] In fact, he found the inner fjords of western Greenland to be fertile and suitable for grazing livestock, as they are today—to say nothing of the wealth of birds, fish, and sea mammals there. His Greenland colony survived for 500 years.

About 985 or 986 Eirík returned to Greenland, leading a flotilla of twenty-five boats of which fourteen are said to have reached Greenland. Some of the fleet may have been lost and some may have turned back. Eirík probably sailed northwest across Denmark Strait, using Snæfellsjökull, the great glacier on Iceland's Snæfellsnes peninsula, as a stern mark. Most probably he headed for the Blosseville coast of Greenland and sighted the blue glacier, *Blåserkr* (Blue Shirt). This glacier was later called *Hvítserkr* (White Shirt), and it seems to me that the name-change may have come about because Eirík sailed during a period of climatic warming, which probably exposed the glacier's blue ice; later, after the climate had deteriorated, it would have carried a mantle of snow.

From a point halfway into Denmark Strait it is only about eighty miles to Iceland or Greenland, and during times of exceptional visibility and refraction—the *hillingar* (upheaving) effect—both may have been visible simultaneously. [53] In fact, with its coastal mountains rising in one place to more than 12,000 feet, the Blosseville coast might have been visible from as many as 150 miles. Then Eirík would have followed the coast southward to *Hvarf* ("turning point")— Kap Farvel (Cape Farewell), the southernmost point of Greenland— at last turning west and then north for a short run up the coast, to the deep and fertile fjords of southwest Greenland.

'Do not under any circumstances attempt to approach the southern coast of Greenland.'

~

I planned to cut the corner. I hoped to head directly for Prins Christians Sund, the east-west fjord behind Cape Farewell. I knew that the only impediments to my plan would be weather or the presence of ice on the east coast of Greenland. The East Greenland Current, flowing south out of the Arctic Ocean, carries quantities of heavy polar pack ice (*storis*) along with it. This *storis* can be very dangerous indeed: it is often very thick and hard, having survived several summers' melting, and, to make matters worse, it is usually heaving up and down in the sea swell and could easily crush a boat.

To take advantage of the best weather of the year in a high-latitude crossing of the Atlantic, a sailor is basically faced with the inconvenient situation that the best of the ice season always lags behind the best of the weather season. In some years it can take quite a long time for the *storis* to retreat up the East Greenland coast. So, heading there "blind" would have been foolish. I hiked up to the Keflavík Post Office and phoned Ice Central in the Danish Meteorological Institute at Narsarsuaq, in southern Greenland. The news wasn't good. "Do not under any circumstances attempt to approach the southern coast of Greenland," came the crackling voice on the telephone. "I repeat, it would be very dangerous." As I will explain later, I had been in *storis* before, in 1989, off southwest Greenland, and it had been an unsettling experience, to say the least, so I didn't have any trouble taking his advice.

~

It turned out that not only was there a thirty-mile-wide band of *storis* on the east coast, but it went right round Cape Farewell and a couple of hundred miles up the west coast as well. It was obvious that, unless I chose to spend a lot of time at sea keeping well clear of Cape Farewell (a notoriously nasty place for storms) and then moving several hundred miles north into Davis Strait, I had better scrub the idea of seeing Greenland in 1993.

Belvedere in Keflavik, Iceland, with the U.S. Coast Guard icebreaker Polar Sea. *The Polar Sea's commander, Captain Lawson Brigham, is in the foreground. Aboard her, in company with the Canadian icebreaker* Louis S. St. Laurent, *Brigham later achieved the first surface traverse of the Arctic Ocean, from the Bering Sea to the Greenland Sea, via the North Pole.*

I was digesting this information while I walked back to the harbor, just in time to see the huge red bulk of the U.S. Coast Guard icebreaker *Polar Sea* (one of the two most powerful icebreakers in the United States fleet) maneuvering onto the quay. The *Polar Sea* was under the command of my old friend Captain Lawson Brigham, who is both a skillful northern mariner and a widely published scholar of the North. Soon I was aboard, and Lawson confirmed Ice Central's advice. "You're right, John. I wouldn't try it this year. That *storis* is awfully heavy. You could wait here for a month to see if it changes, but by then you'll probably be in an autumn weather pattern, and the going could be rough." I agreed with him; then and there I discarded what was to have been my millennial *homage* to Eirík the Red.

With Greenland out, about the only real option was to head directly for northern Newfoundland, so we hauled out a new set of charts and began to revise our plans. It would be about 1,200 miles from Keflavík to St. Anthony, Newfoundland, and our track would take us somewhat more than 100 miles south of Cape Farewell, "the cradle of storms," so we had to plan carefully. I walked back to the post office and yet again phoned Bob Rice in Massachusetts. "How long will it take you to cross in reasonable conditions, John?" he asked. "About seven days, I guess. Maybe seven and a half," I offered.

"Well, for once this summer, you've gotten lucky. I estimate that in about thirty-six hours the weather will moderate over the northwestern North Atlantic, and it should stay fairly well settled for about a week." That was good news. I talked it over with the crew, and we agreed to be ready to leave before midnight on July 15.

The decision made, I now had some time on my hands, so I set off with two Icelandic friends, Oli and Helge Johnsson to visit Þingvellir (*Thingvellir*, "The Plains of the Assembly"). This is the great series of fissures and lava fields in southwest Iceland, where the *Alþing (Althing)*—the Icelandic General Assembly—met a thousand years ago. About twenty-five miles from Reykavík, Þingvellir is another artifact of the crustal movement of the Mid-Atlantic Ridge, the plates of which are moving apart and thus have created the vale where the ancient parliament was established in A.D. 930 on the bank of the Öxará (Axe River). The river was named, it is said, because an axe was thrown into its waters to underscore the fact that the assembly was to be peaceful and without weapons.[54]

By that date, the "Age of Settlement" (land taking) was over: all good land had been claimed, and it had been cleared of wood and the soil had been degraded.[55] In fact, only about 20 percent of the island's 40,000 square miles was usable for crops and pastures, and the population of Iceland is estimated to have stood then somewhere between 20,000 and 45,000 souls. Social stability was needed, and Þingvellir was the place where the *goðar* (chieftain-priests) came together to settle disputes. Consequently, Iceland has been called the first American republic,[56] but it was not a democratic republic in the modern sense of the word; rather it was a plutocracy, wherein the landholders, the *goðar*, met to maintain civil order. Because the code of laws was not put into writing until early in the twelfth century, at each assembly the *lögsögumaður* (law-speaker), who held his appointment for three years, would recite one-third of the laws from memory. Looking up at Lögberg (Law Rock), the raw lava wall from which the law-speaker addressed the *Alþing*, it didn't seem very long ago that this land had risen from the ocean, and even less since those men had acted to establish order in their society.

On the way back from Þingvellir, Oli Johnsson and I began talking about historical Icelandic whaling. He knew that for ten years I had been a curator at the New Bedford Whaling Museum in Massachusetts and that I had specialized in the history of nineteenth-century whaling in North America's western Arctic. I then asked him about recent Icelandic whaling.

"Icelanders have been hunting whales here for a thousand years,"[57] he said, "but in 1985 we stopped whaling, except for a small catch for scientific research. Then in 1989 we declared an outright moratorium on all whaling."

"Why was that?" I asked.

"Well, you remember that in 1982 the International Whaling Commission [IWC] banned commercial whaling because of the worry that many whale species were being driven to extinction. That may be true, but the whales we were hunting weren't at all threatened."

"Then why did you stop?"

"It's simple," he said. "Iceland's only major export is fish. Our fishing catch makes up 70 percent of our export earnings. The environmental groups in Europe and North America threatened to boycott Iceland fish, the way they had done with Japanese goods. There are only 275,000 of us in Iceland. Unlike Japan, we have no diversity in our export products. That boycott would have really hurt us. Nevertheless, we thought the IWC ban was temporary, but it soon appeared to us to be permanent, so, in 1992 we withdrew from the IWC."

Their self-confidence must have grown, because on March 10, 1999, Iceland's *Alþing* adopted a resolution in favor of returning to whaling and annulling its 1983 resolution. Because Iceland, like Norway, is not now a member of the IWC, and because Iceland is not a member of the Convention in International Trade in Endangered Species (CITES), it upholds its self-proclaimed sovereign right to harvest its resources.[58] Referring to the whale, Steingrimur Hermannsson, a former minister of fisheries in Iceland, said, "We don't see it as a holy animal, as some wealthy ladies in the U.S. do. We think it should be eaten, like lamb. And whales eat more fish than we catch."[59]

We left Keflavík's harbor, as planned, at 11:30 P.M. on July 15. At first we kept a very careful lookout ahead because we were surprised to find a large number of drift logs bobbing about in the water. Before the Age of Settlement, Iceland was as much as one-third covered by woodland, but these trees were soon felled for ships, houses, and charcoal for forges. From then on driftwood was the only source.

This driftwood, like the logs we had seen in northwestern Spitsbergen, originated from the rivers of the White Sea and western Siberia. Flushed into the Barents and Kara Seas, it is then carried by the Transpolar Current through Fram Strait, between Spitsbergen and Greenland. That current continues as the East Greenland Current, which carries the wood to Jan Mayen Island and then to Iceland. Dendrochronological studies have revealed that this driftwood (spruce, pine, larch, birch, poplar, and willow) is at least six years old.

The fact these logs normally would have become waterlogged and would have sunk in less than a year and a half indicates that the sea ice must carry them in a frozen matrix for much of their journey.[60]

Some of this flotsam continues onward and fetches up in southwestern Greenland, and both the Norse and Inuit made use of it. In fact, pieces of the Arctic exploration vessel *Jeannette*, which was crushed in the ice northwest of Bering Strait in 1881, were found in southwestern Greenland in 1884, indicating the existence of a transpolar current. This in turn stimulated Fridtjof Nansen to drift across the Arctic Ocean, from eastern Siberia to the Atlantic (1893 to 1896) with the ice-strengthened research ship *Fram*.[61]

Aboard *Belvedere* we enjoyed a good, fast run southwest from Iceland with moderate seas and following winds, passing more than a hundred miles south of Cape Farewell and then entering the Labrador Sea. As we rolled along, I thought about Bjarni Herjolfsson's voyage of a thousand years before. He and his crew were quite probably —and accidentally—the first Europeans to see North America, and his track across the seas was probably quite similar to ours.

Bjarni Herjolfsson was the son of one of Iceland's early settlers, Herjolfr Bardarson. According to the *Grænlendinga Saga (The Greenlanders' Saga)*, which was put into writing in the late twelfth century, he must have been both a skilled mariner and a merchant, for he used his summers to do business in Scandinavia and spent alternate winters there and with his father in Iceland. In 985 or 986, on his return to the southwestern peninsula of Iceland late in the navigation season, he discovered that his father, Herjolfr, had sold his landholdings and had departed for Greenland with Eirik's fleet of emigrants. The saga continues:

Driftwood between Iceland and Greenland—from Olaus Magnus, Historia de Gentibus Septentrionalibus, *Rome, 1555*

[Bjarni] was taken heavily aback by the news, and had no mind to discharge the ship's cargo. His shipmates asked him what he proposed to do, and he replied that he meant to carry on as usual and enjoy winter quarters at his father's home. "I shall steer my ship for Greenland, if you are prepared to go along with me." They all said they would abide by his decision. "Our voyage will appear foolhardy," said Bjarni, "since no one of us has entered the Greenland Sea." Even so they put out the moment they were ready, and sailed for three days before losing sight of land.[62]

Three days out, Bjarni's fair wind died; a northerly and fog took over. For "many days" they had no idea where they were, while they were driven southwest by the wind and ocean currents. Aboard *Belvedere*, we, too, lost our visibility as soon as we entered the very cold water of the south-flowing Labrador Current. In fact, the fog was so thick that the first land we saw in North America was when we were *inside* the harbor of St. Anthony, near the northern tip of Newfoundland.

We, of course, got there by using GPS and radar. Bjarni was simply a highly competent mariner. For Bjarni, however,

> This continued over many days, but eventually they saw the sun and could then get their bearings. They now hoisted sail, and sailed that day before sighting land, and debated among themselves what land this could be. To his way of thinking, said Bjarni; it could not be Greenland. They asked him whether he proposed to sail to this land or not. "My intention," he replied, "is to sail close in to the land." Which they did, and could soon see that the land was not mountainous and was covered with forest, with low hills there, so they left the land to port of them and let their sheet turn toward the land.[63]

Where was Bjarni's landfall? It seems to me that Bjarni probably sailed into one of the famous low pressure systems that regularly cross North America and then are deflected around Cape Farewell by the high pressure system over the Greenland Ice Cap. If that was indeed the case, then a strong northeasterly gale would have driven Bjarni southwest. Working backward from where Bjarni's voyage ended, and considering the presumed set and drift of his vessel by wind and current, it is well within the realm of possibility that the land he saw first was either the north-facing coast of Newfoundland or, possibly, southeasternmost Labrador. I have sailed along those coasts many times. Both areas could be considered "not mountainous" and—remembering that he arrived during a more favorable climatic episode—"covered with forest."

Then Bjarni sailed north, presumably parallel with the Labrador

The land he saw first was either the north-facing coast of Newfoundland or, possibly, southeasternmost Labrador.

coast, for two days, when he saw another country. The crew was perplexed. "They asked whether Bjarni thought this in its turn was Greenland. In his opinion, he said, this was no more Greenland than the first place—'For there are very big glaciers reported to be in Greenland.' They soon drew near to this land, and could see that it was flat country and covered with woods."[64] As I will explain later (in Chapter Six), the only flat, wooded country that I have seen on the coast of Labrador is Porcupine Strand, between Sandwich Bay and Hamilton Inlet. This remarkable, twenty-mile stretch of beach is backed by a dense spruce forest.

The wind died then, and Bjarni's crew wanted to go ashore to take on wood (which was scarce in Iceland and Greenland) and water. The crew bridled when Bjarni retorted, "You lack for neither." But Bjarni, who was apparently a no-nonsense and practical merchant-seafarer, uninterested in exploration for its own sake, ordered the sail hoisted. They stood offshore for three days, sailing before a southwesterly.

Just north of Hamilton Inlet, at Cape Harrison, the shore falls away to the west, and Bjarni, heading north on a good point of sail, a broad reach, probably made good time. "Then they saw the third land, and this land was high, mountainous, and glaciated. They asked whether Bjarni would put ashore there, but no, he said, he had no wish to. 'For to me this land looks good for nothing.' So without so much as lowering their sail they held on along the land, and came to see that it was an island."[65]

In my opinion Bjarni and his men had seen the bare rock mountains of northern Labrador, had crossed Hudson Strait, and had seen the glaciers and forbidding landscape of southeastern Baffin Island. To mariners, tired of gray seas and skies, and longing for green fields and gentle lands, it would have been a logical decision to bypass this rugged place and keep on. "Once more they turned their prow from the land and held out to sea with the same following wind.... This time they sailed for four days, and then saw the fourth land. They asked Bjarni whether he thought this was Greenland or not. 'This is very like what I am told about Greenland,' replied Bjarni, 'and here we will make for the land.'"

To stand offshore from southeastern Baffin Island with a southwesterly wind, Bjarni would have had to change from a port tack to a starboard tack, and this would have brought him to southern Greenland. "So that is what they did, and came to land under a certain cape in the evening of the day. There was a boat on the cape, and there too on the cape lived Herjolf, Bjarni's father.... Bjarni now went to his father's, gave over his sailing and stayed with him for the rest of Herjolf's life, and later lived there as his father's

The only flat, wooded country that I have seen on the coast of Labrador is Porcupine Strand.

successor."[66] So ended one of the great accidental voyages of discovery in world history.

~

Aboard *Belvedere*, after waiting out a gale for a couple of days in St. Anthony, we continued our homeward voyage. First, we ran north a few miles and rounded Cape Bauld, the northern tip of Newfoundland, then crossed the mouth of Epaves Bay near Great Sacred Island. Onshore, near the tiny village of L'Anse aux Meadows ("L'Anse aux Medée," where there once was a seasonal French fishing station) we saw a few low, grass-covered mounds. These were replicas of Norse sod-covered houses that had stood on the site a thousand years ago, for it was here that the first European colony was established in the New World. The remains at L'Anse aux Meadows constitute the only authenticated Norse archaeological site in North America.

On one of these southern expeditions the men discovered wild grapes, and Leif named the area Vinland.

About fifteen years after Bjarni Herjolfsson returned to Greenland, his report of new lands to the west stimulated Leifr heppni Eiríksson (Leif Erikson or Leif the Lucky), the son of Eirík the Red, to go in search of Bjarni's discoveries. He bought Bjarni's boat and departed, with a crew of thirty-five, more or less following Bjarni's route in reverse: first to Baffin Island, then to Labrador, and then, it seems to me, to the northern tip of Newfoundland. There his men built houses before heading south to explore farther. On one of these southern expeditions the men discovered wild grapes, and Leif named the area Vinland (Wineland).[67] At L'Anse aux Meadows they were about 1,500 miles, by their route, from the settlements in Greenland, and there they carried out the first European over-wintering in North America.

But in fact, it may be said that the Norse discovery of the New World was inevitable—because the distances are so short between

The reconstruction of the Norse buildings at L'Anse aux Meadows, Newfoundland

land masses. It is less than 200 miles from Norway to Shetland, a little more than 200 from Shetland or Orkney to the Faroes, less than 200 from the Hebrides to the Faroes, less than 300 from the Faroes to Iceland, about 600 from Stadlandet in Norway to Iceland, less than 200 from northwest Iceland to the nearest point in Greenland, about 600 from southern Greenland to Labrador, and a bit more than 300 from western Greenland to southeastern Baffin Island. From southeastern Baffin Island the rest is entirely a coastal voyage (with the exceptions of crossing Hudson Strait and the Strait of Belle Isle) to northern Newfoundland and farther south.[68] If one assumes, as many do, that in *very favorable* conditions a Norse boat could cover about 150 miles per twenty-four-hour day (a *døgr*), then it is easy to imagine that the distances would hardly have been insurmountable.[69]

After one winter, Leif returned to his home on Eiríksfiord in southern Greenland. Several years later, about A.D. 1010, Thorfinnr karlsefni Thordarson, a wealthy Icelandic merchant who had married Gudridr Thorbjörnsdottir, the widow of Thorsteinn, one of Eirík the Red's sons, returned with about 160 men and women to establish a colony. The experiment lasted three years and involved bloodshed with the native population they encountered. During that time, however, Gudridr bore Thorfinnr a son, Snorri Thorfinnsson, the first child of European descent to be born in North America.[70] A few other winterings took place, but none were successful. The Norse occupation of North America was brief: this Late Iron Age society of hunters, farmers, and husbandmen was simply too far from home and too threatened by the local inhabitants to maintain a long-lived settlement there.

As we lay off Epaves Bay in *Belvedere* I could understand the logic of establishing an advance base here. The bay was shallow, hence boats could be dragged ashore easily. Wood and water were available. The ecosystem was roughly similar to western Norway's, the land was uninhabited, and, most important, the settlement was sited, not as a typical Greenland Norse farm would have been—deep in the protection of a fjord. Instead the buildings were placed right out on the coast, where they were exposed to the northerly winds, but their location was a perfect jumping-off place for explorations farther south.[71]

At L'Anse aux Meadows, our voyage of 1993 aboard *Belvedere* was almost complete. Having returned to North America, it was time to head for home and plan future voyages in the wake of the Norsemen. We headed down the west coast of Newfoundland, and along the coast of Nova Scotia to New England. I left *Belvedere* on September 1 at a boatyard in Maine to begin a refit. And I felt greatly satisfied that in the past three seasons we had completed a 13,000-mile loop in the North Atlantic.

The Northwest Passage Again (1994) and Homeward from Greenland (1989)

O N THE VOYAGE back to New England I had made up my mind that in 1994 I would take my first non-Arctic summer since 1969. Nevertheless, I didn't plan to abandon sailing in the wake of the Norsemen; on the contrary, I wanted to poke around in Canada's Maritime Provinces and try to get a feeling for what the Norse explorers must have seen a thousand years ago. It was not to be so.

Almost as soon as *Belvedere* had been hauled out of the water for a winter of repairs and maintenance, my friend Bill Simon, the former secretary of the Treasury, phoned me. He was excited and energetic as ever. Bill announced that he'd just bought a sturdy yacht that would allow him to travel in high latitudes and that his primary objective would be to traverse the Northwest Passage. "I know you've already done it twice, John," he said, "but would you like to come with me aboard *Itasca*?"

This was catnip. I immediately put my plans for the Canadian Maritimes on hold. "You bet I would. When do you want me?"

I felt at once that this voyage would allow me to gain a better understanding of Norse activities in Canada and Greenland and would help to enrich the perceptions I had gained when *Belvedere* was in Greenland in 1988 and 1989.

As Bill described *Itasca*, she sounded fascinating: a 175-foot ice-strengthened former North Sea oil field tug/supply vessel that had been brought up to yacht standards by her previous owner. With her single, deep, eight-foot propeller, her twin 1,250 shaft-horsepower diesels and a 292-ton fuel capacity, *Itasca* was capable of a fast, safe traverse. Her only minor drawback was her deep draft of sixteen feet, which might make close-in ice work difficult in the shallow waters of the western Arctic; nevertheless, her strength, I felt, would fully offset this.

At the beginning of August 1994, we flew to Nome, Alaska. On landing we learned that a strong gale had forced *Itasca* to find shelter about sixty miles away. However, we quickly overcame this problem. I found Bonnie Hahn at home, and needless to say, we were grateful for her kindness when the next day she took us all in her van to Port Clarence.

Passing through Bering Strait into the Chukchi Sea, we then rounded Point Barrow into the Beaufort Sea and worked among drift ice for several days before winding our way through the straits between the mainland shore and Canada's Arctic Islands. When *Itasca* reached James Ross Strait, however, between King William Island and

The Sir John Franklin *cleared our way into Larsen Sound.*

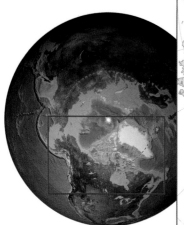

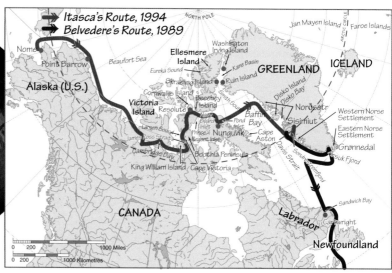

Itasca's route of 1994 and Belvedere's *route of 1989*

the Boothia Peninsula, we found ice blocking the passage north, just as it had when I was at precisely the same spot in 1980, 1987, and 1988.

But *Itasca's* powerful engines thudded rhythmically along, pushing us forward, and soon the lens-like silhouette of Cape Victoria, at the north end of the strait, rose ahead to starboard. We then cautiously entered the drift ice, moving slowly among the floes, which covered three-quarters of the water's surface. I heard the hiss and deep grinding as the floes scraped past the hull, and occasionally *Itasca* would jump sideways as we glanced off an especially heavy piece.

As I had found in 1987 and 1988 aboard *Belvedere*, Cape Victoria can be a difficult place to get past. It is essentially the eastern shoulder of a choke point, a narrow gut through which the current carries ice south out of Larsen Sound, something like squirting toothpaste through the neck of the tube. The ice became thicker and thicker as we approached the cape, and nearing the point, we saw massive ice pressure ridges where the winter's winds had forced the floes to pile over one another against the shore. The largest of these ridges was twenty-five to thirty feet high and grounded in fifty feet of water.

As the ice grew heavier we backed and filled and twisted in the narrowing spaces between the floes, and, I would guess, made progress northward at only about a mile an hour. The ice finally brought us to a standstill just before midnight. We spent the next day, August 17, essentially motionless, beset by very heavy floes that were at least two years old. Sea ice that is more than a year old has lost almost all of its salt and thus has essentially become fresh water; hence old sea ice, without its salt content, is much harder than salty young ice, making it much more difficult for a ship to break through.

Bill wanted to push on, however, and asked the Canadian Coast Guard for permission to follow an icebreaker northward. At about eight o'clock that evening, with a spooky mist rising off the ice, suddenly the massive silhouette of the Canadian Coast Guard icebreaker *Sir John Franklin*, bright red and more than 300 feet long, loomed out of the murk. After a certain amount of back-and-forth discussion on the radio and a faxed waiver of indemnity to the government in Ottawa (via the satellite telephone), we agreed to be ready to go the next morning.

August 18 turned out to be very different from the calm and silence of the day before. The *Franklin,* with her twin screws and 1,400 shaft horsepower, took off at eight knots through the tight pack ice. Thudding and juddering, *Itasca* barged through the floes behind her. We had to keep as close as possible to the *Franklin*'s stern because in places the ice was under pressure from the wind and the floes closed back in behind her quickly. *Itasca* was rarely more than a hundred yards behind and sometimes as close as fifty feet. It was a continuous thundering chorus of screeching, banging, moaning, and scrunching as the floes tore past our hull. At times the *Franklin* forced large floes over on their sides, rolling them over as we passed; at other times she charged right through them, leaving deep parallel propeller slashes gouged into the massive chunks of hard blue ice.

Often we would close on the stern of the *Franklin*, and, thinking she was slowing, we would all relax a bit. Then a huge black belch of soot would shoot out of her stack and, from beneath her stern would burst an explosion of white, churning, ice-filled prop wash, and off she would charge—again and again. In one especially tricky moment a particularly heavy floe stopped her dead. We were right behind her, and the only thing our helmsman could do to avoid crashing into her stern was to put the wheel hard to starboard, throw the transmission into neutral, and run smack into the ice beside her.

After twelve hours of this we broke into clearer water in northern Larsen Sound, and the *Franklin* left us to return to her duties. Everyone was thankful for her help, but exhausted.

The next morning we closed in on the western entrance to Bellot Strait. I was on the bridge with Allan Jouning, *Itasca*'s skillful and supremely competent captain. "I wonder if you'd come along with Bill and me in the helicopter to do some recon?" Allan asked me.

"Sure," I said. "When do you want to leave?"

"In about an hour."

The great British explorer of the Antarctic, Sir Ernest Shackleton, said (and here I paraphrase) that planning is *everything*; that a *well-planned* expedition has already gone halfway toward accomplishing its objective, even before it has set out. It was obvious that Allan and

We were right behind her, and the only thing our helmsman could do to avoid crashing into her stern was to put the wheel hard to starboard, throw the transmission into neutral, and run smack into the ice beside her.

Bill had really done their homework in preparing for the voyage. I had met with Bill several times during the winter and had outlined some of the difficulties in the traverse, as I envisioned them. Bill and Allan had foreseen that they might need some means of aerial reconnaissance in the difficult part of the passage, which would essentially be the leg between King William Island and Baffin Bay.

Because of this, Bill had chartered a helicopter for a couple of weeks, and it now sat like a very welcome, large, red dragonfly on the upper deck, aft. "We could save a hundred miles or more if we can go through Bellot Strait, but from what you've told me, I want to be very careful before poking in there," Allan added.

"I couldn't agree with you more," I replied, remembering my 1980 bypass of it in my umiak and my 1988 traverse in *Belvedere*.[1]

There aren't any tidal tables for the strait itself, but it's not too difficult to run up a graph by using the records of the tidal range at either end. It only took me an hour or so to do this, and by then Bill and Allan were ready to go. It was a murky day, so we had to fly low, under the cloud cover. As we entered the twenty-mile strait, the tall cliffs on either side were lost in the clouds, and it seemed as if we were flying down an enormous bowling alley. Halfway through, with visibility swiftly deteriorating, we found a large ice pan jammed wall-to-wall, athwart the strait and held there by the strong current. Behind it was a fog bank.

I had brought along a copy of what is colloquially called "The Arctic Pilot," the sailing directions for Canada's northern waters. Over static crashes and rotor noise I read to Bill and Allan on the intercom: "Tidal streams run with great strength through Bellot Strait.... In 1977 the survey ship *Baffin* entered Bellot Strait ... at 0715 Eastern Standard Time.... A reconnaissance flight by the ship's helicopter at 0400 had reported mostly open water throughout the strait.... Three hours later when the *Baffin* entered the strait there was $9/10$ coverage of second-year and multi-year ice. About 0.6 mile east of Halfway Island, *Baffin* encountered $10/10$ multi-year ice under very strong pressure. *Baffin* became beset in ice ... and required full engine power to hold her position. Very little forward movement was made until 1000, at which time the tidal flow reversed thus relieving the pressure.... From this experience it appears that ice reports cannot be relied on unless they are less than thirty minutes old...."[2]

Bill and Allan looked back at me with slightly saucer-shaped eyes. Allan recommended bagging it. Bill agreed—and I certainly didn't object. We flew back to *Itasca* and kept on north, up Peel Sound, toward Lancaster Sound and the tributary waters of the Atlantic.

It didn't take long to find ice again: it was waiting for us near Prince Leopold Island at the northeastern corner of Somerset Island.

As we entered the twenty-mile strait, the tall cliffs on either side were lost in the clouds, and it seemed as if we were flying down an enormous bowling alley.

We crunched along, banging and slamming sideways with the now familiar grinding and thudding, as we worked our way across the north end of Prince Regent Inlet.

Toward evening on August 20 the temperature dropped suddenly and soon a fine granular snow began to fall, just as a thin skim of ice started to form between the floes. Soon the visibility was so poor that we shut down the engines and drifted until about 6:00 A.M. *Itasca* then crept along the north coast of Baffin Island's Brodeur Peninsula under a low overcast, accompanied by the whine of the bow thruster and the usual sideways jolts as we zigged and zagged among the floes.

By noon we had cleared the pack ice and then turned south into Navy Board Inlet, with Bylot Island to port, heading for the settlement of Pond Inlet. I had passed this way in 1988 with *Belvedere*, but I had forgotten its beauty: the jagged, raw peaks, the glaciers descending in the valleys, the gleaming white of the ice cap on Bylot Island, and the warm green of the Pond Inlet shore.

Bill also wanted to see the northern islands of the Canadian Arctic Archipelago, so we flew off from Pond Inlet in a chartered DeHavilland Twin Otter, a reliable and sturdy short-takeoff-and-landing bush plane. It is arguably the workhorse of the Arctic, being perfectly suited to the gravel airstrips of the region. It was a fascinating two-day loop that took us, first, west to Beechey Island to

Itasca and Sir John Franklin in Larsen Sound

visit the graves of some of Sir John Franklin's men; then to the town of Resolute on Cornwallis Island; and onward, to Eureka Sound and the north end of Ellesmere Island. On the way back we flew down Ellesmere Island's east coast. Looking out of the plane's port side window, I glimpsed the waters of Smith Sound. Smith Sound is not really a sound at all, but rather, the narrows at the north end of Baffin Bay, where Greenland and Ellesmere Island most closely converge.

Those desolate shores, too, have yielded astonishing evidence of Norse activity. It was once generally thought that the Norse probably hunted only as far north on the coast of Greenland as Disko Bay, about 70°N. This is the region the Norse called *Norðsetr* ("northern sojourn"), their northern hunting grounds.[3] And it was there, near the massive Disko Island, an area teeming with wildlife, that they took walrus, bears, seals, caribou, gyrfalcons, and other birds, some of which were exported to Europe. Here they also probably traded with the Inuit for narwhal tusks. (The Norse lacked toggle-headed harpoons and drag-float technology, which the Inuit possessed, and without which the Norse hunters most probably would have been unable to capture the whales themselves.[4]) The white gyrfalcons, narwhal and walrus tusks, and polar bear skins would have been traded as luxury items, whereas the walrus hides, being extremely tough and durable, would have been sliced up to make very high-quality lines, far stronger than plant fiber or other types of rope.

The walrus ivory was probably the Greenlanders' most important export item, for it was extremely valuable in northern Europe.

The walrus ivory was probably the Greenlanders' most important export item, for it was extremely valuable in northern Europe. The tusks would have helped pay for their imported goods—grain, iron, and timbers, among other things. Equally important, the ivory would not only have allowed them to pay taxes to the Norwegian crown if exacted (Iceland, and possibly Greenland, were absorbed by the kingdom of Norway in 1262), but also to pay the Holy See's tithes and other taxes: Peter's Pence to build St. Peter's Cathedral in Rome and the "six years' tithe" to pay for the Crusades. In fact, one scholar believes that it was precisely because of their access to walrus ivory that Greenlanders received their first bishop in 1124.[5] Today, from studies of museum collections, it is clear that the amount of European-carved walrus ivory increased after the settlement of Greenland.[6]

But there is good evidence that Norse hunters worked even farther north than the Disko region. In 1824 a Greenlander discovered three cairns near Kingigtorssuaq, at nearly 73°N, one of which contained a small, flat stone fragment with a runic inscription: "Erling Sighvatsson and Bjarni Thordarson and Eindridi Jonsson on the Saturday before Minor Rogation Day piled these cairns...."[7] The stone is thought to date from about A.D. 1300.[8] The Minor Rogation

Days take place just before Ascension Day, which itself is forty days after Easter.[9] Thus it is quite likely that Erling, Bjarni, and Indridi had wintered over in the area to take advantage of the richness of the fine spring hunting season. Helge Ingstad, the discoverer of the Norse habitation at L'Anse aux Meadows, Newfoundland, wrote of these cairns: "Raising cairns was an ancient Norwegian and Icelandic custom; these particular cairns may have served as beacons, or perhaps these three men raised the cairns and cut the inscription as a token of their having sailed so far north."[10]

Even more astonishing about the Norse penetration of the High Arctic are the discoveries near Smith Sound. In the 1930s Erik Holtved, a Danish archaeologist, excavated the remains of three ancient Inuit houses on the Greenland side. There, on Ruin Island, he uncovered some amazing artifacts: a scrap of woven woolen cloth, a fragment of chain mail, and board game pieces, among other things—all of them obviously of Norse origin. At that time the logical conclusion was that they were probably intrusive objects from a later time, having been traded, hand-to-hand, up from the Norse settlements in southern Greenland.[11]

That was the generally accepted view of Norse-Inuit archaeological interpretation until 1978. Then Peter Schledermann, a Canadian archaeologist, was excavating an ancient Inuit house, not far from Holtved's site, but across Smith Sound on Skraeling Island, on the east coast of Ellesmere Island. It is now thought that the house is evidence of the very first entrance of the modern Inuit into the High Arctic[12] and a waypoint on their journey from northern Alaska to southern Greenland. "I was carefully removing greasy black soil around a stone-lined meat pit in one of the old houses," wrote

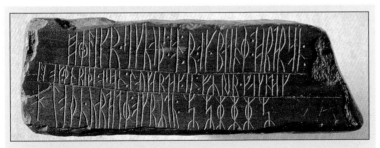

The Kingigtorssuaq rune stone was discovered in 1824 on the northwest coast of Greenland amid some cairns that stood at nearly 73°N. It is the record of three Norse hunters who probably wintered there about A.D. 1300. The inscription reads, "Erling Sighvatsson and Bjarni Thordarson and Eindridi Jonsson on the Saturday before Minor Rogation Day piled these cairns…"

Schledermann. "I was getting very close to floor level when my trowel suddenly hit a hard object that gave off a strange sharp metallic sound. Carefully I lifted a fist-sized heavy object from the ground, brushed some of the dirt away and realized on closer inspection that I was holding a rusted lump of joined rings—a piece of medieval chain mail. Hardly had the find been packed away before another Norse item came to light for the first time in many centuries. In the bottom of the meat pit I uncovered a perfectly preserved ship rivet."

Equally fascinating is the discovery of the remains of two Norse cairns fifty miles north of Skraeling Island, on Washington Irving Island.

During the next few days other team members found similar items of Norse origin in other houses—more ship rivets, a knife blade, and the tip of a large spear point.[13] To the Inuit of the region, who hitherto had enjoyed only limited supplies of meteoric iron, no doubt iron itself was viewed as a precious metal. The presence of ship rivets (used to clinch a vessel's overlapping planking) may indicate a shipwreck.

Over the next three field seasons, the archaeologists found many other Norse objects: fragments of woolen cloth, a carpenter's block plane (lacking its blade), knives, rivets, and a piece of copper.[14] A bronze beam balance arm, suggesting trading activity, also came to light at another site, and a fragment of a bronze bowl was discovered on Cornwallis Island, while Schledermann's team unearthed two barrel bottoms and an ivory figurine, most likely carved by an Inuk,[15] that probably represents a Norseman. Radiocarbon analyses of the house ruins and cloth sample have yielded dates from the late twelfth to early thirteenth centuries, as has a piece of oak spliced into the gunwale of an umiak frame found in northernmost Greenland.[16]

Recently, the Canadian archaeologist Patricia Sutherland has put forward the tantalizing hypothesis that trading contacts between the Norse and the Inuit of Canada's Eastern Arctic were frequent in the late thirteenth and early fourteenth centuries: "There was more than just in-and-out trading and 'Goodbye, we won't be back.'" On the basis of her careful reanalysis of many Dorset (a pre-modern Inuit culture) archaeological collections from the same region, particularly from a site at Nunguvik, in Navy Board Inlet on northern Baffin Island, she feels that the Norse may have set up shore stations on the island.[17]

Equally fascinating is the discovery of the remains of two Norse cairns fifty miles north of Skraeling Island, on Washington Irving Island, at 79°33′N, beyond Smith Sound, in the Kane Basin. There, in August 1875, George Nares, leading the British Arctic Expedition in hopes of reaching the North Pole, spotted a small object protruding above the flat top of the 600-foot cliff on the mesa-like island. When his men scrambled up the mesa's steep rear slope they found two cairns covered in lichen. Lichen grows so slowly in the High Arctic that its presence indicated great age.[18] Recently, archaeologists have concluded that these cairns (and possibly many stone eider duck nesting boxes and several large stone bear traps nearby) are likely the work—or influence—of Norsemen. Peter Schledermann estimates that the cairns were built late in the thirteenth century.[19] "At 194 meters above sea level," Peter wrote to me recently, "I'm convinced that they were not built by Inuit, who would have had no reason whatsoever to climb all the way up to the plateau and construct two cairns."[20] And, it is also worth noting that two cairns of unknown origin were discovered on the hill behind the Norse site at L'Anse aux Meadows, Newfoundland.[21]

∽

On returning to Pond Inlet, we boarded *Itasca* again and set out across Baffin Bay for Greenland. Once we had left the protection of Pond Inlet's steep, glacially scoured cliffs, we found a strong northwesterly driving a big sea onto our port quarter. Rolling heavily, we carried on for a while, but when we neared Greenland, Allan Jouning dog-legged *Itasca*'s course to starboard, thus paralleling the coast and damping the roll by putting the seas more on the stern. Passing outside Disko Island, we cleared Danish Customs just north of the Arctic Circle at Sisimiut (formerly Holsteinsborg), a modern town of 5,000 inhabitants that is Greenland's northernmost year-round ice-free port and the center of the Greenland shrimp industry.

We kept on south under a low overcast, but in the evening, as we turned northeast into Sondrestromfjord (Southern Current-Fiord), the overcast vanished, as it usually does in the fjords. We then began the eighty-five-mile run to the airport at the end of what is one of the world's longest fjords, while the temperature rose and the evening descended.

As the dusk deepened, the sky slightly backlit the great, ghostly gray cliffs towering above us on both sides, and the twilight faintly illuminated the vertical snow streaks in their crevices. At the same time, the northern lights danced above us in vast, undulating ribbons of green, while a half-moon peeked out here and there between the jagged cliff tops as we moved deeper into the fjord. The sparkle of the stars in the velvet sky made it all more the vivid: Altair, Vega, and Deneb astern and Sirius and Polaris to port. A satellite passed overhead and several shooting stars raced by. There is indescribable beauty in the Far North.

∽

Our voyage aboard *Itasca* in 1994 ended close to where *Belvedere*'s earlier Greenland voyage began. In 1988, after *Belvedere* exited Bellot Strait, we rounded the northern end of Baffin Island and headed down its mountainous and glacier-topped eastern coast. Off the low flatlands of Cape Aston we steered directly for Sisimiut, on the other side of Davis Strait. I hauled *Belvedere* out on Sisimiut's marine railway and left her in the shipyard for the winter.[22] Homeward bound the following summer, 1989, we stopped for supplies in Nuuk, Greenland's capital. Nuuk (*point of land* in Inuktitut), formerly Godthåb, lies at 64°10´N, squarely in the fjord system that the Norse called *Vesterbygd*, their "Western Settlement." Like their "Eastern Settlement," *Østerbygd*—the fjord system about

In 1988, on the northeast coast of Baffin Island, Peter Semotiuk looks out over Coutts Inlet.

400 miles to the southeast, where Eirík the Red settled—these fjords offered protection from the punishing Arctic wind and weather, thus sheltering almost all of the arable land in Greenland.

More than 300 Norse farms have been identified in Greenland, as well as seventeen parish churches, one cathedral, an Augustinian monastery, and a Benedictine convent. Because the economy of these farmer-immigrants was based on the Icelandic tradition of animal husbandry, all of the farms were located in areas of abundant pasturage: grasses, shrubs, and small trees. On the other hand, there were basic differences between the livelihoods of the two settlements. As might be expected, the Western Settlement, lying farther up the coast—hence cooler— but much closer to the rich hunting grounds near Disko Island (*Norðsetr*), had a greater reliance on game than did the Eastern Settlement, which was more traditionally pastoral.[23]

How many Norse lived in Greenland, and why had they apparently abandoned it entirely by the sixteenth century? The enduring mystery of the "lost" Norse colony has fascinated scholars and laymen for 300 years. The *Konungs skuggsjá (King's Mirror)*, a mid-thirteenth-century Norwegian text that takes the form of a dialogue between a father and son states, "The people in that country are few, for only a small part is sufficiently free from ice to be habitable."[24] Estimates of the size of the Norse population have varied between a high figure of about 5,000 to, most recently, about 2,000, with an absolute maximum of 2,500. Clearly theirs was a very small population.

The enduring mystery of the 'lost' Norse colony has fascinated scholars and laymen for 300 years.

We know that sometime before 1349 a priest, Ivar Bárdarson, visited the Western Settlement and found it deserted: "When they arrived there, they found nobody, either Christians or heathens, only some wild cattle and sheep, and they slaughtered the wild cattle and sheep for food...."[25] Some scholars see this as evidence of a hasty abandonment of the settlement while giving no reason or other evidence for it. On the other hand, Kirsten Seaver makes the point that Ivar was the Bishop of Greenland's *officialis* and therefore probably went to the Western Settlement to collect taxes. It is possible, of course, that the settlers there had learned of his visit in advance and had simply headed for the hills until the taxman sailed away.[26] Others have estimated that the Church had acquired, by frank almoign (the free donation of landholdings to the Church), ownership of as much as two-thirds of the pasturage in Greenland, thus reducing the population to marginal areas and "alms status." This seems unlikely, and the theory has been challenged.[27]

Nevertheless, recent archaeological investigations have revealed that by the mid-fourteenth century the Western Settlement was in trouble, and the soil had been badly degraded through over-grazing. In fact, the economy of those settlers was probably shaky even at the beginning: many of the men there must have had to travel to the Disko region early in the summer to hunt both for their own subsistence and for marketable trade goods. Those who remained in the Western Settlement—women, children, and older men—cared for the livestock, probably driving them to shielings in the valleys of the interior. On the hunters' return from *Norðsetr* it was time to stock up on fodder for their animals. Then, as winter approached, they would have rounded up their cattle, sheep, and goats and kept them in byres until spring.

Some scholars have speculated that the Norse lived close to the margin of survival in the Western Settlement, without the capacity to build up large stores of fodder.[28] Thomas McGovern, a principal proponent of this school of thought, states, "Unlike the grain-based economies of contemporary Europe, however, the herding and hunting Greenlanders had little ability to store surpluses accumulated in good years to offset hardship in bad."[29] Thus, he thinks that several poor growing seasons in a row could have put them in dire straits. Whether or not this chain of events actually took place is a matter of conjecture.

From a global perspective, Sir Crispin Tickell has written, "In pre-industrial times people could always react, however painfully, to climatic deterioration by going somewhere else. . . . But the limits within which climatic changes or short-term variations in weather can be exploited or tolerated are much narrower for some than for others. . . . First are the marginal areas between climatic zones (polar, temperate, desert and tropical). In such areas a very small shift can have very big consequences."[30]

Climatological analyses of the cores from the Greenland Ice Cap have shown that there were four multi-year cold periods in the fourteenth century, the longest of which spanned the years 1343 to 1362. The deterioration of the climate that began about 1300, after the end of the medieval warm period (about A.D. 800 to 1300) probably forced the Norse to gradually abandon their farmsteads. As the conditions worsened, at some point each landholder must have reached his individual limit of tolerance and accordingly made the rational decision to leave. It seems likely that the Norse population would have trickled down the coast, gradually and orderly, to seek opportunities in the Eastern Settlement, which was temporarily enjoying better conditions.

But one farm, at least, seems to have been abandoned in a hurry. A little more than fifty miles east of Nuuk archaeologists have found "The Farm Beneath the Sand" (*Gård Under Sandet*). This well-preserved frozen site was uncovered under a layer of glacial silt. Most astonishing was the discovery of a loom that still held unfinished cloth.[31] To some this is seen as evidence of a hasty withdrawal from the Western Settlement. It is more likely, however, that, in this case, inclement weather caused a river to change course, flooding the farm.[32]

Aboard *Belvedere*, we left Nuuk, southbound, on June 14, 1989, threading our way among granite islands that still had lots of snow caulking their crevices. Although the temperature was about thirty-eight degrees F, it was a beautiful, cloudless day with a moderate following wind. Soon, however, we picked up a gale warning from Nuuk radio, and almost at once the wind began gusting to thirty knots, sending up a sea that gave us an uncomfortable roll. Because we weren't in much of a hurry, we decided to go into the nearest shelter, Kangerluarsoruseq (formerly Faeringehavn), an abandoned Faroese fishing harbor.

We tried to anchor in front of the old settlement but quickly found that the bottom there was so overgrown with kelp that our heavy anchor just skated across the weedy ledges. Each time we raised it for

Belvedere *on Greenland's west coast, in the harbor at Kangerluarsoruseq (formerly Faeringehavn), 1989*

another set, three or four bushels of long-strand kelp hung from its bill. After a half-dozen tries, a fisherman aboard a small halibut boat at the settlement's dock motioned us to raft alongside. We gratefully accepted his offer, and, to pass the time until the wind died, my son Johnny, Terry Vose, Peter Semotiuk, and I (Bonnie Hahn was sleeping off some seasickness) walked up over the low, rocky hills for a better view of our surroundings.

The contrast with the comparative warmth deep in the fjords behind Nuuk was dramatic. Here, out on the coast, the wind had a real bite to it, and the sparse tundra vegetation was hunkered down in the shelter of the rocky crevices. Below us, at the harbor's edge, were a number of abandoned shacks and a few derelict boats. To the west the strong, cold wind milled up the waters of the Labrador Sea, while to the east, between the huge gray rock peaks, glowed the white halation of the Greenland Ice Cap.

"Does this remind you of home?" Terry asked my old friend Peter, who had joined us for a "busman's holiday" from his home in Cambridge Bay, on Victoria Island in the Canadian Arctic.

"It sure does," said Pete, "but we don't have an ice cap on Victoria Island."

"And you certainly don't have as many rocks," I added, remembering the sandy glacial tills of the western Arctic.

As we moved on south, keeping several miles offshore to avoid the innumerable rocky skerries close in, the coast was magnificent and deeply indented with fjords. From five miles off we saw the glow of Frederikshåb Isblink, the great fan-shaped glacier that pushes toward the sea. Its wide front was so massive that I could almost feel the huge weight of the Ice Cap—700,000 square miles in area and nearly two miles deep at its thickest—slowly forcing its way out between the coastal mountains, turning the ice into a ductile mass.

I wanted to wait for a good patch of weather to cross the Labrador Sea, so we closed with the coast not far from Cape Desolation in southwest Greenland. Then, winding our way through the shoals and islands into Arsuk Fjord, we motored to Grønnedal, the Danish Naval Base that lies well protected near the headwaters. The Danish naval personnel welcomed us warmly and offered us every kindness, including the use of their washing machines, but best of all was getting access to their weather reports.

While waiting out two gales, we took the opportunity to hike in the steep rocky hills. From the tops, the view down the fjord—cerulean waters rimmed by jagged, overhanging mountains—was dramatic, and far below us, at the naval pier, *Belvedere* was but a speck.

"Jesus! Look at the size of that pit," Terry blurted out, while simultaneously Peter added, "It's right at the water's edge!" The rest of us swung around to follow their pointing arms, and there on the south shore of the fjord, at Ivigtut, was indeed an enormous pit, with most of the cliff behind it blasted away. Late that afternoon, when we reached the naval base I asked Henrik Skolemose, the *Borgmester* (mayor), about the hole in the ground.

"That's our cryolite mine," he said.

"What's that?" I asked.

The view down the fjord—cerulean waters rimmed by jagged, overhanging mountains—was dramatic.

"It's also called Greenland spar. It's been mined here since the middle of the nineteenth century. It melts at a low temperature and can be used as a sort of solvent to dissolve impurities in metals. Its value really skyrocketed at the end of that century, though, when scientists discovered that it could be used to refine aluminum. It's the electrolyte that was used to extract aluminum from bauxite ore. They've synthesized it now, but Ivigtut was the only large source of cryolite until a few years ago. Fleets of freighters used to call here to carry the ore to Europe and America."

"The mine's played out now, but during the Second World War it was so crucial to the war effort for making aircraft that the U.S. stationed troops here to guard the mine." I remembered that after Germany invaded Denmark, U.S. President Franklin Delano Roosevelt had invoked the Monroe Doctrine, taking responsibility for Greenland's defense. In view of the importance of aluminum production to defense industries, no doubt the cryolite mine at Ivigtut helped him come to that decision.[33]

When I returned home I found a book by Fullerton Waldo, a young American who had visited Ivigtut in the 1920s. He wrote:

'You discover with something like a thrill of horror that these ladders only reach down part way into the pit, and there is a sheer drop of 150 feet or so beneath them...'

> There is a fence all the way round [the mine pit], and that means almost half a mile. Peering over the fence into the abyss, you see ladders hanging over the banks of the opposite wall. There is a lift, with two cars constantly ascending and descending, but this is only for that luxurious passenger, the kryolith. The ladders that you see are for the workmen. You look more closely and you discover with something like a thrill of horror that these ladders only reach down part way into the pit, and there is a sheer drop of 150 feet or so beneath them where they tail off into space. Between them are hanging ropes that swing loose and may be seized to go lower still. The workmen nonchalantly descend these ladders, grab the ropes, and pirouette off to the right and left after looping the ropes about their waists, while like sea-birds they stand on what seems to be nothing at all....

> Here the man on the line may dangle foot-loose, till with a crowbar weighing perhaps fourteen pounds he has excavated a toe-hold. Then with a compressed air drill weighing at least thirty pounds he must bore into the rock directly before his face, raising a cloud of white dust, and thinking nothing of the distance overhead or underfoot, or of the dizziness....

> But even these miners are not super-men: and sometimes they climb up over the rim of the pit at eventide white and shaky, and come to the superintendent...and tell him that something happened that took their nerve, and they will never go down again.[34]

～

An even more remarkable mineral has been discovered a few miles away in the next fjord south of Arsuk. In 1963 Hans Pauly, a Danish geologist, was picnicking in Ikka Fjord with some officers from the Grønnedal base. A navy diver had brought up from the bottom of the fjord pieces of what looked like whitish stalagmites, and he left them on the deck of their vessel. When they returned after lunch, to their astonishment they found that the pieces had melted, leaving only a puddle of water and some grains of a sandy material. Pauly named the mysterious mineral ikaite. It is now known that ikaite is a form of calcium carbonate that is formed only under high pressure. It precipitates out around underwater springs that seep through igneous basement rock in the unique conditions of pressure and temperature on the bottom of the fjord. Some of the stalagmites are sixty feet high and are visible through the very clear water of the fjord.[35]

These pillars of calcium carbonate are also an element in an ancient Inuit folk tale that, indirectly at least, hints at what may have been one of the factors contributing to the abandonment of the Eastern Settlement. The Norse had been in sporadic contact with the Inuit since, probably, the twelfth century. The *Historia Norvegiae*, a composition of the late twelfth century, relates that the Norse had met a foreign people, small in stature, that they called "skrælings." It may have been that they first met in the *Norðsetr*, near Disko Island, where the north-traveling Norse hunters intersected with south-migrating Inuit.

In the mid-nineteenth century Hinrich Johannes Rink, the director of the Royal Greenland Board of Trade, and a scholar of the Inuit language, spent more than twenty years collecting native folktales throughout Greenland. His book, published first in Danish in 1866, is a compendium of 170 tales, four of which relate to the *Kavdlunait* (Norse), and all of which involve violence or death. These accounts must be used with caution, however, because Rink was very eager to acquire tales about the Norse settlers and quite likely unwittingly encouraged his informants to embellish—or even to fabricate outright—descriptions of Inuit-Norse encounters. "At Ikat, the Kavdlunait living there were also taken by surprise by the Kaladlit [Inuit], and four fathers fled with their children out on the ice, which, however, being too thin broke through with them so that all were drowned; and it is said that only a few years ago they might be seen at the bottom of the sea. It is a common tradition at Arsut, that whenever they become visible it is a sure foreboding that one of the people will die."[36] Three Norse farm sites have been located in Ikka Fiord.

Similarly, there is an Inuit tale about their attack on, and burning of, the farm at Hvalsø (Whale Island), which lies not far to the east of Ikka Fiord. It said that the Inuit leader, Kaissape, killed the Norse leader, Ungortoq (probably *Yngvardur* in Greenlandic Norse).[37] And, a report in the *Icelandic Annal* of 1379 reads, "Skrælings assaulted the Greenlanders and killed eighteen men and captured two."[38] However, we must remember that to date no archaeological evidence has been unearthed that suggests an attack by the Inuit against the Norse.[39]

But not all incidents between the Norse and the Inuit were antagonistic. The *Reisubók Bjarnar Jorsalafara* relates that Björn Einarsson ("Jerusalem-Farer"), heading for Iceland, was blown off course on his return from visiting the Holy Land. He fetched up in

Greenland, where he rescued two Inuit children from a rock in the ocean, and they stayed with his family while he remained there.[40]

There were about twenty Norse farms in Arsuk and nearby fjords, and this concentration composed the western fringe of the Eastern Settlement. As we walked on those highlands above Arsuk Fjord, it wasn't difficult to pick out the few spots where Norse farms had been: not surprisingly, they were all on small, low, green plateaus near streams. A day or two later when we took *Belvedere* up the fjord toward the face of the glacier, Arsuk Bræ, these bits of land seemed pitifully small and marginal.

With Belvedere *at the face of Arsuk Fiord's glacier, Johnny Bockstoce retrieves ice on the port rail. Terry Vose is on the starboard side.*

As we worked through the slushy brash ice toward the fifty-foot-high blue glacier's face I saw that the lichens had been cleanly scoured from the cliff sides for about a mile on either side of the fjord. Evidently Arsuk Bræ was now in swift retreat. If that was true, it occurred to me that it may have been much closer to the Norse farms during the fourteenth and fifteenth centuries, and perhaps it was growing even then. I wondered what it would have been like to dwell near an advancing glacier, and whether these farms might have been among the first to have been abandoned in the Eastern Settlement.

It is thought that the demand for walrus ivory probably ceased during the fifteenth century.

We know from archaeological evidence that, although the Norse deserted the Western Settlement by the end of the fourteenth century, or somewhat earlier, the Eastern Settlement was inhabited longer. The styles of clothing and headgear found in graves in the Eastern Settlement indicate that contact with Europe continued well into the fifteenth century. A chaperon (hood) with a long liripipe ("tail") and a cylindrical flat-topped cap are evidence of mid-fifteenth-century fashions in Europe, if not later.[41]

It seems to me that, once the Norse had abandoned the Western Settlement, it would have been far more difficult for the men to reach the hunting grounds more than 700 miles to the north. Thus it may not have been possible to acquire marketable raw materials (gyrfalcons, tusks, bearskins, and walrus-hide rope) that the sailing merchants wanted for the European market. There is also speculation that at the same time in Europe, because the Crusaders had retaken the Holy Land, trade with Africa and the Levant might have made elephant ivory more accessible, reducing the value of walrus tusks. Whether or not this is an accurate assessment, it is thought that the demand for walrus ivory probably ceased during the fifteenth century.[42] In any case, reliable supplies of elephant tusks only reached Western Europe after the Portuguese reached the Ivory Coast about 1450.[43]

Furthermore, it is possible that in a time of climatic deterioration, the *storis* may have been heavier and reached farther up the West Greenland coast, making it more difficult for the ships to reach the Eastern Settlement. Sea ice reached Iceland occasionally during the eleventh, twelfth, and thirteenth centuries, several times during the fourteenth century, and frequently in the fifteenth.[44] In fact, the *Konungs skuggsjá (King's Mirror)* indicates that the old method of approaching Greenland—by heading west from Iceland to the glaciers of East Greenland, then following the coast south to Cape Farewell—was no longer tenable. Instead, ships now had to stay well offshore and sail south of the cape before approaching the coast from the southwest or west.[45]

The ships that reached Greenland in the colony's later centuries came from Norway, not Iceland. The first settlers in Iceland had "brought with them many ships, but later generations were unable to replace them," Jesse Byock points out. "As the centuries passed[,] the number of seagoing vessels steadily decreased.... Most of the Icelanders who became full-time international merchants moved abroad, operating principally out of Norway."[46]

Thus, it seems that events in Europe may also have contributed to the abandonment. By the thirteenth century it was rare for an Icelander to own a ship. Iceland, and possibly Greenland, had come under Norwegian rule in 1262, and the island was declared a trading monopoly for the crown, a restriction that probably reduced, but likely did not eliminate, other trading vessels touching there. As time wore on, however, the Norwegian crown sent fewer and fewer ships to Greenland. In 1393 German ships attacked and razed Bergen, Norway, the principal port of trade with Iceland and Greenland, and shortly thereafter the Black Death (bubonic plague) and smallpox ravaged Norway and Iceland, disrupting shipping. Norway probably ceased trade with Greenland altogether early in the fifteenth century.[47]

English ships seem to have filled the Norwegian void because the *Icelandic Sagas* of 1412 announced the first visits by English fishing vessels and reported that "no news came from Norway to Iceland.[48] Since the mid-1300s dried cod had been an export commodity from Iceland, when vessels from Norway, Germany, and England began trading there.[49] But during the fifteenth century the power of the

A fifteenth-century liripipe chaperon, found in a Norse grave in Greenland's Eastern Settlement, is evidence of contact between Greenland and Europe near the end of the Norse colony's existence.

National Museum of Denmark

German commercial organization, the Hanseatic League, grew, effectively strangling Norwegian shipping and thus cutting the country off from her overseas possessions.[50]

English traders may have been on the west coast of Greenland in the late 1300s too.[51] And, in fact, English fishing vessels had certainly been operating in the waters near Iceland since the early 1400s,[52] when their presence brought on an Anglo-Icelandic "cod war." This circumstance, in turn, may well have encouraged the English to work in less hostile waters: the fishing banks of southwest Greenland. By the 1420s or 1430s they controlled the waters there. And, later, in the 1460s, the vigorous efforts of the Hanseatic League to monopolize trade with Iceland reinforced this shift, as the English sought fishing grounds that were free of this competition.[53]

"Both fish liver oil and stockfish were essential to the fifteenth century English, not only for their domestic economy, but also for foreign trade," writes Kirsten Seaver. "Oil was used everywhere for food as well as for heat and light, and cheap, high-quality fish protein was sorely needed all over Europe as populations were finally recovering from the Black Death. . . . The lean flesh of codfish lasts up to several years when dried, which was what made stockfish such a desirable commodity, particularly in southern Europe, in an age when refrigeration did not exist."[54] Dried cod, *skreið*, was created by splitting the fish and hanging it on a wooden *stokkr* to air-dry, hence the name stockfish in English.

Whereas Norway, through its own actions, became increasingly isolated from Iceland and Greenland toward the end of the fourteenth century, the Icelanders had almost certainly begun to shift their trade to English ports, particularly Bristol. The Icelanders provided the English with stockfish, among other things, in return for salt, woolen cloth, and grain. And several items of English manufacture have been found in the latest settlement strata in Greenland habitation sites. Four pieces of iron, a table knife, and a pewter cross pendant among other things, all strongly suggest an English origin.[55]

It is worth noting that the last *recorded* Norse voyage to Markland (Labrador) from Greenland took place in 1347; hence it seems likely that English fishermen and traders acquired a knowledge of the fishing banks of Labrador and Newfoundland, *and of the Norse coastal route to get there*, from the Greenlanders, who may have accompanied them to those waters. In fact, the English fishermen may have followed the cod to Labrador and Newfoundland. Cod are very sensitive to temperature, and Brian Fagan believes that as the climate cooled during the fourteenth and fifteenth centuries, the increasingly cold water temperatures in Greenland may have forced the cod to move southwest to more

> 'High-quality fish protein was sorely needed all over Europe as populations were finally recovering from the Black Death.'

favorable waters.[56] Thus, the fact that the earliest *recorded* Bristol fishing voyages to Newfoundland, in the 1480s, went directly west across the Atlantic shows that the mariners had confidence in the existence of fishing grounds on the far shore of the ocean.[57]

In Greenland, of course, it may have been that the eastern population was simply too small to maintain itself and that the deteriorating climatic conditions encouraged a small and gradual emigration to Iceland, where land may well have become available once again because of the plague epidemic of 1402. Perhaps some left, too, for England. Some say that the population of the Eastern Settlement would not have been able to sustain itself with less than 500 individuals, citing that the emigrants to Iceland probably would have been young adults, the most energetic and productive segment of the population.[58] It has been estimated that a Norse population of 2,000 could become extinct in 200 years if only fourteen or fifteen persons were to emigrate annually.[59]

The last clear contemporary record of the Greenland Norse is the confirmation of a wedding at Hvalsø church on September 16, 1408, between Sigrid Björnsdottir and Thorstein Olafsson. The

Hvalsø church, located in the Eastern Settlement, is the site of the last recorded Norse marriage in Greenland, which took place in 1408. The artist William Bradford photographed its ruins in 1869.

couple then returned to Iceland. But at that date there is no evidence, archaeological or otherwise, to suggest that the Eastern Settlement was in trouble; indeed the Norse had recently built a number of festal halls in their communities.[60]

The last, murky, report of the Norse in Greenland is from about 1540, when a sailor called Jon "Greenlander"—because he had once been blown off course on a trading voyage between Hamburg and Iceland—entered a fjord that must have been in the Eastern Settlement. Going ashore, he found buildings and fish-drying racks, and the body of a man lying face down on the ground. He wore a cloth hood, but some of his clothes were made of sealskin. On the ground near his body was a knife with a blade so worn from repeated sharpening that almost nothing remained.[61]

It strikes me that an analogous situation exists today in the coastal communities of Labrador. There, many of the "out port" fishing settlements have been abandoned in favor of consolidation in towns where government services are available. Nevertheless, many of the former inhabitants of the out ports return to their settlements each summer for the fishing season, and, most interestingly, one or two old people have chosen to remain alone, year-round, in the out ports.

The Norse themselves probably did not consider that they had abandoned Greenland. After all, they didn't "keep score" on historical precedence—because they had no conception of such things. They were, simply, opportunistic Late Iron Age farmers and pastoralists, and, later, fishermen. Their view of what had taken place may have been, as Niels Lynnerup puts it: "Perhaps the Norse did not give up Greenland—they gave up some land and fjords that had become less and less profitable for their way of life and moved back to auspicious shores where new opportunities had arisen."[62]

Aboard *Belvedere* we departed Grønnedal on June 20, 1989, and ran down Arsuk Fjord under lowering, gray clouds. After about two hours we cleared the outer headlands and shaped a course for southern Labrador, 600 miles to the southwest. Leaving Cape Desolation behind us, for a short time we thought we were clear of the ice, having worked through a couple of strips and patches without difficulty. Right there I learned how the *storis* could have blocked access to the coast of southwestern Greenland.

Just when I thought things were going pretty well, we found the *storis*, and it was a powerful experience. It was a mixture of bergs and big, blue, bashed-up pieces of multi-year ice that was rafted up and tortured. It was heaving up and down and grinding in the Atlantic's swell—definitely not a friendly sight. As I mentioned earlier, this ice had been carried out of the Arctic Ocean and down the coast of East Greenland, then around Cape Farewell at the southern tip of the island and up the west coast—and it certainly showed the wear and tear of the voyage. Naïvely thinking that we could work through it, we kept on for a while, but, as the concentration of the floes became denser, and hence more dangerous to *Belvedere*, we were forced to turn around and work our way back out. And none too soon either, because the wind sprang up and began consolidating the pack.

As darkness approached, it turned foggy. The visibility dropped to about a tenth of a mile or less. On the helm it was a nightmare of quick glances into the radarscope, tight turns, glances at the compass and dials, then back to the ice in front of us. It was exhausting, just standing a short, two-hour watch, and it took us nearly twenty-four hours to get clear of the *storis*. By then we had run more than 100 miles to the north, paralleling the Greenland coast.

During that night the temperature fell below freezing, and the fog turned to ice as it coated the rigging, lifelines, and stays with a covering one-quarter-inch thick. Then, the next day, when the temperature made it up to thirty-three or thirty-four degrees, the ice started falling with tinkles and crashes onto the pilothouse and deck, where it remained most of the day.

Finally the seas flattened out and the ice and fog thinned. We then turned back to a course for southern Labrador. Most of that run was easy and pleasant, with the exception of one near-gale that came on our port beam, making us roll and pitch, and sending Bonnie and Peter Semotiuk to their berths for twenty-four hours. When it was over, we found the ice again. This time, however, it was flowing south in the Labrador Current, and it was mostly flat, loosely packed sea ice. This sort of ice deflects the wind off the water, calming the seas, so we ran into the pack for half a mile or so to take the opportunity to enjoy the flat water and change our fuel filters.

On the evening of June 24, 1989, we entered Sandwich Bay, Labrador, and motored toward the town of Cartwright to clear customs at the local Royal Canadian Mounted Police detachment. On the way up Sandwich Bay, in the distance of only half a mile, the temperature shot up from forty degrees to ninety-five. To us, who were now used to the cold North Atlantic, it was like sailing into a furnace, and the ice, which once again had coated the rigging, crashed onto the deck. Ashore, the flies jumped us so aggressively that we were all eager to get back aboard *Belvedere* and continue our voyage home to New England.

The fog turned to ice as it coated the rigging, lifelines, and stays with a covering one-quarter-inch thick.

CHAPTER FIVE

Up Iceberg Alley (1995)

IN 1995, WITH *Belvedere* again thoroughly refitted, it was time to begin sailing in search of European expansions to the western shores of the North Atlantic. Labrador was the place to start.

Rising from the ocean in a 700-mile procession of granite shoals, islands, cliffs, and mountains, Labrador's unforgiving coast runs from the scrub-covered islets of Quebec to the jagged Torngat Range in the north. Its warped and scoured escarpments form a severely beautiful palisade that testifies mightily to the violent and complicated geological history of the region. The coastline is made of some of the oldest rocks on earth, so raw and bold that it hardly seems that the region could sustain life. Nevertheless, less than ten millennia ago, once the land was released from the crushing weight of the great continental glacier, the ancestors of today's Inuit (Eskimos) and Innu (Naskapis) spread throughout Labrador.

European colonists have also wrung a living from Labrador's lands and waters. A thousand years ago Norse voyagers from Greenland probed the region, settled briefly, and then returned to the coast for four centuries to harvest its dense stands of timber. Not long after came the explorers and fishermen of England and Portugal, then Basque whalemen, and later, settlers from France, England, and Ireland for the fisheries and the fur trade.

I sent *Belvedere* ahead, fully stocked, to the town of Baddeck in the Bras d'Or Lakes on Cape Breton Island, at the northern end of Nova Scotia, while I remained in New England to attend my mother's memorial service. Bonnie Hahn and I then flew from Boston to catch up. Clearing customs in Yarmouth, Nova Scotia, proved to be a bit trickier than I had anticipated. Because I had sent my sailing clothes ahead on the boat, all I had in my suitcase were some last-minute fruits and vegetables that Romayne had sent with me—and the replacement medications for *Belvedere*'s medical kit. When the customs inspector opened my suitcase, all he saw was a huge assortment of prescription drugs and a couple of dozen hypodermic syringes. "Where are your clothes?" he asked with narrowing eyes. I suddenly realized that this did look pretty fishy: Here I was standing at Canadian Customs with a suitcase full of drugs and vegetables, no clothes, a wallet full of money, and a big bruise on my forearm that I had picked up when wrestling with an outboard motor a few days before. The vegetables alone were enough to arouse suspicion.

After much raising of eyebrows, close questioning, and consultations with superiors, the inspector allowed me to proceed, but my suitcase was in bond. Fortunately, when I reached Sydney Airport, near Baddeck, it turned out that Agent Ethel Poole, who met me there, remembered having cleared *Belvedere* inward a few days before and released my suitcase to me. My old friend Henry Fuller, a

We found a peaceful anchorage in Woods Island Harbour, Bay of Islands, Newfoundland. (Belvedere is on the right.)

Belvedere's Voyage of 1995

lanky, raw-boned ocean sailor who owns the Cape Breton Boat Yard where *Belvedere* was presently berthed, suggested to Agent Poole that I looked fairly shifty and should be deported at once. Ignoring this bit of blatant jingoism, she welcomed me to Canada.

We left Baddeck on July 17, heading north through Great Bras d'Or Channel between the bold, forested hills of Cape Breton Island. Aboard in 1995 were Andy Rowe, Bonnie, Peter Semotiuk, Julian ("Jules") Underwood, who had been with us in 1992 in Norway and Spitsbergen, and a newcomer to *Belvedere*, Nick Smith ("Smitty"), a sailor from Maine, who had already made several voyages to Labrador.

Our first challenge was in crossing Cabot Strait. Lying between Cape Breton Island and Newfoundland, it is the main shipping channel into the Gulf of St. Lawrence and the Great Lakes, and it is exposed to long, open-water fetches from three directions. Sure enough, just as we reached the narrows at the northern end of the Great Bras d'Or Channel, we ran into a nasty, steep chop setting in against the current that was carrying us into Cabot Strait. We discovered that the northeasterly wind, which was forecast to die, still had quite a bit of life in it. The swells were very closely spaced, and some were five feet, causing a violent hobby-horsing motion that drove Peter and Bonnie straight to their berths.

Our course toward Labrador led us past the southwest corner of Newfoundland. Unfortunately, this took us right into the wind, so we had no choice but to motor ahead. Once we had some sea room, however, we began to "tack" across the course, thus taking the swells more on our beams, and making the motion quite a bit easier. Later that night the northeasterly did indeed die to a flat calm, which was then replaced by a twenty-five-knot southeasterly that allowed us to set the mainsail and jib, giving us better than eight knots over the ground.

Our only cause for concern was that the marine weather reports were full of gale warnings for most areas, and this situation was further complicated by the expected arrival of tropical storm Chantal on the southeastern coast of Newfoundland the next day. Cabot Strait is close to seventy miles wide at its narrowest, and the west coast of Newfoundland is more than 300 miles long. But our direct course from the Great Bras d'Or Channel toward Labrador took us up a stretch of the west Newfoundland coast where there were no suitable harbors. For us, this meant that it would be closer to 200 miles from the shelter of Cape Breton Island to reach the safety of Lark Harbour in Bay of Islands, Newfoundland.

The williwaws gouged into the water, blowing plumes of spray forty feet into the air.

Still, our hunch was that we could reach Lark Harbour before the gales reached us, so we kept on. The next day, as we continued northward, the cliffs of Cape St. George, at the tip of the long, triangular Port au Port Peninsula, stood out in the clear afternoon light. The tan, warped metamorphic rock, topped by a brilliant green covering of turf, contrasted sharply in the orange light with the ochre sandstone bluffs of Red Island, just offshore.

In the far distance we saw South Head at the entrance to Bay of Islands, thirty miles away, and because of the exceptional visibility it seemed to take ages to arrive there. In fact, it wasn't until well after dark that we even got close, entering the bay in pitch black, and anchoring in Lark Harbour at 11:45 P.M. with bold, dark cliffs towering above us, while ever more dire predictions of gales came over the radio from the Newfoundland Weather Centre.

By 7:30 the next morning it was blowing thirty-five knots from the southeast. We quickly decided to move across the bay to Woods Island Harbour because Lark Harbour's high hills and fjord-like valleys are notorious for sending williwaws—stiff bursts of wind, rolling over the peaks, then roaring down onto the water.

It didn't turn out be as easy as that. Eyeing the 2,000-foot tops of the Blow-Me-Down Hills in the east, and the clouds swooping down over them, I remembered that early explorers had referred to the "indescribable winds" in Bay of Islands. As we pounded our way out of Lark Harbour, the williwaws gouged into the water, blowing plumes of spray forty feet into the air.

Woods Island Harbour was only a few miles away, but we knew that worming our way in there wasn't going to be a piece of cake. The entrance is only about fifty feet wide, and two ledges force a boat to zigzag on the way in, requiring a hard right turn, followed by a quick hard-left. The strong winds made it even trickier because *Belvedere* has bilge keels jutting out from either side of the hull. This allows her to have a shallow draft, which for a boat of her size one central keel would not allow.

The trade-off for having bilge keels is, however, a loss of the lateral resistance that a central keel would provide. This required us to side-slip toward the harbor mouth, and at the last minute to throw in the turns. Andy Rowe was on the wheel and pulled off the maneuver flawlessly, while Smitty and I were on the pilothouse roof helping with steering instructions. Fortunately we reached the entrance at low water, so we could easily read the surf on the ledges. It was, "Steady, steady... Now! Hard to starboard!" and a few seconds later, "Hard to port!" and then we slipped into the stillness of a totally enclosed hurricane hole a quarter of a mile in diameter.

Woods Island Harbour is a gem. Surrounded by green fields of wildflowers and stands of small spruce trees, it was dotted here and

Williwaws from the Blow-Me-Down Hills pummel the water in Bay of Islands, western Newfoundland.

there by a dozen colorful small houses and their outbuildings. In front of each cluster of buildings was a boat ramp made from spruce poles, and piles of wooden lobster traps with hoop-shaped tops.

We moved to the top of the harbor while the wind howled above us, but it did not disturb the water. Still, we put out two anchors into the sticky black mud of the bottom. By afternoon the wind was down somewhat and patches of blue sky appeared. Andy and Jules and I took the dinghy ashore, landing near the remains of a massive iron-fastened ship's rudder that we assumed was from a wreck.

Moving up from the beach, we walked through meadows full of buttercups, daisies, Queen Anne's lace, irises, fireweed, and lupines. We found lots of strawberry plants and raspberry bushes too, as well as little, perfectly formed, fat and lush balsam firs. From the top of a low saddle on the island we saw that the williwaws were still tearing up the water near Lark Harbour, making us very thankful to be where we were.

As I looked out over the waters of Bay of Islands, with flocks of sea birds swooping above schools of fish, I remembered that Captain James Cook had spent five summers charting the coasts of Newfoundland in the 1760s, before his three famous voyages in the Pacific. He made the first accurate hydrographic surveys of this coast, and of Woods Island Harbour.

But long before Cook's voyages, the west coast of Newfoundland had once been called "*La Côte des Basques.*" In the 1500s Basque fishermen set up fishing stations all along the west coast, as far north as the Strait of Belle Isle, and this harbor had been one of them. From early in the sixteenth century the ships of many nationalities had fished and traded in Newfoundland's waters—French, Portuguese, Basque, English, and Dutch. But by the latter half of the seventeenth century only the English and French remained in significant numbers. After the Treaty of Utrecht in 1713, which ended Queen Anne's War (1701–13) and resulted in large colonial gains for England, the entire western coast of Newfoundland became the "Treaty Shore," when England gave France the right to take, cure, and store fish there. Later, English fishermen settled on the coast, and in the nineteenth century large fleets of schooners made annual voyages from there to fish in Labrador's waters.[1]

'This is a fine place to lay up, not like Lark 'arbour down sout'. Yer as safe 'ere as if yer in God's pocket.'

The next morning was gray and misty, but the wind had gone light, so we hauled up our anchors and headed out for the next harbor, Woody Point in Bonne Bay, forty-five miles to the north. We motored almost all the way over calm seas through fog, with only a quarter of a mile's visibility, but the piloting wasn't difficult and the fog lifted as we came round the high headland at the entrance of the bay, revealing spectacular scenery. Before us were green-topped vertical cliffs flecked with snow banks. Their sheer rock faces plunged into gorges, while white floccus clouds sped overhead and accented the blue waters, where porpoises were breaching.

Before long we were secured to the disused ferry dock, and Bill Roberts, one of Woody Point's friendly elders, hobbled out to greet us. "This is a fine place to lay up, not like Lark 'arbour down sout'. Yer as safe 'ere as if yer in God's pocket." Not only were we in God's pocket, we were also in Gros Morne National Park, a Luxembourg-sized realm of immense beauty and raw granite that was thrust up from the earth's mantle, then scraped clean of vegetation by continental glaciers, making it a nirvana for geologists.

The small town was much as I remembered it during our southbound voyage from Greenland in 1989. Alongshore were a handful of fish houses fronted with rock-filled cribwork piers and boat ramps built from spruce-pole latticework. Ashore were friendly people, quiet streets with a few crafts stores and poorly stocked grocery-hardware stores. We stopped to buy a few postcards in one of them. Tacked to the wall was a notice written on a piece of cardboard: "$500 reward for information leading to the arrest and conviction of person or persons involved in the theft of lobsters on the night of May 15, 1995."

The water was full of jellyfish, some of the red ones trailing dangerous-looking tentacles six to eight feet long.

It was clear that when the highway had gone in east of the bay, bypassing Woody Point and thus putting the ferry out of service, the town had slowed down. "That's the same Pyrex dish that I saw here in '89," said Peter, looking through one of the dusty storefront windows. Now, without long lines of cars waiting for the ferry, we learned that they had even removed the pay telephone from the local bar. Nearby, the fish plant didn't seem to be doing much business either. A few small crab boats and a couple of herring seiners were unloading their catches. But we saw no cod or halibut, formerly the staple of the Newfoundland fisheries. They had been fished close to extinction, and the Canadian government had closed the fishery, putting many people out of work and on the dole.

Two days later we were off Point Riche, the tip of the Port au Choix Peninsula (*Portucho Çaharra* in Basque is "the old little port") when it started to blow twenty knots from the north, sending a steep chop right at us. All at once we were slamming into the waves, so we abandoned our plans to reach the Strait of Belle Isle that day and instead turned into St. John's Bay, where, on St. John's Island, we found a pretty little anchorage in St. John's Harbour.

The island was covered with surprisingly lush green woods, and the shores were lined with horizontal gray ledges that had been undercut by wave action and then carried up by the slowly rising land. The water was full of jellyfish, some of the red ones trailing dangerous-looking tentacles six to eight feet long.

Peter and I took the dinghy ashore and walked among the ledges. All along the shore were orderly stacks of lobster pots with several hundred traps in each pile. An arctic tern fluttered above the tide pools, occasionally diving, while gulls milled above the harbor and, inexplicably, an owl flew about amidst the spruce trees.

To the south we saw Port au Choix a few miles away. I had visited there in 1989 to inspect some ancient archaeological remains in the small museum. Port au Choix has been an excellent fishing and sealing site for several millennia, and it was in the little harbor on Benie Island where, more than four centuries ago, the Basques held a trading rendezvous with the Inuit each August. This was one of the southernmost sites that the Inuit reached. Because each group feared the other, they avoided direct contact by shuttling a boat loaded with trade goods across a piece of water between them. The Inuit put skins in the boat and shoved it across to the Basques who put in "Bread, Brandy, Needles, Thread, Shooes, Stockings, Shirts, Jacketts, Pipes, Tobacco, etc."[2]

The weather was very clear that day, and to the north I also saw the lighthouse at Ferolle Point, the beginning of the Strait of Belle Isle. In Basque it was called *Ferrol Çaharra*; its harbor is thought to have reminded them of the harbor of Ferrol in Galicia at the northwestern corner of the Iberian Peninsula.

〜

We were off the next morning at 6:00 A.M., helped along with the north-flowing tidal current. By noon we saw the lighthouse at Point Amour on the Labrador shore and farther to the west, the twin hills that Captain Cook called "Our Ladies Bubbies."

As we moved deeper into the Strait of Belle Isle (in Basque, *el canal de Granbaya*) our view of the Labrador shore was interrupted by fog patches. The strait, separating Newfoundland and Labrador by about ten miles at its narrowest, is roughly eighty-five miles long. It is a place that mariners respect because of the winds that funnel through there from north and south, gaining strength by the Bernoulli effect as the slowly converging shores constrict the air flow.

There are also two currents that flow there: a warmish north-flowing one on the Newfoundland shore, and a very cold south-flowing one on the Labrador shore—and these currents are slowed or accelerated by the tides flowing in and out of the Gulf of St. Lawrence. When the wind blows against these currents, it can generate a nasty, steep sea, especially during the time of the greatest tidal flow. So, our southerly wind that day had picked up moisture from the north-flowing current, and as it traversed the cold south-flowing water on the Labrador side it turned to fog, first giving us an intermittent view of that coast, then, no view at all.

Later, as we crossed the strait and felt our way through the thick fog toward the shelter of Red Bay, Labrador, we kept our eyes on the radar scopes and the depth sounders, and had an ear cocked for the mournful double hoot of the fog horn on Saddle Island, at the harbor's entrance. We certainly did not want to find either of the harbor's two outlying submerged rocky ledges, affectionately called "*the Louse*" and "*the Scab*."

All at once we burst out of the fog into fine, clear air, right in the harbor's mouth. Suddenly Saddle Island, with its lighthouse, was on

We certainly did not want to find either of the harbor's two outlying submerged rocky ledges, affectionately called 'the Louse' and 'the Scab.'

A flourishing potato garden in Red Bay, Newfoundland

our starboard side. Ahead were high bluffs covered with stunted spruce, and while the harbor was dotted with colorful and carefully tended houses, round the shore stood much evidence of the passing Labradorean cod-fishing culture. It was sad to see abandoned and dilapidated fish houses and broken-down cribwork piers.

As soon as we had secured to the town pier and washed *Belvedere* down, Peter and I walked up the road through the quiet, tidy town. We passed among well-tended potato patches. Their neat raised beds were fenced and surrounded by thick cow parsley, which, Peter told me, was planted there to help cut the force of the cold wind. At the end of the road we came to the small but excellent museum that commemorates the Basque whale fishery and the fact that in the later 1500s Red Bay was the "world whaling capital."

Scholars have known for a long time that sixteenth-century Basque whalemen hunted in the waters of Newfoundland and Labrador, but it was my friend Selma Barkham who put flesh on the bones of historiography. Burrowing diligently away in archives in Valladolid and Oñate in the Basque region of Spain, she uncovered manuscript evidence confirming that Basques had operated a thriving shore whaling industry in more than a dozen harbors on the Labrador coast of the Strait of Belle Isle. The earliest document dates from 1536, but the whalemen were certainly there well before that.

Historians had puzzled over the location of the Basque place names *Butus*, or *Buteres*—later *Les Buttes* (in French)—which Selma reasoned had to refer to Red Bay's red granite cliffs. In 1977 she led a skeptical party of archaeologists and historians there and confirmed her hypothesis, pointing to the quantities of bowhead and right whale bones along the shore of the harbor, as well as to masses of broken terra cotta roof tiles. These U-shaped tiles were exported from Spain and France to cover the whalers' tryworks, where the whale blubber was rendered into oil over fire pits.[3] On Saddle Island archaeologists quickly uncovered low stone walls encrusted with a thick black substance that was burned whale blubber. The following year divers discovered the remains of the galleon *San Juan*. Laden with a thousand barrels of whale oil, she had foundered in the harbor during a gale in the autumn of 1565. Two other wrecks were found later.

Standing high on the shore, looking out into the strait over Saddle Island, Peter Semotiuk pointed to the rusty careened hulk of a collier that had been driven ashore in the 1930s and said, "I can almost see a fleet of seven or eight ships at anchor in the harbor and tryworks all along shore belching greasy black smoke. I'll bet the *San Juan* went down in a gale just like the one that drove that rust bucket ashore."

Basque whaling on the coast of Labrador continued well into the 1600s, with an average of fifteen ships a year hauling their cargoes back to Europe, but the fishery had begun to wane at the beginning of

The wreck of a collier off Saddle Island in Red Bay reminds visitors of the strength of autumn winds in the Strait of Belle Isle.

the 1600s. Several factors probably contributed to this: The demand of the Spanish crown for Basque ships; the opening of the Spitsbergen fisheries in which the Basques were closely involved; and perhaps the southward expansion of the Inuit, who are recorded to have killed several Basques. It seems that the Basques gradually returned to the cod fishery and moved deeper into the Gulf of St. Lawrence.

Equally important, by the time the Basques ceased whaling operations they had probably reduced the right whale population to such a low number that the species has been unable to recover to this day. Scientists, examining whale bones found under the *San Juan*, believe that the right whale population had become so suppressed that the species lost its genetic diversity, which reduced the live-birth rate. There are only about 300 northern right whales left in the Atlantic Ocean, and although the population is fully protected, it is not increasing.

Red Bay served as a fishing harbor from then on. In 1715 a merchant from Quebec set up a fortified trading post on the bay, but the Inuit burned it down three years later. It was quickly rebuilt. In the early 1800s fishermen from Newfoundland began using the harbor for drying their cod catches, and eventually they settled there permanently.[4]

We saw the faint outlines of the earthen foundations of the six-pointed star fort that withstood an Indian raid ten years after it was built.

❦

We left Red Bay at 8:30 A.M. on July 25 and drove right back into the fog bank that had been hanging off Saddle Island. We turned northeast, paralleling the coast, and for the next thirty miles we at no time could see more than fifty feet ahead. Eventually we tired of this and turned into Chateau Bay. As we emerged from the fog wall again, the damp fifty-five-degree weather was replaced by a blazing sun, eighty degrees, and horseflies. After a tour of the large, well-protected embayment, we anchored at Pitts Harbour. Its tree-covered slopes bore the scars of past forest fires.

Andy, Smitty, Bonnie, and I took the dinghy to Barrier Point, through thirty-knot gusts of wind from the southwest. Crossing some lovely green tundra cover, we walked to the remains of Fort York, which was built by the British in 1766, shortly after the end of the Seven Years' War (the "French and Indian War" in North America) to protect the fishing community in Pitts Harbour. We saw the faint outlines of the earthen foundations of the six-pointed star fort that withstood an Indian raid ten years after it was built. Apart from those, the only discernible remains consisted of a pile of stones and bricks where the central fireplace had stood. To seaward lay Henley Island with its reddish, flat-topped mesa of columnar basalt, looking very much like the "castle" (*Xateau* in Basque) that gives the bay its name. Red terra cotta roofing tiles are found at its base too. Offshore, beyond the massive mesa, lay the gray wall of fog, but glowing through it and rising above it were the brilliant white, almost fluorescent tops of two large icebergs.

~

Two days later, at the north end of the Strait of Belle Isle, we threaded *Belvedere* through the narrow tickle into Battle Harbour. In Labradorean parlance a tickle is a strait so narrow that it's ticklish to enter—and the twenty-yard-wide southern entrance to Battle Harbour would certainly qualify for that. Fortunately, its northern entrance is much wider.

This surprisingly cozy village was first settled by the English in 1775, when a trading company set up shop on the ledges at the water's edge, serving the local *Liv'eres* (so named because they "live here") whose severely arduous lives revolved around the fisheries, seal hunting, and fur trapping. In the nineteenth century an Anglican church and a Grenfell Mission hospital were established as well. The world first paid attention to Battle Harbour, however, when in 1909 Commander Robert E. Peary stopped there on his way south from Greenland to use the Marconi wireless facility to broadcast his claim to being the first man to have reached the North Pole. His claim was immediately challenged by Frederick E. Cook, who reported that he had reached the Pole the year before.[5]

This controversy has provided fodder for hundreds of writers ever since, and a large body of opinion now exists that neither man reached the Pole, although Peary probably got much closer to it. In fact, the first men to stand at the North Pole were probably twenty-four members of a secret Soviet expedition that landed there in three aircraft in April 1948.[6] But the first person to attain the Pole on the surface, by crossing the ice, was most likely Ralph Plaisted, who got there in 1968 on a snowmobile.[7] The following year, 1969, Wally Herbert, using dog teams, crossed the Arctic Ocean from Point Barrow, Alaska, via the North Pole.[8] In 1994, two icebreakers, the U.S. Coast Guard cutter *Polar Sea* and the Canadian Coast Guard ship *Louis S. St.-Laurent*, reached the North Pole together, en route to completing the first surface traverse of the Arctic Ocean by ship.[9]

In Battle Harbour, as the twentieth century wore on, however, the fish stocks dwindled and the government centralized its services elsewhere. The people gradually moved to the mainland, leaving Battle Harbour only as a pleasant summer camp, but with many of its three-dozen buildings more or less intact. The Battle Harbour Historic Trust is now restoring the wharves, processing buildings, stores, church, and houses, maintaining them as a living monument

The first men to stand at the North Pole were probably twenty-four members of a secret Soviet expedition that landed there in three aircraft in April 1948.

Belvedere *enters Battle Harbour, Labrador, through the narrow southern tickle.*

to the life and work of the Labradoreans of the last three centuries.

Peter and Bonnie and I walked up over Battle Harbour's smooth granite ridges and spongy tundra moss to the top of the island. In beautifully clear weather I gazed down at the little village, while near shore a couple of minke whales romped around the ledges, feeding on schools of herring. I was drinking in this lovely sight when suddenly from behind us came a deep, thunderous KERWHUUUUUMP!—like the slow explosion of several tons of TNT. Bonnie let out a low "Holy mackerel." I knew what must have happened as I spun around.

Off to the north, out in the perfect blueness of the Labrador Sea, sparkled several dozens of brilliant white icebergs, and a mile away, a violent froth of white water and chunks of broken ice milled around two huge pieces that were slowly rolling over. An iceberg had just calved, throwing up a wall of water that raced across St. Lewis Bay. It reminded me that we were at the beginning of "Iceberg Alley."

Southern Labrador's coast runs about sixty miles due north from Battle Harbour, and it is here that the very cold Labrador Current, running south from Greenland, passes closest to shore, carrying along icebergs in a majestic procession that averages about ten miles a day. Most of these icebergs are created by the glaciers of west Greenland, which themselves are squeezed forward into the ocean by the awesome pressure of the Greenland icecap. The icecap forces the glaciers outward, between the coastal mountains, to the sea. The bergs are not the result of freezing sea water, but rather are formed from snow that was deposited on the icecap and then compressed for thousands of years as more and more accumulated. "Submariners in the Arctic can always tell when they are below a berg," Vice Admiral George Steele, who commanded USS *Seadragon,* the first submarine to traverse the Northwest Passage, told me.[10] "Their hydrophones pick up the hiss of the berg's compressed air escaping as the ice melts." On the surface we found that when we put pieces of berg ice in our drinks, they bubbled and snapped and crackled like puffed rice.

On the average the west Greenland glaciers calve about 27,000 icebergs each year. They then begin a two- to three-year voyage of about 2,000 miles, melting and calving as they travel, first north along the Greenland shore to Baffin Bay, then south, past Baffin Island and Labrador. On average, about a thousand bergs per year reach Belle Isle, and a few find their way into the Strait of Belle Isle, but most are borne down the east coast of Newfoundland to the Grand Banks, where they meet the sixty-degree water of the Gulf Stream and vanish quickly.

As soon as they break off from the face of a glacier, the melting of their submerged part (about nine-tenths of their mass) begins, and this melting is, of course, faster or slower according to the temperature of the water. The deterioration time for a medium-sized berg (say, rising 150 feet above sea level and 300 feet long) in six-foot seas varies widely according to the water temperature. In thirty-degree water it would be about 180 days; in sixty-degree water it would be about five days. Because the vast part of an iceberg is underwater, the bottom melts more quickly than the top. The melting, combined with the oscillation of the ocean swells, creates stresses and makes them unstable. The result is calvings and roll-overs because large chunks can break off from the bottom, which

The nineteenth-century village at Battle Harbour has been preserved as a monument to Labrador's settlers.

makes the berg top-heavy, capsizing it. In fog the presence of lots of small bits of sloughed-off ice (brash ice) usually indicates that an iceberg is nearby, usually upwind.

Icebergs come in all shapes and sizes. A very large Atlantic berg may be more than 250 feet high and 700 feet long. A *bergy bit* is a small piece of an iceberg the size of a big house, and a *growler* is a piece smaller still, the size of a shipping container or grand piano.[11] It is impossible to predict when a berg will calve, but some bergs are less stable than others: Those with twin or triple pinnacles, hence with greater internal stresses, are more prone to break apart than large flat-topped bergs. The pinnacled and steeple-topped bergs, and bergs with arches and holes, are the least stable but the most photogenic, and some boats venture far too close to these in the quest for dramatic photographs. But when a berg calves—or, for that matter, when *any* object of hundreds of thousands, or millions, of tons is in motion—it is a good idea to keep one's distance.

And for anyone who wishes to sail in those waters at night, it is worth remembering that the radar returns from icebergs are about sixty times weaker than for ships of similar size above the waterline. And, smaller pieces, bergy bits and growlers, are very difficult to detect at all, especially in heavy seas.

"Bergy" years seem to come in pulses. The year 1993 was very busy; 1999 was unusually light, with northeast winds stranding many bergs on the Labrador coast. In 1995, for instance, about 1,500 bergs made it south of 48° N, roughly the latitude of St. John's, Newfoundland. Some bergs, however, have drifted well into, and even across, the Gulf Stream. A number of them reach 42° N (not far above the latitude of Boston) at the southern end of the Grand Banks. In the early decades of the twentieth century, during what must have been several exceptionally icy years, bergs were sighted near Bermuda, Ireland, and even the Azores.[12]

It was the most famous iceberg of all—the one that sank the RMS *Titanic*—that brought about the creation of the International Ice Patrol. For four centuries icebergs have been a hazard to shipping near the Grand Banks, lying as they do athwart the great circle route between northeastern North America and northern Europe. But as everyone knows, on the night of April 14, 1912, the White Star Line's *Titanic*, nearly 900 feet long and 11 stories high, with 2,220 persons aboard, at the latitude of Providence, Rhode Island, glanced off a berg southeast of Newfoundland, opening her starboard side and sending her to the bottom, with 1,513 dead.[13]

Almost at once U.S. military vessels began patrolling the area to warn of the iceberg danger. After the Safety of Life at Sea Convention (SOLAS) of 1913, the International Ice Patrol was formed, and since then the U.S. Coast Guard has carried out its operations. Today eighteen nations contribute to the cost of running this service, which flies spotter planes (currently HC-130H Hercules) from St. John's, Newfoundland, over the Grand Banks. Data from the planes' observations are then transmitted to the headquarters of the International Ice Patrol at the Coast Guard Research and Development Center in Groton, Connecticut, which plots their locations and, in close cooperation with the Canadian Ice Service, establishes a boundary for the limit of all known ice (LAKI), which

It was the most famous iceberg of all—the one that sank the RMS Titanic—that brought about the creation of the International Ice Patrol.

is then transmitted to Atlantic shipping.[14] For a vessel to pass within this boundary—without specific exemptions in its insurance policy—risks voiding the policy if the ship suffers ice damage.[15] "Since the inception of the International Ice Patrol," Lieutenant Alfred T. Ezman of the U.S. Coast Guard has written, "there has not been a single reported loss of life or property due to collision with an iceberg outside advertised limits of all known ice in this area."[16]

Today, with the threat from icebergs mostly contained, and ice-strengthened drilling rigs in place on the Grand Banks,[17] these formerly fearsome things have gained an exotic charm in the minds of much of the public. Boat tours advertising "up-close" encounters with icebergs are offered to tourists at many towns in eastern and northern Newfoundland. And in fact, two entrepreneurs there, Ronald Stamp and Paul Benson, formed the Iceberg Corporation of America and are using a barge, fitted with heated tanks—which had formerly transported molasses—and a crane and grapple to produce bottled water from icebergs. "Imagine the marketing possibilities within the $30-billion-a-year worldwide bottled water industry," wrote Nathan Vardi under the headline of "With the Cod Fished Out, What's a Newfoundlander To Do?"

Two entrepreneurs . . . are using a barge, fitted with heated tanks . . . and a crane and grapple to produce bottled water from icebergs.

As Vardi explained, a tugboat more or less lassos an iceberg, maneuvering it next to a barge where a grapple bites off about a half ton and crushes it into the heating tank. When it has collected a quarter of a million gallons it heads to the company's plant ashore.

"The enterprise was goofy enough to attract one of those doomed government efforts to create jobs," Vardi continues. "The Atlantic Canada Opportunities Agency, desperate to improve Newfoundland's 15 percent unemployment rate, lent the company $400,000 interest free. It bought them 35 jobs. . . . Icebergs may be free, but they are a long way from the customers. Despite steep retail prices —$4.75 for a six-pack of 12-ounce bottles—Iceberg Corp. lost $1.7 million on revenues of $500,000 in the nine months ended Mar. 31."[18]

Two days later, sixty miles farther north and still in Iceberg Alley, the weather was brilliant. We were running easily with moderate winds from the northwest and seventy-degree temperatures. The warm, dry air distorted the icebergs, raising some above the horizon. We saw one of them on our radar about eighteen miles ahead, and it looked huge. We motored toward it, taking about three hours to get there. During our approach it appeared alternately above or below the horizon, elongated horizontally, divided into two layers, stretched vertically, and domed in the center. When we got close, we were somewhat disappointed. We estimated it to be about 100 to 110 feet high, about twice the height of *Belvedere*'s mast, but certainly not the behemoth that we had anticipated.

That done, we motored toward Hawke Harbour, passing red granite ledges and hills covered with green moss. We were not prepared for what we found there.

The powerful silence of Hawke Harbour was almost overwhelming. In the evening stillness a soft fog washed over the spruce-topped granite hills surrounding the anchorage, while outside the harbor's heads, past the rocky ledges, sea birds rested on the slick tops of growlers, swooping

and diving above pods of minke and humpback whales. Ashore, the silence was broken only by the swash of waves amid the seaweed-covered rocks and the occasional eerie call of a loon.

Yet amid this serenity was a jarring reminder of a half-century's noise and violence. The head of the harbor was a mass of wreckage. Rusty tanks, smokestacks, conveyor belts, boilers, firebrick, and twisted metal rails lay in a wild confusion. At the water's edge decomposing whalebones—vertebrae and ribs—were jumbled together with all sorts of industrial junk and exploded bits of harpoon heads and small railroad wheels. Above, on a low granite bluff, were the tortured, imploded remains of two large oil storage tanks, and below them great black streaks of charred oil smeared the cliff face.

The wreckage of the whaling station in Hawke Harbour, Labrador

A couple of hundred yards away the half-submerged hulks of two catcher ships listed against one another at unnatural angles. On both sides of the hulks five pairs of large holes pierced their bulwarks—and testified to the violence of the whaling industry. These were fairleads, through which lines were run from the whales' flukes. After the whales had been killed with exploding grenade-tipped harpoons fired from the ships' ninety-millimeter cannons, the carcasses were collected and towed to the station. There, winches hauled the whales up a slipway to the flensing deck, where workers with long-handled knives stripped off the blubber and meat and separated the bones. The pieces were then drawn up a conveyor belt for processing: The blubber was rendered into oil in "steam digesters" and the bones were ground up for fertilizer.

As I have mentioned, commercial whaling began in North America early in the sixteenth century, when Basque whalemen set up stations on the Labrador coast near the Strait of Belle Isle and produced a valuable harvest of bowhead and right whale oil for the European market. This intensive hunting severely reduced the whale populations in the strait, but, as we have seen, at the very end of that century the discovery of even richer whaling grounds near Spitsbergen drew the commercial whalers there. With the exception of a small American pelagic whale fishery in the eighteenth and nineteenth centuries, the Labrador coast was essentially left to fishermen, seal hunters, and fur trappers.

Events in Norway were, however, to end this. In 1868 the birth of the modern whaling industry took place when Svend Foyn and his Norwegian associates began using steam-powered catcher ships that were fitted with heavy guns firing grenade-tipped harpoons. These innovations allowed them to take the larger, faster-swimming whales that had hitherto been very difficult to capture.

After quickly depleting the stocks in northern Norway, the Norwegians cast their eyes farther afield and perceived new opportunities in the western Atlantic. With Newfoundland investors, they incorporated a shore-whaling venture and began operations in 1898, catching 91 whales that year. The boom-and-bust cycle continued, and by 1904 there were ten catcher ships serving fourteen shore stations. That year the combined effort resulted in the capture of 1,275 whales.

The Hawke Harbour station began operations in 1905 and operated on and off, depending on market conditions, until 1959. The station took a wide variety of whale species: in 1928, for instance, it processed 59 blue whales, 280 fin whales, 15 humpback whales, 23 sei whales, and 22 sperm whales, for a total of 399.[19]

Hawke Harbour's final, appropriately apocalyptic moment

occurred on September 12, 1959, when a spectacular fire swept through the station, destroying everything. Today the profound silence of Hawke Harbour reminds me of the feeling of a great battlefield—Gettysburg, Culloden Moor, Omaha Beach. There are ghosts here, and the presence of mortal contest and slaughter is palpable.

The Canadian government banned commercial whaling in 1972. Since then the only Canadian harvest of large whales has been a few bowheads, taken by the Inuit, for subsistence.

CHAPTER SIX

An Icy Summer on the Labrador Coast (1996)

T HE FOLLOWING SUMMER, 1996, we pushed farther up the coast in search of early European contacts in Labrador. When we arrived near Hawke Harbour, we found ourselves with a big, uncomfortable swell setting in from the Labrador Sea, so instead of going on, we took a fishermen's route, locally called *Squasho Run*, up the inside passage behind Venison and Hawke Islands. As soon as we had land between us and the swell, the water went to a flat calm, and we headed up the narrow waterway. High granite cliffs on either side were studded with stands of black and white spruce and a few birch. Elsewhere the slopes were covered in a thick layer of yellow-green reindeer moss.

After about fifteen miles in this lovely run, we emerged into the Labrador Sea and back into the big *lop* (a ground swell in Labradorean) on a sparkling morning. The enormous swells broke dramatically on all the outlying ledges and *sunkers* (submerged rocks). As we moved out into the ocean, we passed amid the dull booms of the breakers. These were accompanied by great white explosions of foam and spray that stood out against the deep blue of the sky and the sea. Each of these *sunkers* was well known to the fishermen of the nineteenth century, and each had an evocative name: *The Squire, Old King, The Feather Bed, The Ravens, The Pippies, The Cobbler, The Planter,* and *Mad Moll.*

Our fresh water supply was getting low, so we decided to duck into the town of Black Tickle, on Island of Ponds, to top up our tanks from the local fish plant. From seaward the town did not have an attractive countenance. Two black cylindrical oil tanks and the skeleton of a rusty red International Scout, ca. 1982, marked the approach. Once we were secure to the pier we discovered that the fish plant was closed for the season; hence no water was available. Later we found that the town's fuel hose would not reach to our berth. The only solution would have been to move to a fully exposed part of the pier where a twenty-five-knot southerly was putting an ugly swell right against the pilings. It made sense to wait out the blow right where we were.

The following day, July 10, 1996, the *Northern Ranger*, the coastal passenger-and-freight ship, arrived on its scheduled visit, and I went aboard that fine vessel to talk with the captain and to learn what might lie ahead for us. We had heard from a number of people that there was plenty of ice up ahead on the central Labrador coast, and the captain confirmed it: "We weren't able to get into the two northern towns on the coast, and we had difficulty getting into the next two below them. You'll definitely see ice this summer."

Belvedere entering Sandwich Bay, Labrador

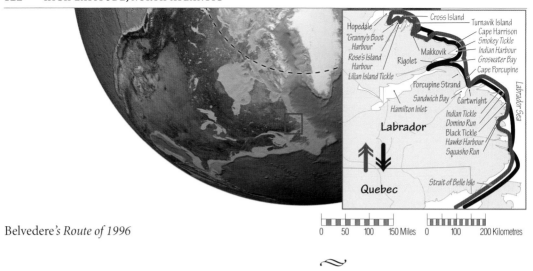

Belvedere's *Route of 1996*

Belvedere *and the*
Northern Ranger
at the dock in Black
Tickle, Labrador

We left Black Tickle that morning and headed inside the islands, through the protection of Domino Run and Indian Tickle, toward the town of Cartwright in Sandwich Bay. A few hours later I was on deck, taking photographs, and we had almost reached the point to turn into Sandwich Bay, when suddenly, a dry offshore breeze swept over us and the air temperature shot up. I remembered our arrival from Greenland at exactly the same spot in 1989, when the hot wind had quickly loosened the ice in *Belvedere*'s rigging, and right away pieces began raining down onto the deck. This time, however, the wind produced a fierce mirage.

Around us were twelve good-sized icebergs, one of them with two large vertically elongated spires. The mirage, too, distorted the outlines of the islands nearby into tall, narrow objects, and occasionally produced an upside-down image that hovered above the horizontally distorted lower one. At the same time the horizon seemed to swim upward, as if made of jelly.

We were encountering one of the most dramatic of the Arctic's mysteries, the superior mirage, or *fata morgana*. The name derives from the Italian name for King Arthur's magician half-sister, Morgane Le Fay. Such phenomena are common in the Strait of Messina. A *fata morgana* arises when a layer of warm air rests over a cooler one; in this case, from the warm offshore breeze flowing over the cooler air that lay just above the cold Labrador Current. "Light travels slightly faster through warm air than through cold," the Arctic naturalist E. C. Pielou has written, "causing a light ray, as it passes from cooler to warmer air, to curve back toward the cooler air. This means that to somebody observing a distant object, say an ice floe, through air that is warmer above than below, the floe will seem higher than it really is; it will also be elongated vertically, making it seem taller than it really is . . . ."[1]

And at certain times the cooler air can act as a duct between layers of warmer air, bringing images to the observer's eye of objects that are actually below the horizon, a phenomenon variously called *hillingar* in Old Norse, "looming," *nauscopie*, or "the Novaya Zemlya effect." The latter name derives from Willem Barentsz's experience when wintering at the northern tip of Novaya Zemlya in 1596–97. In the spring his men saw the sun rise two weeks before it would have been above the horizon at their latitude of 76°15' N.

An extreme example of this occurred on July 17, 1939. The famous Newfoundland mariner and Arctic explorer, Captain Robert A. Bartlett, was aboard his auxiliary schooner *Effie M. Morrissey*, halfway between the southern tip of Greenland and Iceland. With Bartlett was the geographer, Professor William H. Hobbs. Hobbs reported, "At 4 P.M. with the sun in the southwest the remarkable mirage appeared in the direction of southwestern Iceland. The Snaefells Jökull (4,715 feet) and other landmarks well known to the captain and the mate were seen as though at a distance of twenty-five or thirty nautical miles, though the position of the schooner showed that these features were actually at a distance of 335 to 350 statute miles. . . . Captain Bartlett writes: 'If I hadn't been sure of my position and had been bound for Rejkjavik, I would have expected to arrive within a few hours. The contours of the land and the snow-covered summit of the Snaefells Jökull showed up almost unbelievably near.'"[2] If a superior mirage were not in effect, "Snaefells Jökull would not have been visible beyond 93 miles."[3]

Perhaps this mirage had a role in the Norse expansion across the northern North Atlantic: the *hillingar* effect occasionally allows the Faroese to see the southeastern coast of Iceland, 240 miles away. It seems possible, too, that Gunnbjorn's Skerries, the sight of which helped draw the Norse to Greenland, may have resulted from the *hillingar* effect.[4]

A third type of mirage, the inferior mirage, can occur when warm air is overlain by cooler air and a distant object may appear upside down. This may explain the phenomenon of the "Flying Dutchman," a legendary spectral ship that heralded disaster. The "Flying Dutchman" was occasionally observed sailing upside down in the region of the Cape of Good Hope. But on July 24, 1822, William Scoresby, Jr., a whaleman-scientist and explorer, saw a "Flying Dutchman" on the east coast of Greenland.

Warm air over cold creates a superior mirage, or fata morgana, *on the Labrador coast.*

The most extraordinary effect … was the distinct inverted image
of a ship in the clear sky … the ship itself being entirely beyond
the horizon. … It was so extremely well defined, that when
examined with a telescope … I could distinguish every sail, the
general 'rig of the ship,' and its particular character; insomuch
that I confidently pronounced it to be my Father's ship, the
Fame, which it afterwards proved to be; —though, on
comparing notes with my Father, I found that our relative
position at the time gave our distance from one another very
nearly thirty miles, being about seventeen miles beyond the
horizon, and some leagues beyond the limit of direct vision.[5]

A few days later, after a crew change in Cartwright, *Belvedere* was
at Cape Porcupine, surely one of the most surprising sights in all of
Labrador, and my photographs do not do it justice. Here, instead of
bold granite headlands and lurking ledges are twenty miles of gentle
pink sand beaches backed by dense stands of black spruce. We
anchored a quarter of a mile from shore and took the dinghy to the
mouth of a stream that flowed between two grassy meadows. The
beach was covered with caribou tracks, and near the stream I saw
paw prints where a black bear had been fishing. I'm sorry to say that
the list of fauna didn't end there: we were attacked by clouds of
mosquitoes and black flies and, worse, some of the biggest horse flies
we had ever seen.

I think there is a sort of savage hierarchy among these vexatious
bugs. Mosquitoes are fairly easy to deal with: they merely want to have
a bit of your blood, and then they are off to breed, like—well—flies. In
the North, mosquitoes are fairly slow and somewhat aimless; hence
they can be neutralized by a head net, thick clothing, insect repellant
(which doesn't really repel them, but rather makes you invisible in an
olfactory way), and, of course a good swat always does the trick.

Like the mosquito, the black fly's game is based on massive
numbers: too many to swat so you'd better be well covered. Black
flies, however, also have a sinister stealth approach: they crawl down
your socks or up your sleeves and bite you, causing little pain—that
is, until you take your socks off an find little bloody tracks where
they have been feeding contentedly.

But the heavyweight division is certainly ruled by the horse fly,
which might well be called the mascot bird of Labrador or the
warthog of the insect world. A week earlier, aboard *Belvedere*, when
one had sunk his fangs into my neck, it felt as if I had been hit by a
pellet from a BB gun. Fortunately, these ugly brutes are pretty slow.
I gave my neck a hellacious swat and came up with the thing still

The horse fly, known as the "mascot bird of Labrador"

wriggling in my fist. It was so big, that I felt as if I were holding a miniature *Tootsie Roll*. Slowly opening my hand, I marveled at its aggressive second wind and asked a Labradorean "What's that!" His reply: "Oh, we call 'em Stout Flies. They're so big and mean that when one of 'em gets a bite on ya, he tears a strip off and drags it up in the woods, where the rest of 'em fight over it." To conclude this encounter, Smitty finally put the stout fly's lights out with a shot of spray from our engine-starting ether. We thought we should send it to the Boone and Crockett Club (which is the registrar for record-sized hunting trophies) to check whether it was a world-class trophy fly.

A little later the same Labradorean pulled my leg really hard. He described his first encounter with a motorcycle. When he was a young lad, he told me, he had gone out hunting with his Uncle Bill near the road that had only recently been punched through to his village. Suddenly they heard an ear-shattering roar: "RRRRRRRRRRRRRR."

"What's that, Uncle Bill?" the boy asked. "I dunno," Uncle Bill replied. Terrified, the lad ran off into the woods and hid. Then he heard a BLAM from his uncle's gun, and he ran back to the road. "Did ya kill him, Uncle Bill?" "Nah, he's over there growlin' in the ditch somewhere, but at least he let go of that fella he had hold of."

The Norse visited Cape Porcupine, Labrador, a thousand years ago. In fact, these beaches are mentioned in the *Saga of Eirík the Red* as an important waypoint on the route to Vinland, making it just about the only pre-Columbian European place name in North America that is both readily identifiable and generally accepted by scholars. Describing Leif Eiríksson's voyage to Vinland, the saga relates their journey along the Labrador coast: "After two days they sighted land again and held in towards it; it was a promontory they were approaching. They tacked along the coast, with the land to starboard. It was open and harbourless, with long beaches and extensive sands. . . . They called this stretch of coast *Fudurstrands* [*Fuðurstrandir*, "Wonder Beaches"] because it took so long to sail past it. Then the coast became indented with bays and they steered into one of them."[6] I assume they steered into Sandwich Bay, which contains a number of embayments and lies just south of Porcupine Strand.

I could well imagine the awe of those early explorers, newly arrived from treeless Greenland and the barren shores of Baffin Island and northern Labrador, as they drank in the warmth of the

*Labrador mosquitoes
are slow but plentiful*

spruce scented wind, the soft beaches, the richness of the rivers and the thick timber. To the Norse, these strands were square in the middle of Markland, the wooded land where the Greenlanders went to cut their timber. The last *recorded* voyage to Markland took place in 1347, and they probably went on longer than that.

Later that summer, on our return voyage to the south, we worked our way inland, into Groswater Bay and stopped in Hamilton Inlet at the village of Rigolet, one of the oldest Hudson's Bay Company posts on the Labrador coast. There, away from the coastal winds, we found ourselves inside the tree line and amid the dense boreal forest. Soaking in the silence of the forest, I could almost hear the ringing axe strokes of the Norse as they harvested timber for building their boats and houses and to make charcoal on the spot to take back to Greenland for their smelters. Here we certainly were in the wooded Markland of the Norse sagas, and we weren't far from the Wonder Beaches near Cape Porcupine.

The *Grænlendinga Saga (Saga of the Greenlanders)* also reports that somewhere nearby the Wonder Beaches was the site where Thorvald Eiríksson, Leif's brother, on a voyage from Leif's winter camp, broke the keel of his boat and went ashore to repair it. "They ran into a fierce gale off a headland and were driven ashore; the keel was shattered and they had to stay there for a long time while they repaired the ship. Thorvald said to his companions, 'I want to erect the old keel here on the headland, and call the place Kjalarness.'"[7] If the story is true, this mark on "Keel Cape" may well have been the first European navigational aid in North America. Cape Porcupine juts into the Labrador Sea with a low smoothness that is readily visible for a good distance from both north and south. It isn't difficult for me to believe that Cape Porcupine could be the *Kjalarness* of the Norsemen.

Soaking in the silence of the forest, I could almost hear the ringing axe strokes of the Norse.

∾

I would have loved to stay on Porcupine Strand longer, but it was great sailing weather, and we had to keep on to the north. We continued along the coast in clear air and calm seas past the mouth of Groswater Bay and worked our way through the narrow tickle called Indian Harbour, where one of the Grenfell Mission's hospitals had stood, then rounded the island and entered Smokey Tickle. We wanted to secure to the government pier, but winter ice had torn some big planks off its face, and it looked a bit shaky. "Is this pier strong enough to take us?" I asked one of the caretakers on the dock.

Belvedere crew stroll The Strands at Cape Porcupine, Labrador. These beaches are mentioned in the Saga of Eiŕik the Red *as an important waypoint on the route to Vinland. In the* Saga *they are called Fuðurstrandir, "Wonder Beaches."*

"Sure is," he replied. "It's stronger 'n hog's breath."

The men were busy dismantling the fish plant there to send the equipment north to an area where some crab fishing was still going on. Except for them and for one family at their fish camp on a ledge above the harbor, the place was deserted. All the weather-beaten houses, sheds, and docks stood empty. A few decaying trap boats with old "one-lunger" engines were slowing going to pieces on the shore; yet Smokey Tickle and Indian Harbour had once been thriving "out-port" fishing communities. As I have explained, for 500 years cod was one of the main food sources of Europe. Because they are slow swimmers, cod were relatively easy to catch, and their low-fat white meat was easy to preserve by air-drying and light salting, thus creating a highly transportable source of protein for growing human populations. Later, after Clarence Birdseye invented his method of freezing food, and the mechanical filleting machine was introduced by the fish processing industry, the demand for cod accelerated again in 1962 when McDonald's restaurants produced the Filet-O-Fish sandwich. This intense pressure finally destroyed the bulk of the cod population in the seas off Labrador and Newfoundland and in many areas of the North Atlantic. More than a decade ago the cod had mostly vanished and the Canadian government closed the fishery entirely and thus ended a way of life that had persisted for three centuries.[8]

In the evening a couple of the men came aboard *Belvedere* for a beer. You could see the hardness of their lives etched in their faces; yet, with it, their utter kindness, decency, and acceptance of others, qualities that are found throughout the whole of Labrador's population. We began talking about the old days at Smokey and Indian Harbour, and it was easy to see that the men fondly remembered an earlier, simpler time, when the resources of the land and sea, if not plentiful, were at least adequate, and everyone helped everyone else through the hard times.

It was easy to see that the men fondly remembered an earlier, simpler time, when the resources of the land and sea, if not plentiful, were at least adequate.

Having worked for the Grenfell Mission in 1962, I was curious about the hospital that had stood, and later burned down, at Indian Harbour. The men were full of quiet praise for Dr. Wilfred Grenfell, who had come to the coast from England in 1893 as a young medical doctor of only twenty-seven years. He spent the rest of his life providing medical aid and other services to the people of northern Newfoundland and southern Labrador.[9]

Smitty told me about a conversation he had had with an old man on the dock in one of the communities we had just visited. Eyeing *Belvedere*'s stars and stripes ensign, he asked, "That Doctor Grenfell, 'e was an Hamurican wuddn' 'e?"

"No," said Smitty, "He was English."

"Well, I heard tell they got him up to St. Ant'ny. 'E's mummified up there under the clifts. 'N if it ain't 'im, it's som'un that looks just like 'im!"

The next day, too, was wonderfully clear. As we moved north from Smokey Tickle, the air temperature was 46 degrees and the water 32.1 degrees. As Cape Harrison rose above the horizon, without binoculars I counted more than a hundred icebergs in sight. The cape is big, bold, barren, and brown. This jagged basalt peninsula juts northeast into the Labrador Sea, and, like Capes Makkovik and Harrigan to the north, it acts as a large hook to snag the ice that the Labrador Current carries south.

Sure enough, as soon as we rounded Cape Harrison and turned northwest, we began to find bits of sea ice, and as we moved on, they grew more and more compact, forcing us to zigzag, until we were brought to a halt by a big patch of densely packed floes. The next day brought more of the same weather and ice. It was a beautiful day, with the blue sea and sky contrasting with the white ice floes. The water was absolutely flat, but off to starboard, a mile or two out in the Labrador Sea, we saw an unbroken line of pack ice.

'Lard Jesus! I hain't never seen nuthin' like it. Everywhere ya look there hain't a stick o'water.'

As we worked our way on up the coast, first to the friendly village of Makkovik, and then to Hopedale, with its eighteenth-century Moravian mission church, we saw more and more ice to seaward. The elders of Hopedale, all savvy old fishermen of immense practical experience, told us to be on the lookout for pack ice. Pack ice is sea ice, and sea ice differs from berg ice in being formed from salt water, not the fresh water in glaciers. Thus sea ice is generally low, and even if the wind has forced it against itself into pressure ridges, it rarely exceeds thirty feet above the water. Either way, it can be a real problem for a boat of *Belvedere's* size.

I knew that a big strip of sea ice had recently surged out of Hudson Strait, at the northern tip of Labrador, and that the Labrador Current was carrying it south. This worried me. Easterly winds had been blowing for several days, and it didn't take a genius to figure out that it would push the ice toward the coast. In fact, the fishermen offshore were reporting a wide band of closely packed ice that was giving them plenty of trouble. On *Belvedere's* radio we heard one particularly evocative report from the skipper of the *Atlantic Storm*, one of the sturdiest fish boats on the coast: "Lard Jesus! I hain't never seen nuthin' like it. Everywhere ya look there hain't a stick o' water."

I climbed a high hill behind Hopedale and through my binoculars looked north, toward Cape Harrigan. Sure enough, I saw a lot of drift ice to the north and east, and some of it had almost reached the islands off the harbor's mouth. I had been chased around by the pack ice enough times in Alaska and in Canada's western Arctic to know that the best thing to do was to get out of there right away and head south to avoid being bottled up in Hopedale. This was confirmed by a rather alarming ice chart that we received on our weatherfax: it showed that the ice had closed in behind us to the south, all the way to Cape Harrison, with floes covering between four-tenths and nine-tenths of the water's surface.

Then the fishing supply boat *Catherine Anne* of Gaspé, Quebec, pulled into the town dock. The captain had rammed her through the four-tenths ice cover and had torn most of the sheathing off her hull on the way in. Soon the *Northern Ranger* arrived, and the captain reported having forced his way through extremely close pack ice composed of heavy old floes. This was "multi-year ice," meaning that it had survived at least one summer's melt. Because sea ice gradually sheds its brine over a winter, this old sea ice would have become essentially fresh water; hence very blue, and much harder than first-year ice.

The old fishermen in Hopedale understood our problem. They knew that with all this ice we didn't have a hope of getting far enough offshore to reach the usual shipping track, the "recommended route" with its well-marked soundings. Hunching over our charts, a couple of veterans drew from memory the track of the local "inside route" among all the rocks and islets and ledges, telling us that in the old days the fishing schooners had gone this way when the ice was close on the off-lying islands. There were few, if any, soundings on this entire sinuous route, but they assured us that, with one exception, it was very deep and that we would mostly carry fifteen to thirty fathoms (90 to 180 feet of water) the whole way.

We woke at 6:30 A.M. on July 20, 1996, to find thick fog and Hopedale Harbour full of three- to four-tenths ice cover. We were off at seven, using the radar to help pick our way through the floes. We took the old schoonermen's route, and at times the fog lifted enough to allow us a view of the gray, rounded islands that were often topped with one or two stunted black spruces so tortured by the punishment of the winter wind that their few branches grew only on the leeward side of their spindly trunks. The air temperature hovered in the low forties.

At about 2:00 P.M., just as we were approaching Turnavik Island from the west, the temperature dropped, the fog set in thick, and the

The Moravian church and Hudson's Bay Company buildings at Hopedale, Labrador

ice became very closely packed. We twisted and turned, and backed and filled, and we couldn't see more than a hundred yards in any direction. The drift ice, coming down from the north, was piling up on the shoals there. Apart from one or two, none of these shoals had been charted, thereby delivering a triple problem to us: tight ice, rotten visibility, and uncharted, reef-strewn waters.

We probably could have coped with one or two of these challenges, but with all three at once we had to accept *force majeure*. With strong easterly winds forecast, plus the very "iffy" probability of being able to push ahead to reach a harbor that was secure from ice and easterlies, we decided that it would be best to retreat to a bullet-proof harbor that we

A Belvedere crew member views the approaching sea ice that threatened to trap us in Hopedale Harbour, Labrador. We left in a hurry.

had noted along the way on our schoonermen's route.

We made it back without too much trouble and tucked into an unnamed harbor (55°17.1' N, 60°04.7' W) south of Cross Island, shaped like an old-fashioned high-button shoe. Smitty christened it "Granny's Boot Harbour." It was completely enclosed by high rounded cliffs, similar to Hopedale's, and, like Hopedale's gray granite, it was shot through with vivid pink quartzite veins. There, out of the prevailing wind, the leeward fissures in the cliffs were filled with green tundra moss and the occasional stunted spruce.

With that, we settled in to wait out the expected gale. The temperature was forty-four degrees and the ceiling was not over 200 feet, yet everyone was in good spirits. "John," said Smitty, "I reckon we're only an hour and a half from Hopedale, but we've covered something like sixty nautical miles today."

"I guess it comes with the tour package," I replied.

We spent two days in Granny's Boot Harbour, waiting for the easterly to die down. Then we pushed on about twenty miles through fog and scattered floes to Rose's Island Harbour to wait for better visibility. To our surprise, we awoke on the morning of July 23 to find that we actually could see five miles and that the temperature was a balmy forty-eight degrees.

Because we were in poorly charted waters at best, we sent two of the crew ahead in the dinghy with a hand-held depth sounder and a VHF

Because we were in poorly charted waters at best, we sent two of the crew ahead in the dinghy with a hand-held depth sounder and a VHF radio.

Wind-battered spruce on Rose's Island

radio to help us work through the narrows of Lilian Island Tickle, which we knew was shallow and a little tricky. Then we towed the dinghy past Drunken Harbour, following the one thin line of soundings that lay just inside the margin of the pack ice.

But the ice floes grew thicker and thicker again, forcing us to weave more and more. Finally it came to this routine: slow down, dead slow, neutral, reverse, wheel hard over, forward, hard-a-port, hard-a-starboard, and so on. I climbed to the lower spreaders to help us work through the pack ice, and after what seemed a very long time, and just when it seemed as if we couldn't go any farther, through my binoculars I saw an open lead a quarter of a mile ahead.

We barged on, slowly worming our way along, and eventually

worked into more open pack, only to find that farther along, in a stretch of very deep water, the pack ice was solid against the cliffs near Makkovik. Here we were lucky. When we reached the barrier, the tide started to fall, and a fifty-foot-wide ribbon of ice-clogged water opened at the foot of the cliffs.

In Makkovik, the wonderful elders there, Jim Andersen and Bertie Winters, also took care of us. We pulled out our charts and they showed us the "inside route" behind the islands (where the charts showed no soundings at all) to Cape Harrison, where they thought we should reach open water. We were off again as soon as possible, grateful for their unfailing generosity.

We left Makkovik on a calm and clear day, with the ice sparkling against the blue of the sea and the brown of the small rocky islands. As we carefully threaded our way along we passed the spotlessly clean and flawlessly operated coastal supply ship *Duke of Topsail*, northbound. She was owned and commanded by the most experienced skipper on the Labrador coast, the late Captain Lloyd Bugden.

A Newfoundlander, Captain Bugden was "a fine upstanding man, a man that you would admire." He had been a mariner since 1946, when he was fifteen. His voyages had taken him throughout the world, but his abiding love was the North, where his commands reached as far as Igloolik, north of Hudson Bay, and to Thule, Greenland. On one voyage coming back from the Caribbean, he had to amputate his own big toe after it was crushed by a winch brake. "My foot was pinned under the brake and we had to get another man to help lift it off. I ran to the cabin and took off my sock, my big toe was hanging, so I got the scissors, cut it off, and threw it overboard."[10]

Lloyd was well known for his generosity in sharing his vast knowledge of the coast and of the ice. "Hello, John," came over the radio. "*Belvedere*'s looking Bristol fashion."

"Coming from you, that's praise enough for me, Captain. How'd you find the ice?"

"There's plenty of it around, all right. I see you're on the inside route. I'd stick to it. Outside is pretty heavy. You'll have enough on your hands as it is, but you'll be fine."

"Thank you, Captain. Safe voyage."

"Roger that, and to you. *Duke of Topsail* clear. Standing by on sixteen and thirteen."

"*Belvedere* clear. Standing by on sixteen and thirteen."

At once we were back in the ice, and again we backed and filled and twisted and turned. I had done a lot of this kind of ice work aboard *Belvedere* in the Northwest Passage, and we needed the

At other times, when it was necessary to turn sharply amid very constricted floes, we used my western Arctic 'bank shot.'

entire crew of seven to make headway. I and another were aloft on the mast's lower spreaders with binoculars and radios, giving steering instructions to the helmsman, who was usually so busy with the wheel that another person worked the throttle and gear-shift controls. At the same time, Smitty plotted fixes on the chart every few minutes, while two others stood by at the stern, ready with long pike poles to keep the floes clear of the rudder and propeller when we reversed.

Occasionally we had no choice but to push right through the pack ice. In the western Arctic, when the ice was too tight to allow maneuvering, I had learned to pick out a conveniently notched floe and ease *Belvedere*'s bow into the notch. Then I would open up the engine a bit and use the floe, athwart the bow, to take the punishment as we banged along slowly through the pack.

At other times, when it was necessary to turn sharply amid very constricted floes, we used my western Arctic "bank shot" method of turning *Belvedere*. If, for instance, we needed to turn hard right, we would intentionally glance off a floe to the left, thus throwing the bow abruptly to starboard. Those of us at the spreaders had to hang on tightly during that maneuver. When we did use the "bank shot" I would look astern and see a streak of red bottom paint on the floe we had just bounced off.

Smitty, whose previous experience in Labrador had been aboard fiberglass boats, was impressed with the strength of *Belvedere*'s steel hull. His dictum: "From now on for me up here, it's 'steel or no deal.'"

It took us six days of hard work to wend our way the hundred miles south from Hopedale, past Cape Harrison and into clear water, on what would otherwise have been merely a day's run. The irony was that, although the central Labrador coast was for a time very icy, the boats in northern Labrador had a comparatively ice-free summer.

Working through sea ice toward Makkovik. It took us six days of hard work to cover what would have been merely a long day's run in clear water.

Going Counterclockwise:

Around Newfoundland and the Gulf of St. Lawrence *(1997)*

HE NEXT YEAR, 1997, I wanted a break from banging around in the ice floes. Returning to my original plan for the summer of 1994, I decided instead to probe the early European activities on the southern and eastern coasts of Newfoundland and the Gulf of St. Lawrence. The simplest way to do this seemed to be a 2,000-mile loop, going counterclockwise around Newfoundland and the Gulf.

With most of the same crew as the summer before, we began by visiting France. The islands of Saint Pierre and Miquelon, only about fifteen miles off Newfoundland's south coast, are the last bits of the French Empire in North America. Although they were probably discovered by the Portuguese about 1520, the islands were claimed for France by Jacques Cartier during his voyage of 1536 and thereafter became an important outpost for French cod fishermen working the banks south of there. The islands were seized by the British during the Seven Years' War, but later, with Britain firmly in control, they were returned to France after the end of the Napoleonic Wars.

Their lasting fame was secured, however, during the years of Prohibition (1919–33) in the United States. Saint Pierre became a hive of clandestine activity for rumrunners. In fact, Al Capone even visited the place. He went there because Canadian distillers needed a legal export destination and Saint Pierre was the nearest foreign soil. Once the liquor reached the island, locals ferried it offshore to international waters, where boats stood by to carry it to the United States. During the boom they moved as many as 300,000 cases per month.

In 1933, with the passage of the twenty-first amendment repealing the Volstead Act and thus ending Prohibition, the islands reverted to their traditional venue, "living off cod fishing and the kindness of French bureaucrats." That is, until the 1970s, when the islands became

PHOTO, OPPOSITE PAGE

Approaching the eighty-foot-wide Passage Germaine

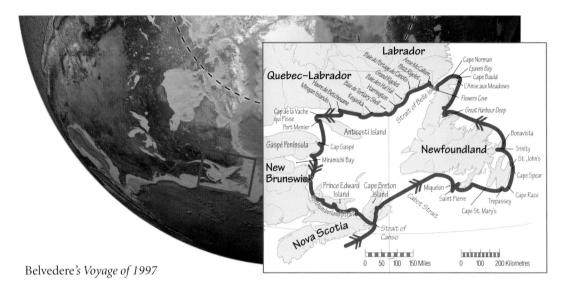

Belvedere's Voyage of 1997

the focus of a bitter dispute between Canada and France during the "Cod Wars," while the two nations waged a war of words over the dwindling stocks of fish.[1] Throughout all, France's overseas department of Saint Pierre et Miquelon has remained resonantly and somewhat defiantly French.

In 1997 we arrived at Saint Pierre, out of the fog, not on Bastille Day, but rather on the Fourth of July. As soon as we had secured to the quay, a pair of friendly and polite customs and immigration officers boarded us for what was more of a visit than an inspection. We had entered the harbor flying the French *Tricoleur* and the yellow "Q" (quarantine—requesting customs and immigration clearance) flag from our starboard flag halyard, and from the port halyard we had the flag of Saint Pierre et Miquelon, which I had bought there in 1991, on our way to Scotland. We offered the men a glass of red wine, which they cheerfully accepted and quickly asked if it was French. When I showed them the bottle—it was Medoc—they looked relieved.

Our greeting was definitely warmer than the one given to a yacht from Boston that arrived just after us. It entered the harbor with the *Canadian* flag flying at the starboard spreader and without a "Q" flag. The officers poked around in their boat for forty-five minutes and, as far as we could tell, did not leave smiling.

In just about the thickest fog I have ever seen we wandered around this resolutely Gallic town (someone called it "France without the jet lag") that houses all but 700 of the islands' 7,000 inhabitants. After a brief stop at the one-room museum devoted to rumrunning, I spent my time trying to conquer the complicated telephone system in the post office, where I discovered that U.S telephone credit cards are *not* accepted. Then I did some window-shopping, but succeeded only in buying a *Saint Pierre et Miquelon* baseball cap for Bonnie.

The next day, just as the fog began to lift a bit, the threat of a gale came over the airways, so we shoved off in a twenty-knot southeasterly for a short run to the nearby town of Fortune, Newfoundland. We headed northeast and soon had the Burin Peninsula abeam. The fog, now blowing over the warm land, vanished, giving us a lovely run as we drank in the beauty of the cliffs which were topped by a covering of greenery so brilliant that it looked like a manicured golf course.

We pulled into the narrow channel at Fortune just as the jet catamaran ferry was leaving for Saint Pierre, and the school children onboard waved and cheered us. We found space at the fishermen's dock at the head of the harbor, where a number of people were digging for clams in the flats at the mouth of the river. Soon we had cleared Canadian Customs and were welcomed by the townspeople, who were gracious and friendly and interested in our voyage.

One of the visitors was Jack Piercey, a craggy and fit seventy-nine-year-old. He told us of his service in Britain's Royal Navy during World War II. Newfoundland was a colony of Great Britain until its confederation with Canada in 1949. Jack, a young colonial sailor from the island, described his first impression of the big city of London: "By God, the doorman at the Odeon Theatre was wearing more braid than Hermann Goering!"

He told us about growing up in a strict Methodist family in Fortune, where, in those days, the only alcohol came from Saint Pierre with the bootleggers. When he joined the Royal Navy he was amazed at the amount of grog—he called it "Nelson's Blood"—that the sailors consumed, because, as he put it, he had been "brought up with the wrath of God, not the love."

He also described his recent surgery for cataracts, which had allowed him to discern colors for the first time in forty years. His doctor asked him, "You mean that you've had cataracts for forty years?"

"Hell no," Jack replied, "I was just drunk for the first thirty-nine!"

Smitty then walked over to the ferry dock to watch the high-speed catamaran return from Saint Pierre. A very large Newfoundland woman disembarked wearing curlers and carrying a big load of duty-free liquor. Her husband, who was rather smaller, asked her how the trip had gone. Her reply: "Fog and rain. Couldn't see a fuckin' thing for two days." All this was said without removing a cigarette from her lips.

∽

A few days later we were roaring across the mouth of Placentia Bay on a wonderful sleigh ride, surging along under cloudless skies, driven by a thirty-knot westerly and following seas. The temperature was sixty degrees. This was a rarity for southeastern Newfoundland, where the warm, moist air from the Gulf Stream usually turns to

We drank in the beauty of the cliffs which were topped by a covering of greenery so brilliant that it looked like a manicured golf course.

An iceberg in the approaches to St. John's, Newfoundland

Europeans discovered the fastness of St. John's Harbour around 1500, and it quickly became a refuge from the Atlantic's storms.

dense fog over the chilly waters of the Labrador Current. In fact, it was so warm and balmy that Smitty blurted out, "Sitting in the lee of the dinghy, it was just like St. Tropez!"

Soon we drew abreast of the famous bird cliffs at Cape St. Mary's, where thousands and thousands of murres, fulmars, gannets, and shearwaters were milling about and diving into the waters below. We were heading for the town of Trepassey when the wind died, but we found "the Texaco breeze" — sailors' lingo for taking the easy way out by keeping your speed up with the engine.

Trepassey's large harbor was quiet, almost eerily so. We saw only a couple of fish boats there, and we learned that the town had shrunk from 1,400 to 600 persons after the moratorium on cod fishing had been imposed. We left Trepassey's dock at 7:00 A.M. on July 8 and motored ahead in a flat calm. Soon the lighthouse at Cape Race, at the southeastern corner of Newfoundland, popped up above the thin surface fog. Like Cape Hatteras, it is one of coastal North America's famous landmarks. There, while porpoises, minke whales, and humpbacks played nearby, we turned north toward St. John's.

Rounding Cape Spear, the easternmost point in North America, we found an enormous iceberg nearly blocking our approach into the rock palisades of St. John's Harbour. As we moved between the high cliffs, Signal Hill towered above us to the north. The hill is the site of the harbor's eighteenth-century fortifications, but in 1901 it became the spot where Guglielmo Marconi flew a kite, 400 feet high in a gale, to receive the first transatlantic wireless signal, the Morse code letter "S," broadcast from Cornwall, England.

Europeans discovered the fastness of St. John's Harbour around 1500, and it quickly became a refuge from the Atlantic's storms for the fishing fleets of many nations. In 1583 Sir Humphrey Gilbert entered the same narrows and announced to the crews of thirty or forty French, Portuguese, Basque, and English fishing vessels that he was claiming Newfoundland for the English crown. Britain and France then competed for control of the harbor for nearly two centuries, but in 1762, British troops, including a detachment from Massachusetts, defeated the French on the slopes of Signal Hill,[2] thus concluding the French and Indian War and winning Newfoundland for Britain.

The ensuing Peace of Paris treaty of 1763 "was one of the greatest territorial carve-ups in history," writes the historian, Paul Johnson. "The French [surrendered] the whole of Canada, Nova Scotia, and their claims to the Ohio Valley.... As part of a separate deal France gave Spain all of Louisiana.... The net result was to knock France out of the American hemisphere, in which it retained only three small Caribbean islands, two in the fisheries [Saint Pierre and Miquelon], and a negligible chunk of Guyana."[3]

⌇

After a couple of days in St. John's for supplies, laundry, and visiting friends, we were off again, running north along the cliffs, looking for a harbor for the night. One place we decided not to visit was Carmanville. The *Cruising Guide for Newfoundland* contains this report from Arthur Chase: "On approaching we ran a range which had the proper bearing, but turned out to be an outhouse and a church which were more visible than the government range."

We finally stopped in Trinity, one of the oldest towns in Newfoundland. We were now on "The English Coast" of the island. In 1497 John Cabot (Giovanni Caboto), sailing for King Henry VII in search of a passage to Asia, discovered Newfoundland, or somewhere nearby, and claimed it for England. Although it is impossible to figure out from the existing documents exactly where he fetched up in the New World, chambers of commerce from Maine to Newfoundland have claimed the distinction of being Cabot's landfall. It seems most likely that Cabot's landfall was somewhere between Cape Breton, Nova Scotia, and Cape Bauld, at the northern tip of Newfoundland. Nevertheless, the town of Bonavista, Newfoundland, near Trinity, recently seized the brass ring and welcomed the replica of Cabot's ship, the *Matthew*, on June 24, 1997, the 500th anniversary of his landfall in the New World.

One thing is fairly certain, however: Cabot knew where he was going because Bristol fishermen had been on the coast of the "Isle of Brasil" since the 1480s.[4] As we have seen in Chapter Four, these English fishermen probably received their knowledge of the coast from other English fishermen and traders who had worked on the west coast of Greenland in the fourteenth and fifteenth centuries—when the Greenland settlements were headed toward their final years—and had learned of lands and fishing grounds to the west from the Norse.

Only three years after Cabot's voyage, Gaspar Corte-Real, an Azorean explorer sailing for King Manoel of Portugal, visited Trinity, and soon thereafter, early in the 1500s, English fishermen permanently settled on the shores of Trinity's beautiful and protected harbor.

'This is a place where old trucks come to die.'

They were accompanied, or were followed within only a few years to Newfoundland, by Portuguese and French fishermen, who no doubt were drawn there by the reports of the vast richness of the fish stocks on the banks nearby.[5] In a letter to the Duke of Milan on December 18, 1497, Raimondo di Soncino described the fishing grounds that Cabot had discovered: "They assert that the sea is swarming with fish which can be taken not only with the net, but in baskets let down with a stone...."[6]

On a foggy and drizzly day we reached the Northern Peninsula of Newfoundland and, with gales forecast, we ducked into shelter amid the towering granite cliffs in the fjord called Great Harbour Deep. A small fishing community lies there, but the steep sides of the fjord have made it impossible to put in a road to the outside world, so it is serviced in the summer by a small coastal ferry that calls several times a week.

Joey Donnelly, an easy-going sailor-friend from Maine who had recently joined the crew, and I walked into Great Harbour Deep's small store. We found Linda Hopkins, the owner, sitting on the freezer with a wooden bat in her hand. "Are you guarding the stuff in that freezer?" asked Joey.

"If anyone tries to take anything, I'll whomp him numb," was Linda's reply.

As we had come to understand about Newfoundland, the people here are unfailingly kind and helpful. She and Bob Pittman loaned us their muffler-free (and somewhat compression-free) pickup truck so that we could tour all two miles of the town's dirt roads. Pointing to the truck, Linda said, "If you scratch it, we'll never know. A car wouldn't last two months here. This is a place where old trucks come to die."

On July 18, again with very murky weather, we rounded Cape Bauld, at the northern tip of Newfoundland, then turned west. The fog was in and out all day. Needless to say, we didn't see much of the coast, but the seas were fairly flat, and in Epaves Bay, just as we approached L'Anse aux Meadows, the fog lifted a bit, giving us a view of the replicas of the Norse turf buildings. They melded with the background landscape perfectly and were difficult to pick out at first.

Seeing the settlement from seaward—and thus from the perspective of a Norse mariner—was interesting. The bay is very shoal, with lots of boulders and foul ground, but the bottom rises gently; hence it would have been fairly easy to land the Norse ships there and pull them ashore. The site also offered the advantage of good visibility of the Strait of Belle Isle, and of course, Black Duck Brook provided the fresh water.

As I have mentioned, the settlement was very probably the site of Leif Eiríksson's wintering camp of ca. A.D. 1000, and three years later Leif's brother Thorvald spent a couple of winters there. The site is called *Straumfjord* (Current Fiord) in *Eirík the Red's Saga* and *Leifsbuðir* (Leif's Huts) in the *Greenlanders' Saga*.[7] It was from here that expeditions went southeast, presumably along the Great Northern Peninsula to the north coast of Newfoundland, and southwest, into the Gulf of St. Lawrence, and north, along the Labrador coast. "L'Anse aux Meadows marks the northern entrance to Vinland," writes the scholar and archaeologist Birgitta Wallace. " It is ideal for a base camp and gateway. It is easy to find from all directions. Its location west of ... Cape Bauld shows that travel in and out of the Gulf held precedence over eastern Newfoundland."[8]

We were again overwhelmed by the kindness of the Newfoundlanders.

We were off again pretty quickly, rounded Cape Norman without seeing it in the fog, and proceeded down the strait with white-sided dolphins playing about our bows. Soon we picked up a fair tide, which carried us along with such force that at times we exceeded ten knots over the bottom as we surged through the mists with our foghorn hooting. In fact, we were going so fast that we reduced the engine revolutions so that we wouldn't overshoot the harbor we were heading for, Flowers Cove.

With visibility down to ten yards we worked our way into the cove, then burst out of the fog bank and secured to the town wharf. Almost at once Edmund Moores, who is a friend of ours and a local fisherman, came down to the boat, bringing scallops as well as bread that his wife, Doreen, had just baked. We were again overwhelmed by the kindness of the Newfoundlanders.

Edmund and I began talking about the old days in Flowers Cove. I mentioned that I had worked here at the Grenfell Mission nursing station in 1962, when I was fresh out of high school. He asked me, "Who was the head nurse then?"

"Elizabeth Bailey," I replied.

"Were you the one who made home brew in the bath tub when she was away?"

"Yup."

On the way into Flowers Cove we had seen lots of dots on our radar screen. They turned out to be small open fishing boats, each with a couple of men jigging for cod. They reminded me very much of the way things were during my summer here. In the evening, after the work was done, we would jump into a dory, row out a short distance, unwind a line weighted with a leaded hook, and jig it up and down, usually with quick success. To a Newfoundlander a cod is a "fish" and everything else that swims is something else: "How'd ya do this evening?" "Not too good. I caught three salmon and one fish."

To a Newfoundlander a cod is a 'fish' and everything else that swims is something else.

It was also somewhat spooky the way those small trap boats materialized out of the fog, less than twenty-five yards from *Belvedere*, then quickly vanished astern. Flowers Cove is the nearest point in Newfoundland to the Labrador shore. It is less than ten miles from there, across the Strait of Belle Isle, to Point Amour, and a lot of shipping exits the Gulf of St. Lawrence via the strait, bound for Europe or points north.

Looking at the thick wall of fog in the strait, I asked Edmund, "Isn't it dangerous out there with big ships coming through?"

"We're always worried about being run down out there in the straits in the fog," he answered. He described how a friend of his, out fishing in the strait in a real pea-souper, once looked up from his cod line to see the side of a ship sliding past only yards away. As if to prove his point, we heard the deep blasts of foghorns from several large ships traversing the strait. I thought of the dangers that nineteenth-century fishermen faced on the Grand Banks when the big passenger liners, running on a great circle course between the English Channel and Nantucket Shoals, came through the fog at flank speed.

Rudyard Kipling described it with chilling immediacy in *Captains Courageous*. In that novel a spoiled American brat, Harvey Cheyne, falls overboard from a passenger liner and is hauled out of the water by the crew of the *We're Here*, a fishing schooner from Gloucester, Massachusetts. Harvey spends the summer aboard her, experiencing all the hardship and danger of the Grand Banks fishermen, simultaneously growing into young manhood. One day the crew of the *We're Here* listened to the sounds of a liner approaching in the fog and tried to signal their location to the big ship:

" Aoooo – whoooo – whupp!" went the siren. "Wingle – tingle – tink," went the bell. "Graaa – ouch!" went the conch, while the sea and sky were all milled up in milky fog. Harvey felt that he was near a moving body, and found himself looking up at the wet edge of a cliff-like bow, leaping, it seemed, directly over the schooner. A jaunty little feather of water curled in front of it, and as it lifted it showed a long ladder of Roman numerals—XV., XVI., XVII., XVIII., and so forth—on a salmon-colored, gleaming side. It tilted forward and downward with a heart-stilling "Ssssooo"; the ladder disappeared; a line of brass-rimmed port-holes flashed past; a jet of steam puffed in Harvey's helplessly uplifted hands; a spout of hot water roared along the rail of the *We're Here*, and the little schooner staggered and shook in a rush of screw-torn water, as a liner's stern vanished in the fog. Harvey got ready to faint or be sick, or both, when he heard a crack like a trunk thrown on a sidewalk, and, all small in his ear, a far-away telephone voice drawling: "Heave to! You've sunk us!"[9]

Sorry to leave Flowers Cove, we motored across the Strait of Belle Isle, westward to the Quebec-Labrador coast in an unusual calm for that blustery place. This seldom-visited, jagged coast runs about 200 miles into the Gulf of St. Lawrence and is dotted everywhere with granite islets and strings of islands that shelter deep bays and long, protected passages. In 1534, when the French explorer, Jacques Cartier, saw the region, he recoiled at its apparent severity, writing that it was made up only of "stones and horrible rocks." He added, "This is the land God gave to Cain." But I was quickly struck by the richness of its rivers and bird life, by the green density of its bushes and spruce stands that blanket its pink granite islands and hills, and, offshore, by the numbers of fish, seals, dolphins, and whales.

There are fifteen small communities and two small Native American reserves along the Quebec-Labrador coast, but no roads to connect it to the rest of the world: the main highway ends west of there, and there is only a short road, linked to Newfoundland by ferry, at its eastern end. In between, the settlements are served in the summer mostly by coastal boats and float planes. The entire population hovers at only 6,000, leaving the vast part of the region almost empty.

At dusk on July 23 we anchored for the night in Anse McCallum, a secure and quiet bay that overwhelmed us with the heady scent of spruce and utterly lacked any sign of mankind. The next day was also calm, allowing us to make more than fifty miles among the hundreds and hundreds of islands littering that complicated stretch of coast. We were "inside" all day, moving among the granite islands that supported thick covers of reindeer moss and juniper bushes as well as increasingly dense stands of black spruce.

Our route took us along Petit Rigolet Channel, which is only 150 to 200 yards wide through most of its twelve-mile span. After a peaceful night in Baie du Portage du Canots, we squeezed through the eighty-foot-wide Passage Germaine, between steep granite islands, thus saving ourselves a long detour outside some ugly ledges in an uncomfortable chop. Continuing southwest through the same lovely scenery in Grand Rigolet, past the mouth of Baie des Ha! Ha! (the origin of the name eludes me), we left the protection of the islands and hurried to Harrington Harbour just ahead of a southwesterly gale.

The island community of Harrington—285 population—is a gem. Friendly people met us at wharfside. Nearby, several well-tended, boulder-ballasted cribwork piers jutted out over the smooth, glacier-scoured ledges; up the hillside, amid the cheerful polychrome of several dozen tidy houses, were large, neat stacks of firewood. The town site is too vertical and fissured to support conventional streets; instead, twelve-foot-wide wooden boardwalks knit together the houses, school, several small stores, and a handsome Anglican church. The four-wheel ATV is the vehicle of choice, and the boardwalk's speed limit is fifteen kilometers per hour.

Once the gale had blown through, we were on our way west again—to another magical anchorage in Baie de Tertiary Shell, which, I assume, can only have been named by a singularly zealous geologist. Under a flaming crimson sunset we tried to set *Belvedere*'s 100-pound anchor, but found the bottom to be very soft, very black, and very smelly mud. Smitty, exasperated by repeatedly raising and lowering the anchor, as we tried to get a good hold, described the bottom: "This damned stuff is just like the Mississippi—too thick to drink and too thin to plow."

We had hoped for a long run the next day, but the weather forecast—or rather what we could understand of the weather forecast, which was read in English by a heavily accented francophone meteorologist—suggested that we might get a thrashing. The only alternative, because the anchorages are sparse the farther west you go on that coast, was to head to the town of Kegaska and secure to the small public wharf there.

Kegaska, with only 155 inhabitants, is the last of the English-speaking towns on that coast, and, like the others in Quebec-Labrador, it was colonized by Newfoundlanders a century and a half ago. One of the locals described the situation: "We're Hinglish 'ere. We're sandwiched between the French and the Hindians!" he said, referring to the Montagnais Indian reserve to the east and the bulk of Quebec to the west.

We waited out the southeasterly gale in Kegaska. While a heavy

The "streets" of Harrington, Quebec

surge rolled into the harbor and slowly ground our fender boards into splinters against the pier, we marveled at the ferocity of the breakers exploding on the ledges and cliffs outside. My friend Peter Stone, a tall, lanky, and supremely skilled sailor—and an acclaimed landscape artist—had joined us in Flowers Cove. Peter is a hard worker, and he lets very little get in the way of his work. When off watch, he would frequently be found on *Belvedere*'s foredeck, covered in a plastic sheet, sketching away, while spray flew over him.

During the gale I walked out to the gulf side of the harbor, over smooth pink granite ledges. Far away toward the gulf I spotted Peter at work. Four or five brushes sprouted from his back pocket while he worked hunched over his easel in the howling wind, right at the edge of the breakers. The pink ledges, white breakers, and gray sea and sky framed him perfectly, reminding me very much of the way the artist Winslow Homer must have looked a century before, when he painted stormy seas from the ledges at Prout's Neck in Maine.

'This damned stuff is just like the Mississippi—too thick to drink and too thin to plow.'

We were also getting low on water but found, to our dismay, that the government fish plant on the dock, which is the usual source of water for boats in all northern communities, had closed after a very brief commercial fishing season. None of us relished the idea of tight shower rationing, but the problem vanished almost as soon as it had cropped up: when one of the townspeople heard of our need, he put a couple of fifty-gallon drums in his pickup and made several trips to the local well. "You'll like the water 'ere," he said. "It's clear as gin."

The tiny island town of Harrington, Quebec, is home to 285 people.

We also liked Kegaska, but with good weather forecast, we had to make some miles to reach the next anchorage, which lay nearly ninety miles to the west. At the end of the day we anchored at Isle La Chasse in Havre De Betchouane. There we were in the Mingan Archipelago National Park. It was a lovely, quiet spot, with very little evidence of mankind's intrusion: limestone islands, some of them sculpted into fantastic shapes by the waves, were thickly covered by dense stands of black spruce. The sun was low, giving deep shadows to the spruce forest and making the gray limestone cliffs stand out dramatically.

Here we turned southwest, heading on another ninety-mile run to Anticosti Island in the middle of the gulf. It was a beautiful, clear day, but hammering into swells, driven by a twenty-five- to thirty-knot headwind wasn't fun. We finally reached the island and rounded a cape unforgettably named *Cap de la Vache Qui Pisse*. We assumed that the breakers splashing upward had reminded an early settler of a cow peeing on a rock. Peter Stone, a man of many talents, penned this doggerel and recited it in an accent that resembled Peter Sellers in his role of Inspector Clousseau in *The Pink Panther*:

> *Isle of endless timbers, caribou muske, et sedge,*
> *Limestone cliffs and black flies, precipitous wicked ledge,*
> *And a northwest wind which bristles, and a sea to spit and hiss,*
> *The gray sun sets over St. Lawrence, et La Cap de la Vache Qui Pisse!*

We entered Port Menier—the only real harbor on the whole of Anticosti's more than 3,000 square miles and 135-mile length—and secured to a steel cofferdam pier that was heaped with spruce logs that were headed for a pulp mill somewhere. It wasn't an attractive spot, and the town was a mile away over a riprap causeway, but still we were very glad to be out of those lumpy seas.

At once a number of people drove out to the end of the pier to look at *Belvedere*. We learned that a hundred years before, Henri Menier, a French *chocolateur*, had made the island his personal domain and had introduced a number of exotic species of animals to the island, among them white-tailed deer, the population of which now stood at 120,000 animals. So, in addition to supporting a timber industry, the island had become a destination for sport hunters and fishermen.

Nevertheless, it was good to get going the next morning, now heading due south, for the Gaspé Peninsula. What a day it was! We departed Port Menier at 7:00 A.M. on July 31 and caught a fair tide and a quartering breeze that drove us along at nine knots, and as soon as Anticosti sank below the horizon the Gaspé rose before us. In the afternoon we rounded Cap Gaspé, a huge, tilted limestone headland topped with a spruce forest and a lovely white lighthouse.

As we entered Baie de Gaspé we were greeted with the strong scent of evergreens. We headed up the bay, toward the town of Gaspé, where, in 1534, Jacques Cartier had erected a cross and claimed the St. Lawrence for France. Simultaneously a dark thunder squall raced toward us with sweeping rain clouds, occasional murk and lightning, blasts of wind, and striated shafts of light—while behind us rose a robin's-egg-blue sky. It was a lovely, luminist scene.

While we waited out a gale in Kegaska, Quebec, Peter Stone worked on a seascape from the ledges.

A squall in
Baie de Gaspé

And two days later, as we motored over calm seas toward Miramichi Bay, the power of the gulf swept over us again. Flocks of gannets, diving after fish, hit the water vertically, like bolts from a cross bow, while a porbeagle shark swam languidly away—all of this against a background of huge, black thunder squalls moving across the water with majestic slowness. We crossed the shallow bar and anchored just out of the channel to Burnt Church, New Brunswick, behind one of the two great sand spits that enclose the bay. As darkness fell, we drank in the warmth and bounty of the Miramichi, while lightning bolts and thunder claps flashed and cracked all around us.

Jacques Cartier had also been here, but before him, the Norse, too, were probably in the Miramichi area. It is well known that the Norse sagas mention Vinland, a land where Leif Eiríksson discovered wild grapes. In the *Saga of Eirík the Red,* one of Leif's men returns to camp after a long absence:

> Leif said to him, "Why are you so late, foster-father? How did you get separated from your companions?"... "I have some news. I found vines and grapes."... They slept for the rest of the night, and the next morning Leif said to his men, "Now we have two tasks on our hands. On alternate days we must gather grapes and cut vines, and then fell trees, to make a cargo for my ship." This was done. It is said that the tow-boat was filled with grapes.

They took on a full cargo of timber; and in the spring they made ready to leave and sailed away. Leif named the country after its natural qualities and called it Vinland.[10]

The location of the Norse explorations in the New World has been the focus of much speculation and conjecture over the years; indeed, it has become more of a lightning rod than a collegial debate. Places as far away as New York Harbor,[11] Narragansett Bay in Rhode Island, Cape Cod, and even the Carolinas have been proposed as places where the Norse explored.[12] And for many years scholars have debated whether there is any truth to this account about wild grapes, which more than a few have considered to be a fable. Nevertheless, "one find at L'Anse aux Meadows is a clear indication that the wild grapes of Vinland were not a segment of Norse imagination," writes the archaeologist Birgitta Wallace, who conducted excavations at the site.

> Among the Norse artifacts preserved in the bog were three butternuts, and one burl of butternut wood. Butternuts . . . are a New-World relative of walnuts. Walnuts were considered delicacies and imported from Europe all the way to Greenland. . . . Butternuts have never grown in L'Anse aux Meadows or even close to the site. Their presence with the Norse artifacts shows that the Norse had paid visits to more southerly areas where such nuts grow. What is particularly intriguing is that their northern limit coincides with that of wild grapes. The northern limit of butternuts as well as for wild grapes lies in the St. Lawrence Valley and what is now northeastern New Brunswick. . . . This means that the person or persons who picked butternuts are likely to have encountered wild grapes as well. The name Vinland must indeed reflect a first-hand experience on the part of the Norse.[13]

As Dr. Wallace explains elsewhere, "In Europe walnuts do not grow north of Denmark, or grapes north of the Rhine valley, but both walnuts and wine were among the luxury goods obtained by chieftains in the rest of Scandinavia, including the chieftains in Greenland."[14]

Eirík's *Saga* also mentions a site called Hóp (tidal lake), where on a subsequent voyage Leif's brother-in-law, Thorfinnr Thordarson (called Karlsefni), tried to establish a permanent settlement. Nevertheless, Hóp was abandoned after one winter because of hostile encounters with natives. The *Saga* continues:

> Karlsefni sailed south along the coast. . . . They sailed for a long time and eventually came to a river that flowed down into a lake and from the lake into the sea. There were extensive sandbars outside the river mouth, and ships could only enter it at high tide. . . . Here they found wild wheat growing . . . and grapevines

on all the higher ground. Every stream was teeming with fish. They dug trenches at the high-tide mark, and when the tide went out there were halibut trapped in the trenches. In the woods there was a great number of animals of all kinds.[15]

I believe that Hóp could very well have been located in the Miramichi area. The Miramichi is one of the world's greatest salmon rivers, the bay is rich in bottom fish, and there are large stands of hardwood there as well. "There is no doubt in my mind," writes Wallace, "that . . . Hóp includes this particular area. Hóp means lagoon by a river estuary protected by sandbars. . . . It should be stressed, however, that the description of Hóp in the sagas includes observations made elsewhere as well. Hóp is the code name for all that is attractive in Vinland."[16]

Hóp is the code name for all that is attractive in Vinland.

Did the Norse probe farther south? Perhaps they did, but we must remember that these Late Iron Age sailors were exploring the shores of the New World from their home in Greenland, not to "see what's on the other side of the mountain," but rather, to acquire valuable commodities. Those things that the Norse sought were readily available in the Gulf of St. Lawrence. From my point of view, it doesn't make much sense for them to have traveled farther when their necessities were at hand.

We must remember too that it was about 1,500 miles by sea from Norway to the settlements in Greenland, and, by the Norse coastal route, it was probably a bit farther than that from Greenland to L'Anse aux Meadows. On top of this, it would have been more than another 600 miles to reach the Miramichi area. At the *maximum* speed of six or seven knots for the Norse ships (and they almost certainly usually went slower than that) it would have been a very long voyage.[17]

The settlement at L'Anse aux Meadows was a short-lived outpost, an experimental base that was used to support probing expeditions that pushed even farther beyond. At the time that it was occupied, about A.D. 1000, "the pastures of Greenland were ample," writes Birgitta Wallace, "and there was no lack of sustenance at the time they became aware of the existence of Vinland. The attraction of Europe was greater. The Norse could get not just lumber, wine and walnuts, but spices, precious metals, glass, honey, grain, salt, silk, velvet and current fashions, news of relatives and friends and staff for the churches. To the end, the Greenlanders kept their eyes on Europe, not on the new lands to the west."[18]

Aboard *Belvedere* in 1997 we continued on, through Northumberland Strait, south of Prince Edward Island, then via the Strait of Canso, between Cape Breton Island and mainland Nova Scotia. Returning to the Atlantic, we then headed southwest to New England.

CHAPTER EIGHT

Belvedere with the Bears in Northern Labrador *(1998)*

*I*N 1998, with my batteries now fully recharged to take on new ice work, I decided to learn more about the European expansions in northern Labrador. With most of my usual crew aboard *Belvedere* we pushed off from Makkovik in mid-July. A few days later we stopped in Nain, the northernmost town in Labrador, long enough to top off our fuel and water, then kept on up the inside passage in murky weather to anchor for the night in an unnamed harbor on South Aulatsivik Island. It reminded me very much of the anchorages in the Lofoten Islands of northern Norway: huge, glacially smoothed cliffs, a glacial rubble of rocks and mud along the shoreline, black spruce growing in the rock clefts, and erratic boulders, deposited by the continental glacier, breaking the silhouette of the ridge line. The difference from Norway was, of course, that on South Aulatsivik we were nearly 700 miles farther south than the Lofotens, and the reason that the vegetation was similar to Norway's was the cold south-flowing Labrador Current, which chills the Labrador coast, and the North Atlantic Drift, which warms the seas around Norway.

For the rest of the month the weather was miserable. Easterlies brought fog and rain and kept the thermometer stuck at forty-one degrees F. As we exited Port Manvers Run into the open ocean, we began to feel the familiar *lop* (ground swell) setting in from the Labrador Sea. Rolling a bit, we moved along the most direct coastal route, outside the Okak Islands and inside Cod Island to Cape Mugford, where we could see only the bottom third (approximately 1,000 feet) of the famous clefted scarp called the Bishop's Mitre. Layers of wispy stratus clouds were cold and gray against the dark, nearly vertical rock faces that were themselves set off by the bergy bits and growlers that were grinding at their base. As if to give us some sense of the truly massive scale of the cape, we spotted a small white dot: a lone polar bear plodding along the lower cliff faces and sniffing the air to catch our scent.

PHOTO, OPPOSITE PAGE

Hebron Harbour, Labrador

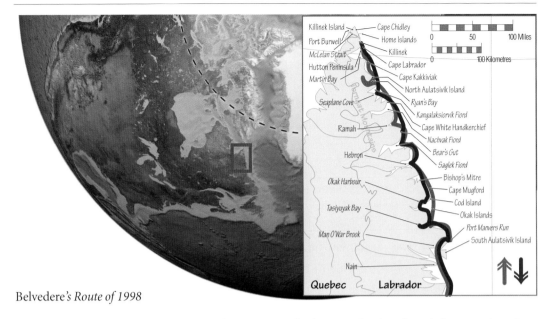

Killinek Island — Cape Chidley
Port Burwell — Home Islands
McLelan Strait — Killinek
Hutton Peninsula — Cape Labrador
Martin Bay — Cape Kakkiviak
North Aulatsivik Island
Seaplane Cove — Ryan's Bay
Kangalaksiorvik Fiord
Ramah — Cape White Handkerchief
Nachvak Fiord
Hebron — Bear's Gut
Saglek Fiord
Bishop's Mitre
Okak Harbour — Cape Mugford
Cod Island
Tasiyuyak Bay — Okak Islands
Port Manvers Run
Man O'War Brook — South Aulatsivik Island
Nain
Quebec   Labrador

0   50   100 Miles
0   100 Kilometres

Belvedere's Route of 1998

Collecting ice near Cape Mugford, Labrador

Late on the evening of July 20, *Belvedere* found the security of Hebron's harbor. In the morning we visited the abandoned town site where the Moravians had once run a thriving community.

One of the oldest Protestant orders, the Moravian Church, the German order of The Unity of the Brethren, was founded in the fifteenth century and by the eighteenth century was sending missions globally to "the underprivileged of the world." In 1752 they made their first attempt to establish a mission in Labrador, near Hopedale, but the Inuit murdered seven missionaries and the effort was abandoned. It was not until 1771 that Jens Haven, a former Greenland missionary, set up a permanent mission at Nain, and from then until 1900 the brethren spread along the coast, setting up seven stations between Makkovik and Killinek, at the northernmost point of Labrador. By 1843 virtually all of the Moravian Inuit were literate.

The station at Hebron began in 1818, and the present main building was put up in 1837 to house both a small chapel and the Moravian brethren who lived and worked there. The brethren closed the settlement, however, in 1959, after the government had consolidated a number of outlying communities in Nain, where a school, a Royal Canadian Mounted Police post, a nursing station, and an airstrip had been established.

Now all was silent. Decay and deterioration

dominated. The wind had torn the metal off the roof in places, collapsed the entryway housings, and damaged the weathervane atop its delicate cupola. Bonnie and I quietly picked chives from the remains of one of the mission's cold frames, and we found the scene incredibly sad, yet beautiful, in the fog's soft gray light. On the hillside a couple of caribou grazed contentedly, and the only sounds were the peeps of a plover that perched on the ridge of one of the outbuildings, the haunting calls of two loons flying overhead, and the gentle swoosh of small waves that moved amid the seaweed on the marbled ledges.

The only sounds were the peeps of a plover that perched on the ridge of one of the outbuildings.

~

Two days later we were at Ramah, having had visibility of little more than a tenth of a mile the whole way. Like Hebron, Ramah was the site of a Moravian mission. Now nothing remained, save the outlines of several semisubterranean Inuit houses and a small grassy graveyard with one red sandstone plaque marking the grave of a German missionary's wife who died in the mid-nineteenth century. The fog lifted briefly, however, to reveal the majesty of the fjord's 3,800-foot-high mountains marked by tortured and warped rock

The Bishop's Mitre, near Cape Mugford, Labrador

veins with dozens of thin waterfalls streaming over the bare faces to the black scree slopes below.

The fog disappeared just after we passed the mouth of Nachvak Fiord, allowing us a glimpse of the beginning of the rugged Torngat Mountains and the 2,450-foot Cape White Handkerchief, with its great blaze of white quartzite. The cape stood out wonderfully against the briefly blue sky and sea, but then the fog shut in again, and it was not until July 25, when we reached Martin Bay (60°05' N, 64°24' W), at the northern tip of Labrador, that things temporarily improved again.

In Martin Bay the ceiling gradually rose, showing us a large, well-protected harbor, with bold cliffs to the west and lower hills to the north and east covered in glacial boulders and rubble. It reminded me of something a Labradorean had said couple of weeks before in Makkovik: "God made the rest of the earth in six days and spent the seventh throwing rocks at Labrador."

We stopped in Martin Bay to search for the remains of an unmanned, automatic radio-transmitting weather station that had been secretly placed there by the crew of a German submarine in 1943. Its existence remained unknown to the Canadians for nearly forty years, until Franz Selinger, an Austrian historian working on a book about World War II German weather reconnaissance in the Arctic, uncovered evidence that a station had been surreptitiously set up from a submarine.

The Moravian mission *at Hebron, Labrador*   The German Meteorological Service established a number of these stations—on Novaya Zemlya, Svalbard, Bear Island, and Jan

Mayen Island—to transmit data about air temperature and pressure, as well as wind direction and velocity. The service also set up manned clandestine weather stations at sites on the east coast of Greenland and on Spitsbergen and anchored weather buoys on the banks west of Scotland. Nevertheless, by far the most audacious project was the one in Martin Bay, Labrador.

Ramah Fiord, Labrador

In what was simply an incredibly skillful feat of piloting, on October 22, 1943, the German U-537 threaded its way southward along the coast from Cape Chidley, between Home Island and the Avayalik Islands, through the myriad uncharted ledges, and stole into Martin Bay on the surface. The captain wanted to be as far north in Labrador as possible and had chosen this site because he thought there would be few Inuit there.

The U-boat anchored just inside the arm of the Hutton Peninsula that encloses the southeast side of the bay. Then, in what must have been twenty-eight very tense and stressful hours, U-537 remained on the surface with all her hatches open, while the crew unloaded more than a ton of equipment and hauled it ashore in rubber dinghies. They "could neither submerge, run for it, nor defend [themselves] if attacked," writes Alec Douglas, who discovered the site in 1981. "Working through the night," he explains, "the crew manhandled ten heavy canisters containing nickel-cadmium and dry-cell batteries, transmitter and weather measuring devices, as well as the tripod and mast, over the beach, and 170 feet up a hill about a quarter mile inland. The U-boat stayed long enough to verify that the station (now called "Kurt") was functioning properly on its frequency of 3,940 kilohertz and then slipped out to sea."[1]

The site of the station was beautifully concealed. Bonnie, Peter Semotiuk, Craig George—an old friend from Point Barrow, Alaska, who had been part of the crew on several voyages in the Northwest Passage—and I spent a couple of hours, armed with a fairly exact map, and still we couldn't find the site. It was only after we had returned to *Belvedere* and consulted our documents again that Craig and Peter returned for another look. They climbed the hill again, and after about ten minutes "Bingo!" came over the radio from Craig. The equipment had been set up in perfect cover on a low plateau, well back from the ridge line, in a position where it was invisible from the water.

If the German Labrador stations had been successful in transmitting weather data, I wonder how this might have affected the D-Day landings.

In 1981 the unit was disassembled and taken to Ottawa, and now the ground was littered only with decaying dry cell batteries, metal plates, and bits of wire. Gazing westward from the site, we could see that *Belvedere* was anchored in almost the same spot where U-537 had been. I could only think of the superior navigational skills of the captain and the *sang-froid* of the crew as they waited, vulnerable, on the surface.

The Germans made two small miscalculations, however. In spite of the captain's desire to erect the station in a seldom-visited area, in fact he chose a location that was not far from the military air route between Fort Chimo (now Kuujjuaq) in northern Quebec and Frobisher (now Iqaluit) on Baffin Island. And, the site at Martin Bay was only about twenty-five miles from the village of Port Burwell on Killinek Island at the northern tip of Labrador, and judging from the condition of the equipment when Alec Douglas found it, the Inuit had almost certainly found the site. The other mistake was in labeling one of the canisters "Canadian Weather Service." No doubt the Germans thought it was a good way to make the unit look official if it was discovered, but in fact, no such organization existed, and, at that time, Newfoundland and Labrador were a colony of Great Britain— they were not confederated with Canada until 1949.

When U-537 left Martin Bay, the station transmitted weather information for two weeks or more, but soon the Canadian military picked up the transmissions and began jamming the frequency, probably assuming that the transmissions were being broadcast from a submarine. The station continued transmitting, however, for about three months. In 1944 a second submarine was sent out to set up a station, but it was sunk on the way and, so far as is known, no other attempts were made. As Alec Douglas points out, the information from Labrador had the potential to aid the U-boat wolf packs in the Battle of the Atlantic.

If the German Labrador stations had been successful in transmitting weather data, I wonder how this might have affected the D-Day landings. During the Second World War, the "war for weather" was crucial in the tactical planning of operations. By June 1944, many of the German weather stations, both manned and unmanned, had been captured or silenced. Group Captain James Stagg, General Eisenhower's meteorological advisor, alerted the general to the small "weather window," during which Ike launched the invasion of Europe on June 6, 1944; the German High Command was unaware of it.

That evening, as we sat on *Belvedere*'s deck, Craig, ever vigilant, spotted a chevron of ripples on the calm water on the far side of the bay. "Nanook, over there!" (*Nanuq* means polar bear in Inuktitut). A glance through binoculars revealed a pair of white, furry ears and a coal-black nose at the apex. The polar bear swam very casually to the boat, inspected us, and then swam off across the harbor—and the next morning we saw another. It reminded me that although northern Labrador is well below the Arctic Circle, because of the effect of the cold Labrador Current it is climatologically, and hence faunally, fully "Arctic."

Craig George inspects the remains of the clandestine autonomous weather station that was set up by the crew of a German submarine in 1943 in Martin Bay, Labrador.

JOHN CRAIGHEAD GEORGE

We were off the next day for nearby McLelan Strait, the narrow alley that separates Killinek Island from the tip of mainland Labrador.

We ran north inside Oo-olilik and Home Islands to Cape Labrador, where, with Cape Chidley visible in the distance, we turned northwest into the strait. I wanted to visit the abandoned town site in Port Burwell at the western entrance. Because the tidal currents are so strong there, we carefully studied the tables so that our arrival at the eastern entrance would coincide with the beginning of the flood into Hudson Strait. Unfortunately the tables proved to be off by a few hours (we checked this a number of times), and instead, we met a ferocious ebb.

For a while we thought that we might be able to buck the current and bull our way through to Port Burwell, but the flow was so strong that we were stopped cold about halfway through—despite running *Belvedere*'s engine flat out and scorching the paint on the exhaust stack. In slack water our engine would have pushed us along at more than eight knots, but with that millrace roiling and boiling around us and throwing *Belvedere* this way and that, the only thing we could do was turn around, and, now with the flow, roar back to the eastern entrance. We anchored there in the upper part of Clark Harbour, where we had the chance to read John T. Rowland's hair-raising account of taking a thirty-foot yawl through McLelan Strait in 1911, when he was on his summer vacation from Yale:

> Advancing up the tickle, we soon noticed the strong current running with us. As we approached the narrow, straight-walled gorge and heard the thunder of waters that issued from it, I think we all experienced a sinking of the diaphragm.... Too late to turn back, the current had *Daryl* in its grip.... I kept *Daryl* going at full speed, the better to maneuver the seething whirlpools which sometimes spun her half around. One curious effect was that the level of the water in the middle of the tickle appeared to be several feet lower than where it frothed against the walls. We rushed down a liquid U-shaped flume— a fortunate circumstance which perhaps saved *Daryl* from butting her brains out against the smooth rock. The worst spot came about halfway through, where the gorge grew narrow and we had to negotiate a sharp turn. Here the current gained even greater speed and hurled itself in fury against the resisting wall. At this point *Daryl* elected to go stern first, and nothing I could do would stop her. Waves broke over her deck, and it looked as if she planned a carom off the wall. We stopped the motor and hung on. In a few moments the current had swept her through, like a chip of wood that is carried down a brook. (You may have noticed that the chip never strikes a rock.) Altogether it was a fast fourteen miles.[2]

As we were digesting John Rowland's story we received a weather forecast that predicted several days of strong easterly gales. Because we were on a fairly tight schedule, I regretfully decided to leave our Port Burwell visit for another year. I should add that the weather forecast wasn't the only thing that we received in the tiny confines of inner Clark Harbour: in the evening polar bears twice swam out to the boat. Polar bears are massively strong and fully capable of boarding boats—occasionally they do. When the first bear got too close for comfort, we drove him away by firing a couple of slugs into the water from my twelve-gauge shotgun, causing the bear to turn and swim away, but without great urgency.

The second bear, however, was much bigger and dirtier, and seemed to me to be more definite in his approach. Because I was low on slugs—we needed to save them for our forays ashore—this time I fired a blank black-powder round from my ten-gauge signal cannon. The great belch of greasy, white smoke and its longer, deeper boom did the trick. The bear headed for shore in a hurry, and a second round sent him off over the hill, with his big shaggy paunch flapping from side to side. A third bear arrived in the morning for a shoreline breakfast of kelp but did not approach us.

When the first bear got too close for comfort, we drove him away by firing a couple of slugs into the water.

July 27 was another of those cold, foggy north-Labrador days, but as we approached Cape Kakkiviak, southbound, the fog again cooperated and lifted for a bit, giving us a "haunted" view of the 1,750 feet of bold veined and fissured granite. All was gray: gray overcast and water, and layers of gray stratus clouds across the face of the massive, dark rock. Clouds billowed over its peak, occasionally parting to reveal the white domed tower of a North Warning System radar station. It reminded me of a 1930s horror film, in which a mad scientist lives in a castle aerie, conducting unspeakable experiments accompanied by spooky organ music.

This powerful scene was repeated several hours later when the clouds suddenly lifted near Eclipse Channel, dramatically revealing its portals, North Aulatsivik Island's 3,050-foot reach and the 2,450-foot peak off Ryan's Bay. By evening we were in Seaplane Cove in Kangalaksiorvik Fiord, where, in 1931, Alexander Forbes, a geographer from Harvard, had based one of his expeditions for mapping northern Labrador from the air. In contrast to the lands farther north, here we saw some green mosses on the boulder-strewn slopes and two polar bears grazing on kelp along the strand.

〜

Our next stop was in the fjord called Bear's Gut. Although fairly small, it is steep and deep, and we discovered that the bottom was quite regular at 300 feet. It was so deep that the only holding ground we could find for the anchor was off a small creek's mouth a couple of hundred feet from shore, where we set the main anchor in 60 feet, then backed around and, for a stern hold, buried a 75-pound anchor on the grassy beach.

The fjord overwhelmed us with its severe beauty. Its smooth, glacially scoured walls rose almost vertically to tops at more than 3,500 feet. Layers of wispy clouds stood out against the wet blackness of the fjord's ancient faces. Onshore, to the south, about a half a mile away, we saw a polar bear taking a nap on his belly with both paws draped over a small knoll; hundreds of eider ducks congregated on the smooth water of the fjord. We were in the midst of the Torngat Mountains, a massif of raw and jagged archaean gneiss and granite which, at 3.8 billion years of age, is among the oldest rock on earth. "This place is so wild and untouched," said Craig, "that we might well be witnessing the end of the Ice Age, thousands of years ago."

One night in Saglek Fjord a polar bear nipped our dinghy.

〜

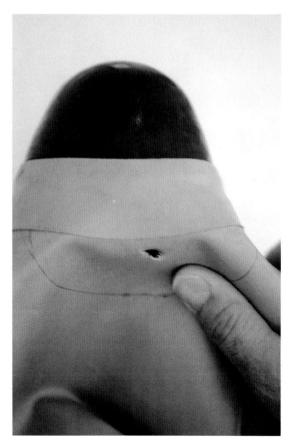

As we motored out of Bear's Gut with, as usual that summer, about a tenth of a mile's visibility, we dodged a few icebergs that we saw only on the radar screen on our way toward nearby Saglek Fjord. There we put the hook down in Anchorage Cove to wait out a rising easterly. The next morning, July 30, we woke to find that my Zodiac dinghy was half deflated on the starboard side. When we pulled it aboard we found one large puncture and several tooth marks at the tip of the sponson: a polar bear had apparently visited us during the night and chewed on the Zodiac.

I shouldn't have been surprised, because many years ago in Alaska a polar bear ate the foam rubber seat off my Skidoo. Craig George inspected the damage. He, as I have mentioned, is a wildlife biologist from Point Barrow, Alaska, where he has had more encounters with polar bears than one would wish. In one incident, a bear ate the corner off a twelve-volt automobile battery he had put on the ice to power a whale-call recording. In any case, the puncture in my Zodiac was at a spot where it was very difficult to get a patch to hold firmly. We spent every morning thereafter pumping up the dinghy and muttering nasty things about that bear. Later that autumn the people at the raft repair center in Rhode Island refused to believe how that puncture hole got there.

Once we had rigged a jury patch on the dinghy we decided to make a few miles by running round the 1,700-foot vertical rock bluff at Cape Uivak. With its huge black diabase intrusion it appeared to be almost the negative image of Cape White Handkerchief. On arriving in Jerusalem Harbour, which is just across an isthmus from Hebron, almost immediately we spotted half a dozen caribou grazing on one of the slopes. Above them a black bear was so busy rooting something out of the ground that it didn't even raise its head when a caribou calf walked by less than a hundred feet away. The bear's coat was so smooth and prime that the sunlight glinted off it.

At last, on July 31, the weather began to improve, and by the time we returned to the Bishop's Mitre we were able to see its magnificent bifurcate top, which was nicely balanced by a large, three-pinnacle iceberg at its base. Soon we entered Mugford Tickle. All at once the temperature jumped from forty-five to fifty-five degrees, and we saw the first trees on the coast—a few lonely, stunted, black spruces scattered about in the shelter of the crevices. Coincidentally the wind went into the west, giving us the first truly clear skies of the summer and starting a run of fair weather that was mostly with us until we reached Baddeck, Nova Scotia, in the latter part of August.

'This place is so wild and untouched, that we might well be witnessing the end of the Ice Age, thousands of years ago.'

∾

On August 1 we continued on the inside route, west of South Aulatsivik Island to a lovely anchorage amid massive sand dunes in Tasiyuyak Bay. We had to feel our way in over three moraines and then anchored almost a mile from shore; even so, horseflies, mosquitoes, and black flies reached us in the evening's stillness. Nevertheless, it was a beautiful place, with the jagged outline of the Kiglapait Mountains to the south and, nearby, the spruce trees and thick reindeer moss covering the lowlands. Two Inuit fishermen rowed out to *Belvedere* and told us that they had discovered a wolf's den amid the dunes.

On our way back to Nain we stopped in Port Manvers Run to take on water from Man O'War Brook, a large stream that cascades in multibraided skeins down the sloping rock face. We anchored close in, then sent the dinghy ashore with a hundred fathoms of line, the end of which we made fast to a large boulder, then winched

A three-pinnacle iceberg near the Bishop's Mitre

Belvedere's stern into ten feet of water. After that it only required taking one end of a 300-foot string of garden hose to a clear pool and letting the washdown pump do the work. Two days later we returned to Nain's dust and feral children.

Taking on water at Man O'War Brook in Port Manvers Run

In Nain we learned that the polar bears had been active everywhere on the north coast all summer and that more than one camping party had been to be evacuated in a hurry because of their frequent intrusions. There are currently about 1,500 polar bears living within Canada's borders, a population that is both healthy and strictly managed. I am glad of that, despite the insult to my Zodiac.

CHAPTER NINE

Closing the Loop:

Belvedere Back to Baffin Island (1999 & 2000)

AFFIN ISLAND has always fascinated me. Rugged, remote, and vast, its nearly 200,000 square miles make it the fifth largest island in the world, and, being 930 miles long, it is the bulwark that long prevented early European explorers from penetrating the inner waters of the Northwest Passage. In 1999 I wanted to see it again—to close the loop that I had begun in 1988, when I was last in Baffin Island's waters aboard *Belvedere,* and thus, in a way, to round out my wanderings in the North Atlantic's high latitudes.

In 1988 I had sailed along Baffin's north and east coasts during my traverse of the Northwest Passage, but in 1999 I wanted to go to the southeastern coast, to rarely visited Resolution Island, in search of a fascinating historical mystery: the site of an Elizabethan "gold mine" (actually a fool's gold quarry) that was worked in 1578.

This mine's origin was the offspring of the post-Columbian race for the riches of the Orient. In the second half of the sixteenth century England found herself blocked from reaching eastern Asia by Spain's control of the southern route, but some entrepreneurs also believed in the existence of northern water passages to the Far East. As a result, in 1576 mariner and privateer Martin Frobisher—"a man whose career balanced precariously upon the edge of legality"[1]—set off with Queen Elizabeth's blessing in two small ships and a pinnace (a very small, two-masted vessel) in search of a northwest passage. Frobisher was, as one of his shipmates wrote, "persuaded of a new and neerer passage to Cataya [China] than by Capo d'Buona Speranza [Cape of Good Hope], which the Portugalles yeerly use."[2]

The pinnace was lost in a gale off Greenland, and the crew of the other ship turned back in fright, leaving Frobisher to head northwest with one ship alone. On July 28, 1576, he sighted what was probably Resolution Island, off the southeast tip of Baffin Island, and then turned north, discovering a "great gutte, bay, or passage, dividing as it were two mayne lands or continents asunder...." Frobisher assumed that it was the water route to Asia; in fact, it was actually Frobisher Bay on Baffin Island.

But according to George Best, one of his lieutenants, Frobisher also found a curious "peece of a blacke stone, much like seacole in coloure, which by the waighte seemed to be some kinde of mettal or Mynerall."[3] This chunk of rock, the size of a "halfe pennye loafe," sparkled with shiny yellow flecks, and in London Frobisher presented it as a curiosity to his principal backer.

Michael Lok, the leader of Frobisher's syndicate, had the black rock assayed for its gold-bearing potential and received three negative reports. In January 1577, however, he at last turned up a "goldfiner" who testified that it did indeed contain gold. "It was a profoundly bad choice" of an assayer, writes James McDermott.[4] When Lok asked John

Razorback Harbour, Labrador

Baptista Agnello, an Italian assayer in London, how he had discovered gold in the sample when no one else had, Agnello is said to have replied, "*Bisogna sapere adulare la natura*" ("It is necessary to know how to flatter nature").[5] Although "the most likely explanation . . . is incompetency or dishonesty,"[6] it is now mooted that the gold may have been accidentally introduced through additives used in the assay process.[7]

With more investors now joining the venture, Frobisher's backers discarded any plans for another attempt at discovering a northwest passage to Asia and instead sent him back to Baffin the following summer, 1577, on a mining voyage to collect the black ore. The next year, 1578, he had fifteen ships under his command and returned to England with 1,200 tons of the stuff. Unfortunately all attempts to render gold from it were fruitless, and the venture collapsed under heaps of mutual recrimination.

It was on that third voyage that Frobisher inadvertently led his flotilla 200 miles into Hudson Strait before turning back to his mines. George Best became separated from the main fleet and anchored his two "leakie," ice-damaged ships in what we now believe to have been Resolution Harbour on Resolution Island. There he discovered a "great blacke Iland" of "such plentie of blacke Ore" that would "suffise all the golde gluttons of the worlde."[8] Although neither ship carried an assayer,[9] his crew began to excavate it, and although they left in haste shortly thereafter, he called the place "Best's blessing." Recently a considerable amount of archaeological work has been devoted to the quarries in lower Frobisher Bay, but the location of "Best's blessing" has remained conjectural.

Belvedere's Route of 1999 and 2000

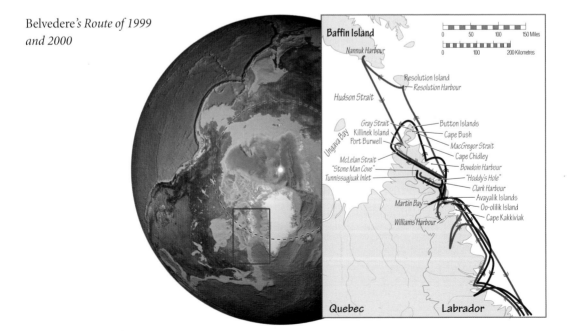

We left Makkovik on July 15 and ran overnight offshore, first through a vast field of icebergs too numerous to count, and later through dense fog, to the town of Nain, where we touched briefly to top off our water and fuel. We arrived at Williams Harbour, near the northern tip of Labrador, on July 21.

Williams Harbour is a large, bleak, and well-protected anchorage that is extremely well charted because it is the supply point for the early-warning radar installation (*LAB ONE*) atop Cape Kakkiviak. In the morning a young polar bear swam a mile across the harbor to us and, before returning to shore, hung nearly motionless in the water, six feet from *Belvedere*'s stern, inspecting us with great curiosity. In the distance we saw another bear having a snooze on the beach.

That day we ran only a short way north, past Martin Bay, to tiny Clark Harbour, at the eastern end of McLelan Strait. Here Smitty and I, along with Hod Hildreth, a sailor friend from Maine and a frequent member of *Belvedere*'s northern crew, took the Zodiac into the strait on a very cold and bouncy run to check on the set and timing of the strong tidal current that had defeated our attempts to pass through there in 1998. Hod had been here on his own boat a few years before, and he showed us a small basin where he had waited out the tidal cycle.

The rising tide swept us right in to "Hoddy's Hole," but we agreed that, safe as it might be, it was too small and tricky for us to use, so we returned to *Belvedere* very wet and chilled and discussed going through McLelan Strait the next day on the flood. Suddenly however, we heard a forecast that predicted settled weather for several days —and that doesn't happen often up there—so we quickly shelved our plans for McLelan in favor of crossing the sixty-mile-wide Hudson Strait to Resolution Island.

Out of Clark Harbour early on July 23, we left Cape Chidley and the Button Islands to port and traversed the strait in conditions that must be the nearest those rugged waters ever come to a flat calm. Ahead lay a real challenge, however. The big tides and strong tidal currents at Resolution Island are, if anything, more ferocious than those in McLelan Strait. John Davis, an English explorer and mariner who visited Resolution less than a decade after George Best, encountered a "furious overfall,"[10] with "the water whirling and roring"[11] near the mouth of Resolution Harbour. And Best described it this way: The "rushling and noyse that the tides do make in this place with so violente a force, that oure shippes ... were turned sometimes round about even in a momente, after the manner of a whirlepoole and the noyse of the streame no less to be hearde a farre off, than the waterfall of London Bridge."[12]

The big tides and strong tidal currents at Resolution Island are, if anything, more ferocious than those in McLelan Strait.

We took these reports seriously. To avoid the problem as much as possible we timed our crossing to arrive right at the harbor's narrow mouth at slack high water. We weren't far off, but although we arrived at the spot only fifteen minutes early, we found a three-knot current still flooding into the strait. Peter Stone was masterful on the helm. We had to line up several hundred yards east of the entrance, and, while the current carried us westward, we motored straight toward the bare rock cliffs.

I am glad to say that we got this exercise right. Just when it seemed as if we might slam smack onto the rocks, we tore through the hundred-yard-wide entrance exactly as planned. I remember a general "phew!" escaping from everyone. Then, as Peter throttled back to idle, we were swept into the gut at eight knots, going slightly

Just when it seemed as if we might slam smack onto the rocks, we tore through the hundred-yard-wide entrance exactly as planned.

downhill on the water's surface at the same time.

Once inside, we had to be very careful. We kept our eyes glued to the forward-looking sounder because George Best had had trouble here. His ship, the *Anne Frances*, "came agrounde uppon a suncken Rocke within the Harborough, and lay thereon more than halfe drye untill the nexte floud, when by Gods Almighty providence, contrarye to all expectation, they came afloate agayne, béeyng forced all the tyme to undersette theyr Shyppe wyth their mayne yarde, whyche otherwyse was lykely to oversette and putte thereby in daunger the whole companye. They hadde above two thousande strokes togyther at the Pumpe, before they coulde

Belvedere in Resolution Island Harbour, at the southeastern tip of Baffin Island

make theyr Shyppe frée of the water agayne, so sore shée was brused by lying upon the Rockes." His other ship, the *Moone*, "came safely, and roade at Ancker by the Anne Frauncis, whose helpe in theyr necessitie they coulde not well have missed."[13]

We found Resolution Harbour to be as George Best described it: "an indifferent place to harborough in" and a tidal range of nearly twenty-five feet. After a couple of tries we managed to set the anchor through a dense forest of kelp, on a ledge, in ninety feet of water. This was too deep for real comfort because it is best to have the anchor line as close to parallel with the bottom as possible, which therefore puts a horizontal drag on the anchor, making its hold most effective. The greater the depth of anchoring, the steeper the angle of the anchor line against the anchor, a situation that gives the line a more vertical pull, allowing the anchor to pop out of its hold more easily. The only way around this problem is to let out more line or to find a shallower place to set the hook. And the safety of the set in any ledge anchoring should be treated as suspect because there is little mud or sediment to help keep the anchor's flukes well bedded. So, we were essentially betting on a good hold in a rock cleft. Fortunately, the set held firm until we departed.

The author going ashore at Resolution Island.

George Best eloquently summarized the problem of Resolution Harbour: "The coast is so much subject to broken ground & rockes, especially in the mouth and entrance of everye harborow, that albeit the channell be sounded over and over againe, yet are you never neare to discerne the daungers. For the bottome of the sea, holding like shape and forme as the lande, beying full of hilles, dales and ragged rockes, suffereth you not, by your soundings, to knowe and keepe a true gesse of the depth. For you shall sounde upon the side or hollownesse of one hil or rocke under water, and have a hundreth, fiftie, or fourtie fadome depth: and before the next cast, ere you shal bee able to have your leade againe, you shall be uppon the toppe thereof, and come agrounde, to your utter confusion."[14]

After a couple of tries we managed to set the anchor through a dense forest of kelp, on a ledge, in ninety feet of water.

The shore was no more welcoming. In 1615 William Baffin sketched it perfectly: "We went on shore, but found no certaine signe of inhabitants, but only the tracke of beares and foxes. The soyle is only rocks and stony ground, hardly any thinge growing thereon which is greene."[15]

My journal entry follows. "This is without doubt the most bleak piece of real estate that I've ever seen in the Arctic: there is not a piece of green; the ledges are scraped bare except for a few snow patches in the rock crevices; and large...frost-shattered boulders litter the raw...landscape."

That evening Peter Stone and I took the Zodiac north, through the narrowing harbor channel, taking soundings (there were none on the chart) every hundred yards or so, and radioing them back to Smitty, who entered them on our chart aboard *Belvedere*. In the deepening twilight the full ebb was running against us, and the water was moving so fast—slick and black, with small whirlpools spinning along in it—that it seemed positively viscous.

Drawing on the excellent geological fieldwork and archival research of Professor Donald Hogarth,[16] who describes the island as "a harsh and uninviting land" with "repellant features," we pushed along in the gathering dark, and suddenly, and just as we rounded a small rock bluff, the great black ore seam loomed above us. The dense blackness of the cliffs was highlighted by narrow snow patches in their crevices. Against the deep gray of the sky it was a powerful scene.

There were also plenty of omnivorous bears on that bleak island, and our foray ashore that evening was spent with our eyes over our shoulders and our shotguns (loaded with both blanks and slugs) firmly in hand as we collected ore samples from the ledges. Peter and I kept close together and small noises made us jumpy. Fortunately there wasn't much to make us tarry there: the light was too poor for him to sketch or for me to take photographs.

The next day, after another inspection trip ashore, we caught the beginning of the flood, which carried us quickly westward along the Baffin Island coast under clear skies and over gentle seas. Along the way we passed several large icebergs, so fresh, flat-topped, and hard-cleaved that they could only have calved recently and nearby, from one of Baffin Island's glaciers, rather than those of Greenland, where the majority of the Atlantic's icebergs are born.

In Hudson Strait an iceberg lies off the Baffin Island shore. The barren flatness of southeastern Baffin Island may have been the inspiration for the Norse place name Helluland, "Flat Stone Land" or "Slab Land," which appears in the sagas as a geographical reference point on the way to Vinland.

A polar bear in Nannuk Harbour, Baffin Island

We slept well that night in the beautiful fastness at the head of Nannuk Harbour's fjord. As I have mentioned, *Nanuq* means *polar bear* in Inuktitut. As if to confirm the harbor's name, on the way into that long, narrow fjord we saw two polar bears on the cliffs: one of them, large and active, craning its neck as it sniffed the air to catch our scent, and the other, small and so lethargic as it napped on the rocks that it barely raised its head as we steamed by and clattered out our anchor chain.

That evening my thoughts returned to the Norse. About a hundred miles west of Nannuk Harbour on southern Baffin Island, archaeologists Deborah and George Sabo unearthed an artifact as fascinating as the chain mail that Peter Schledermann found on Ellesmere Island. They turned up a small Inuit figurine that is thought to represent a Norse person. That figure wears a hooded garment that is slit up the front and falls to the ankles—definitely not Inuit garb. Most surprising is the incised cross on the figure's chest, which suggests to some that it may represent the pectoral cross of a priest.[17] Oddly enough, there is a hazy secondhand report of an English Franciscan (Minorite) friar who, in 1360, sailed from England to Greenland and probably onward, to Labrador.[18] Others have speculated—and it is only speculation—that the figurine may depict a Teutonic knight, an order that, after the crusades ended, was involved with hostilities in northern Europe and consequently might have become involved with the conversion of the heathen *skrælings*.[19] In sum, "All that can be said with any certainty," Kirsten Seaver wrote to me, "is that it represents a European."[20]

Nevertheless, an increasing number of Norse artifacts have been found in archaeological sites on the northern, eastern, and southern shores of Baffin Island. Among them are strands of *spun*

An Inuit figurine found in an archaeological site on southern Baffin Island near Kimmirut (formerly Lake Harbour) most likely represents a Norse visitor. A cross appears to be incised on its chest.

©CANADIAN MUSEUM OF CIVILIZATION (HARRY FOSTER, PHOTOGRAPHER), CATALOG NO. KeDq-7:235, IMAGE NO. S94-6299

fur rope, which is not an Inuit artifact and implies the presence of Norse women. We should not rule out the fact that the figurine may represent a Norse woman who accompanied one of the Norse trading voyages from Greenland into Hudson Strait.[21]

With the fine weather still holding, but a series of gales forecast in less than forty-eight hours, we agreed that it would be best to cross Hudson Strait again, using the favorable conditions in those waters which have a deservedly ugly reputation. As fulmars swooped and soared around us, we headed south in a nearly flat calm with unlimited

In Port Burwell, Killinek Island, Hod Hildreth surveys the cliffs.

visibility amid the uncountable numbers of icebergs that dotted the sea. It was pitch black in the early hours of July 27 when we anchored in Port Burwell on Killinek Island, off the northern tip of Labrador, while in the roadstead on the Ungava Bay side, rode the lights of the big Canadian Coast Guard icebreaker *Des Groseilliers*.

After most of the day at Burwell, spent filling our tanks from a waterfall at the head of the harbor and marveling at the richness of the tundra cover compared to the north side of Hudson Strait, we then caught the ebb and were flushed quickly eastward through the millrace of McLelan Strait. We waited out the gales near there in an unnamed cove in Tunnissugjuak Inlet, which was alive with bears and seals and one minke whale that was making life dangerous for the local fish stocks. Smitty and Peter climbed up to the top of one of the rocky hills and built a stone cairn shaped like a man. It was similar to an Inuit beacon, an *inukshuk* (*like a man* in Inuktitut), rows of which were used in caribou drives to channel the animals toward waiting hunters. We named our anchorage (60°16.5' N, 64°30.3' W) *Stone Man Cove*.

A few days later we reached Nachvak Fiord. The fog had been thick all day, and when we burst out of it, we were awestruck by the grandeur and beauty of the fjord: a deep, glacially scoured valley with walls that rose almost vertically to jagged, toothed peaks more than 1,000 feet high. Delicate streaks of waterfalls cascaded everywhere onto green scree slopes covered with grass and low bushes. Yet the sweet sound of the falls was intermixed with the noisy roar of rockslides that came crashing down the fjord's sides, leaving puffs of rock dust behind them.

As soon as I reached home at the end of August, I sent a piece of the rock that we had collected on Resolution Island to Professor Donald Hogarth at the University of Ottawa, asking him whether we had collected Best's "black ore." The phone rang about a week later. "My guess is you found Best's Blessing, John," said Don. "That rock is the 'black ore,' the same stuff that Frobisher mined. It's a hornblende, no gold at all, but the mica flakes make it sparkle. When they got back to England in 1578 with hundreds of tons of ore, they couldn't produce any gold from it, and they just left it in Dartford, where they had their smelter. You still can see chunks of it built into some of the walls in the town. I've seen it there."

Today, ironically enough, mines on Baffin Island produce lead, zinc, and silver. And although Frobisher's claim of possession for Queen Elizabeth was the beginning of the British control over much of northern North America, the town of Iqaluit (formerly Frobisher Bay) is the capital of the new Territory of Nunavut, "which restores to the Inuit a measure of the sovereignty claimed for England by Frobisher."[22]

A sample of "the blacke ore," with a 20-gauge shotgun cartridge for scale

In April 2000, as I was planning my return to Hudson Strait for the summer, an interesting letter arrived. I've been traveling in boats in the North since 1962, and in most of the waters I've visited, I have pitched a re-corked wine bottle overboard with a note and a business card inside, asking any recipient to get in touch with me. Until recently my return mail has been utterly absent: If anyone did find the bottles on the shores of the Gulf of Alaska, the Bering, Chukchi, and Beaufort Seas; the Northwest Passage, Baffin Bay, or the Norwegian, Barents, and Greenland Seas, they are apparently lousy correspondents.

In 1999 in Hudson Strait I was grousing about this, when Smitty suggested sensibly, "Perhaps you didn't protect those bottles well enough. They may have broken as they washed ashore." That seemed logical enough, so out came another wine bottle, and Smitty wrapped it up with several layers of that Protean sailor's tool, gray duct tape. For good measure he spray-painted it fluorescent orange and wrote "MESSAGE" on it in bold face. The note inside read: "Friday, July 23, 1999. Dear Finder, this message was dropped in Hudson Strait at position 60°37.0' N, 64°13.0' W by the crew of U.S. yacht *Belvedere*. . . . We would greatly appreciate hearing from you. . . ." The bottle went overboard with Cape Chidley in sight and icebergs all around us. With that, we turned our attention back to the rigors of piloting in those poorly charted waters and promptly forgot all about our message in a bottle.

We received our return mail in the spring:

> 14th April 2000, Thurso, Caithness, Scotland . . . If only the wine bottle could talk! I found your message in a bottle a few days ago as I walked along the shore in a little village in the north of Scotland. There it was lying on the rocks waiting to be rescued; I think the grey tape that was wrapped around its body kept it safe from the rocks and the elements. It was so exciting; some people look for rare birds and flowers. I look for a message in a bottle . . . Who knows the journey it endured to get to Bonnie Scotland . . . If you reply to this letter may I suggest by air and not by sea! Ellen Henderson.

I doubt that the bottle drifted directly to Scotland—for that would have required it to fight contrary currents south of Greenland. Rather, I assume it was carried out of Hudson Strait on its strong tides and then was taken south, with the icebergs, in the very cold Labrador Current. It then must have passed east of Newfoundland and over the Grand Banks, where a northerly wind would have pushed it into the warm waters of the Gulf Stream. Then those currents would have drawn it across the Atlantic to Pentland Firth

By that route our message in a bottle would have covered more than 3,000 miles, or a bit more than 12 miles per day.

and ultimately to Skerray on the north coast of Scotland, where Ellen found it. By that route our message in a bottle would have covered more than 3,000 miles, or a bit more than 12 miles per day. Oddly enough, the bottle washed up not far from the harbor of Wick, where *Belvedere* had found shelter from a gale in August 1992.

In July 2000 we returned to where we had posted our "mail" the summer before. This time we were joined by Jem and Maur Tetley, who had been aboard *Belvedere* in 1992 and 1993. Jem is a first-class navigator and helmsman, having honed his keen instincts as a helicopter pilot in the Royal Navy's Fleet Air Arm. And everyone was ready for Maur's excellent cooking.

As soon as we dropped anchor in Martin Bay, Jem said to me, "John, Old Boy, it's really smashing to be here, but I'm a bit concerned about your newest guest," pointing to a large polar bear that was swimming purposefully across the bay directly to us. After some yelling and banging, the bear veered astern of *Belvedere* and climbed ashore not far from the spot where the German submariners must have landed their equipment for the secret autonomous weather station.

"Uh oh, he's back," Peter Stone piped up a little later. I was in my cabin and I heard a tremendous banging and crashing from Jem and Smitty. The bear put both his forepaws on the Zodiac's starboard side and appeared to be about to climb aboard. Thinking fast, Jem threw the contents of our ice-filled cooler at him, but not before he bit down hard on the dinghy. A hiss of air rushed out, and the bear paddled off.

The next morning Smitty somewhat balefully inspected the now limp side of the dinghy. "Now the score is: bears 2, *Belvedere* 0," he said. This time the bear had bitten into the tough fabric, right at the rub rail, which was an equally difficult place to glue on an air-tight patch. As before, we spent the rest of the summer pumping up our leaking boat and growling about that bear's bad manners.

In September the life-raft repairmen, seeing our battle-scarred

The uninvited visitor in Martin Bay, shortly before it bit a hole in the dinghy

J.E.D. TETLEY

dinghy for a second time, now believed our story about how it had
been violated.

~

Our next stop was nearby, in Bowdoin Harbour, on the Atlantic side
of Killinek Island. Donald MacMillan, the famous explorer, used this
bolt hole to shelter his schooner *Bowdoin* many times during his voyages
in the first half of the twentieth century. For him, as well as for us, the
attraction was its protection and its clear, cascading stream of water.

I had planned to jump across Hudson Strait from Bowdoin
Harbour to Frobisher Bay to inspect more of the black ore quarries.
But, oddly enough, in what was otherwise a comparatively ice-free
summer, we learned that Frobisher Bay was clogged with ice so
thoroughly that an icebreaker was at work. None of us relished the
idea of being amid heavy ice floes with a *charging* icebreaker working
nearby, so it wasn't difficult to leave that task for another year.

We also had to think about getting Jem and Maur to Nain for a
scheduled flight back to England, so we decided instead to circumnavigate
Killinek Island. Now having some spare time, we were free to poke
about wherever we might choose in northern Labrador. Smitty carefully
studied the tidal charts and thought we might be able to do it on only
one tidal cycle by first using the flood to help us along into Hudson
Strait and then riding the ebb eastward through McLelan Strait.

We were off from Bowdoin Harbour at 10 A.M. on July 26, 2000.
After running north a few miles we passed under Cape Chidley. For
mariners it is traditionally the northern point of Labrador. Maur
wrote, "It towered above us in all its glorious colours of gray with
pink veins of granite slicing through it."

We soon turned to port and entered MacGregor Strait, between
Killinek Island and Cabot Island. Immediately there were gulls, terns,
and fulmars wheeling all about us as we steered around an iceberg
that almost blocked our path. At the same time a majestic gray
weather front came sweeping through from the west, across Killinek,
just as the tidal current quickly built to five knots from the east.

In the strait—that is, in the cleft between the steep and bold
cliffs on either side—the wind, which was about twenty-five knots
from the southwest, funneled through at more than forty knots,
heeling *Belvedere* past thirty degrees to starboard. "The wind is upon
us with a rush of hot breath," Maur wrote, "and the surface of the sea
boils. Williwaws blast spume across the narrow strait, and Jem at the
helm, has to fight to keep us on course: added to his difficulties are a
pack of growlers ahead which we must avoid yet keep on our track.
A party of seals play nonchalantly on our starboard bow as the birds,
still with us, wheel hectically around; it is a fearsome spot even with

*None of us relished
the idea of being
amid heavy ice
floes with a
charging icebreaker
working nearby.*

the tide with us, and *Belvedere* heels under her reefed main but plows steadily onward."

Later, we entered Gray Strait between Killinek and the Button Islands. The Button Islands and Resolution Island guard the eastern entrance to the turbulent waters of Hudson Strait. Although the Buttons are politically part of the Canadian territory of Nunavut (formerly part of the Northwest Territories), the islands are geographically the northern tip of Labrador.

Jem was on the helm for two critical watches and handled *Belvedere* perfectly, through MacGregor Strait and then Gray Strait. At the time I remember thinking, I hope we have many more voyages together.

Once we had rounded Cape Bush, at the northern point of Killinek, the wind moderated a bit, and it set in murky. I looked west, into Ungava Bay and Hudson Strait, thinking about those mariners who had preceded us centuries ago, and, once again I marveled at their skill and saluted their courage.

Thinking about those mariners who had preceded us centuries ago, I marveled at their skill and saluted their courage.

Although the strait today bears his name, Henry Hudson was not the first European in those waters. As I have mentioned, Martin Frobisher entered what he called "Mistaken Straits" when, in 1578, on his third Arctic voyage, he sailed 200 miles into it before realizing his mistake and turned back to his mines in Frobisher Bay, nearly losing several of his ships to the pack ice in the meantime. At the same time, the way the Inuit had approached Frobisher's party to trade in the previous year—placing their trade goods on the ground, retreating and then returning once the English had themselves retreated— suggests that they had learned this trading procedure from prior contacts with foreigners.[23]

The Norse, who, as we have seen, were probably on the south coast of Baffin Island, may have traveled to southwestern Ungava Bay as well, for several odd-looking cairns there hint to their prior presence. That enigmatic report of an English Minorite friar who, ca. 1360, accompanied an expedition to Greenland and possibly to Labrador, suggests that he may also have been in Hudson Strait: it mentions "indrawing seas,"[24] which strongly remind me of the tidal currents near Resolution Island and in McLelan Strait. Indeed it is possible, too, that John Cabot's son, Sebastian, may have entered the strait in the first years of the sixteenth century,[25] and it is he who "invented the concept of a Northwest Passage around North America."[26]

We know too that in 1586 John Davis was in the strait as well, calling it Lumley's ("Lumleis") Inlet and naming its southeastern promontory, Cape Chidley, but his most important contribution to geographical knowledge is in having delineated Davis Strait, between

Baffin Island and Greenland.[27] A century after Sebastian Cabot was there, George Weymouth, with two ships on a voyage of discovery for a northwest passage, may well have been there, and may have pointed the way for Hudson.[28]

In 1610, Henry Hudson, on his fourth voyage of discovery, and, with only six months' provisions, sailed through Hudson Strait's 450 miles to Cape Wolstenholme and entered the 475,000 square miles of Hudson Bay. The rather strange route that Hudson took suggests to some that he had acquired prior knowledge of the bay and was searching, not for a northwest passage, but rather, for exploitable raw materials. Nevertheless, Hudson believed he had found a northwest passage. He wintered at the southern end of Hudson Bay, in James Bay. After the crew endured a nasty, scurvy-ridden winter on very short rations, the ice released his ship, but on June 23, 1611, the crew mutinied and set him and eight others—his son and the sick and the loyal—adrift in a small boat. They were never heard from again.

The rather strange route that Hudson took suggests to some that he was searching, not for a northwest passage, but rather, for exploitable raw materials.

"Hudson blazed the way... and opened up the vast tract of inland sea beyond," the historian Lesley Neatby has written. "More than that, his colossal effort gave his countrymen such an impetus that, barely five years after his disappearance, the rough chart of his bay was complete..."[29] After Hudson, explorers visited the bay frequently, and in 1670 the Hudson's Bay Company was granted a charter by King James I of Great Britain to exploit the lands of its huge watershed that stretches across a vast part of North America and drains into the bay. Following the voyages of Hudson and Cartier, the European expansion into northern North America started in earnest, and, in a sense, the modern history of that part of the continent began.

As for our part, with autumn's gales approaching, it was time for *Belvedere* to head south once again and to prepare for more northern voyages.

Sable Island *(2001)*

*I*N THE SUMMER OF 2001, because the responsibilities of helping to organize the 150th anniversary of the America's Cup competition forced me to remain in more southern waters, I was unable to visit the North in a boat for the first time in nearly forty years. Nevertheless, I did manage to sail to Sable Island, Nova Scotia, nearly 200 miles east-southeast of Halifax, at the edge of the continental shelf.

The crescent-shaped sand dunes of Sable Island run more than twenty miles east to west and, in one spot, nearly a mile north to south. The island's highest point is only about eighty-five feet above sea level, and its sandbars extend as many as seventeen miles from both ends of the island. Swept by strong ocean currents and located as it is at the confluence of the Gulf Stream and the Labrador Current, the island's dunes and bars are constantly shifting, and fog enshrouds them for much of the year.

Sable Island is known for its wildlife. It is the only recorded nesting place of the Ipswich sparrow, a subspecies of the Savannah sparrow. Terns, black-backed gulls, herring gulls, sandpipers, and

Wild horses graze on Sable Island, Nova Scotia, August 5, 2001.

plovers nest on the island, and, after gales during the migration season, almost any species of bird from eastern North America may be found there.

The island also has the largest breeding colonies of gray and harbor seals in the western Atlantic. And Sable Island is famous for its herds of wild horses, which were introduced in 1738 during an attempt to colonize the island. Today, about 300 horses graze on the marram grass that covers the dunes.

Because it is difficult to see Sable Island from a distance, and because it is close to the shortest route between the northeast ports of North America and the English Channel, its shoals are believed to have trapped 500 vessels since its discovery about 500 years ago. More than 200 ships are known to have been wrecked there since 1800; the last, a yacht, in 1999. Storm-driven waves occasionally expose the bones of a wreck, only to bury them again in another storm. Thus the island has earned the title *Graveyard of the Atlantic*.

On August 5, 2001, as I walked among the horses and seals on Sable's misty beaches I thought about the long sweep of European encounters with those sands and with the shores of the northwestern North Atlantic. It struck me then that because of the richness of this complicated history, for me, there are many expeditions yet to come, probing the waters of the North.

My northern travels are a voyage begun, but not ended.

ca. 700	Irish monks are in the Faroe Islands.
ca. 750	The Norse expansion begins, with seaworthy, ocean-going ships.
790*s*	Viking raids begin in the British Isles.
ca. 795	Irish monks visit Iceland.
ca. 800	Population growth and land shortages occur in Norway.
ca. 800	The Norse settlement of the Faroe Islands begins.
800–1300	A climatic warm period occurs in the North Atlantic.
825	Dicuil writes of Iceland.
ca. 860	The Norse discover Iceland.
ca. 870	The settlement of Iceland begins.
ca. 900	Gunnbjörn Ulf-Kråkuson sights Greenland (Gunnbjörn's Skerries).
930	The first Icelandic *Alþing* (parliament) takes place.
ca. 930	The settlement of Iceland is complete.
978	Snaebjörn Galti winters on the coast of east Greenland.
ca. 982–85	Eirík the Red explores Greenland.
ca. 986	Eirík the Red colonizes Greenland.
ca. 986	Bjarni Herjolfsson sights North America.
1000	Iceland adopts Christianity.
ca. 1000	Christianity arrives in Greenland.
ca. 1000–01	Leif Eiríksson explores Vinland.

ca. 1003–05	Thorvald Eiríksson conducts explorations from Leif's base camp.
ca. 1007–09	Thorfinnr Thordarson (Karlsefni) attempts to colonize Vinland.
ca. 1075	Adam of Bremen writes of Vinland.
early 1100s	South-migrating Inuit reach *Norðsetr* on the west coast of Greenland.
ca. 1124	The Bishopric of Greenland is established.
1170	Norse hunters encounter *Skrælings* (Inuit) in *Norðsetr*.
ca. 1190	The *Grænlandinga Saga (Greenlanders' Saga)* is put into writing.
1194	"Svalbard" is mentioned in literature.
1200s	Iceland's *Lándnamabók (Book of Settlements)* is compiled.
ca. 1260	*Eiríks Saga Rauða (Eirík the Red's Saga)* is put into writing.
1262	Norway absorbs Iceland and possibly Greenland.
ca. 1300	The Kingigtorssuak rune stone is deposited by Norse hunters at 73° N in western Greenland.
1300–1850	The "Little Ice Age" occurs in the North Atlantic.
1319	Norway and Sweden are united. Norway's focus begins to shift from the Atlantic.
mid-1300s	The Norse Western Settlement in Greenland is abandoned.
mid-1300s	Iceland begins to export dried cod to Europe.
1347	The last recorded voyage to Markland (probably Labrador) takes place.
1348	The Black Death ravages northern Europe.
1349	Ivar Bárdarson reports abandonment of the Norse Western Settlement.
1350–1400	Increased drift ice is found around southern Greenland.
ca. 1360	An English Minorite friar may have sailed to Greenland and Labrador.
1378	The last bishop in Greenland dies.
late 1300s	English traders may have begun to work on the west coast of Greenland.
1393	Bergen is sacked by Germans.
1402–04	The Black Death occurs in Iceland.
1406	The last recorded sailing from Greenland appears in the Icelandic *Annals*.

early 1400s	English cod fishermen begin visiting Iceland.
1408	The last recorded wedding in Greenland, at Hvalsø church, takes place.
1412	No Norwegian ships are reported to reach Iceland.
1420s–30s	English fishermen are probably in the waters of southwest Greenland.
ca. 1450	Portuguese reach the Ivory Coast of Africa. Reliable supplies of elephant tusks begin to arrive in Western Europe.
1480s	Bristol fishermen are probably in the waters of the Grand Banks and Newfoundland.
1492	A papal letter on Greenland reports that no ships have gone there for 80 years.
1493	A Demarcation Line is established by Pope Alexander VI between Spanish and Portuguese possessions in the New World.
1494	The Treaty of Tordesillas between Spain and Portugal moves the Demarcation Line to about 1,110 miles west of the Cape Verde Islands.
1497	John Cabot probably lands in Newfoundland.
1500–01	Gaspar Corte-Réal explores the eastern Newfoundland coast.
1500s	Basque fishermen are on the coast of Labrador and west Newfoundland.
early 1500s	Breton fishermen work in the Strait of Belle Isle.
1508–09	Sebastian Cabot may have explored Hudson Strait and Hudson Bay.
1534–36	Jacques Cartier explores the Gulf of St. Lawrence.
1536–1632	Basque whalers are known to have been hunting near the Strait of Belle Isle on the Labrador coast.
ca. 1540	Jon "Greenlander" finds a Norse corpse in Norse Greenland's Eastern Settlement.
1576–77	Sir Humphrey Gilbert claims England's possession of Newfoundland.
1585–87	John Davis explores west Greenland and Baffin Island.
1596	Willem Barentsz discovers Spitsbergen and Bear Island.
1600s	The heyday of whaling in the Greenland Sea takes place.
1604	Thousands of walruses are reported at Bear Island; in a few years none are left.
1607	Henry Hudson visits Spitsbergen.
1610	Henry Hudson explores Hudson Bay.

1610	Whaling begins in Spitsbergen's waters.
1612–13	Thomas Button explores Hudson Strait.
1615–16	Robert Bylot and William Baffin explore Hudson Strait and Baffin Bay.
1618	The Dutch and English divide the Spitsbergen shore whaling fishery.
1630	Whales are scarce near the Spitsbergen shore. The Dutch begin pelagic whaling in the Greenland Sea.
1670	The Hudson's Bay Company is established.
1713	The Treaty of Utrecht results in large territorial gains for Britain in North America, at France's expense.
ca. 1720	The Dutch discover the Davis Strait whale fishery. The British soon arrive.
1763	In the Peace of Paris, France surrenders most of her North American holdings to Great Britain.
1771–82	The first Moravian missions are established on the Labrador coast.
1824	The rune stone (deposited ca. A.D. 1300) is discovered at Kingigtorssuaq, Greenland.
1875	George Nares discovers the remains of two Norse cairns in the Kane Basin.
1897	Salomon Andrée attempts to reach the North Pole by balloon from Danskøya, Svalbard.
1906	Americans establish a coal mine at Longyearbyen, Svalbard.
1906–09	Walter Wellman attempts to fly to the North Pole from Danskøya via dirigible.
1908	Frederick E. Cook, traveling by dog sled, claims to be the first to reach the North Pole.
1909	Robert E. Peary, traveling by dog sled, claims to be the first to reach the North Pole.
1912	R.M.S. *Titanic* strikes an iceberg and sinks southeast of Newfoundland; 1,513 persons are lost.
1913	The Safety of Life at Sea (SOLAS) convention takes place. The International Ice Patrol is formed.
1918–19	An influenza epidemic ravages many communities throughout the Arctic.
1920	The Versailles Peace Settlement recognizes Norwegian sovereignty

	over Svalbard.
1926	Richard E. Byrd claims to be the first to reach the North Pole by aircraft.
1926	Amundsen, Ellsworth, and Nobile fly over the North Pole to Alaska by dirigible.
1932	The Soviets begin mining at Barentsburg, Spitsbergen.
1940	The United States assumes the protection of Greenland under the Monroe Doctrine.
1941–45	Convoy battles take place in the North Atlantic.
1943	A clandestine automated weather station is set up at Martin Bay, Labrador, from a German U-boat.
1948	The Soviets secretly land three aircraft at the North Pole.
1949	Newfoundland, hitherto a colony of Great Britain, joins the Canadian Confederation.
1959	The Moravian mission station at Hebron, Labrador, is closed.
1968	Ralph Plaisted is probably the first person to reach the North Pole over the ice, via snowmobile.
1969	Wally Herbert crosses the Arctic Ocean via dog team and reaches the North Pole.
1978	Peter Schledermann discovers Norse chain mail in an Inuit archaeological site near northern Ellesmere Island, Canada.
1981	The autonomous German weather station is found at Martin Bay, Labrador.
1991	The Soviet Union collapses.
1994	The USCGC *Polar Sea* and CCGS *Louis S. St. Laurent* make the first surface traverse of the Arctic Ocean by ship.

Belvedere

I BOUGHT BELVEDERE in San Diego, California, in the spring of 1982. Having completed my umiak voyages in the Northwest Passage, I needed a sturdy auxiliary-powered sailing vessel for the research and exploration I planned farther offshore in the Arctic, and when I saw *Belvedere* I knew she was right for the job.

George Sutton designed *Belvedere* (ex-*Estrellita*, ex-*Pacifier*) and built her himself at his boatyard in Huntington Beach, California, in 1964. Made of heavy-gauge steel, she was 60 feet overall, with a 15-foot beam and a draft of a little less than 6 feet. She had bilge keels for stability, carried tanks for 1,200 gallons of fuel and 500 gallons of water, and was outfitted with a reliable diesel engine. In addition to having berths for seven and two heads and showers, she was rigged with a robust aluminum mast (taken from a much larger yacht) reaching 70 feet above the waterline. She was intended to be a shallow-draft long-range cruising boat capable of crossing the reefs of Micronesia or of "drying out" on the mud flats of southeast Alaska. Barring a few changes, she seemed ideal for high-latitude work.

I sailed *Belvedere* up the West Coast to Puget Sound for her refit. We added a strongly reinforced pilothouse with double-glazed windows and a "dry" exhaust system for both the engine and the generator (ice can clog a "wet," or "raw water" exhaust system's intakes, causing overheating). We ran the exhaust pipes up behind the pilothouse, forming a sort of *faux* mizzenmast, which also created a place to fix platforms for mounting the radars, radio antennae, and navigational gear. The theory behind this was that, should the mast come down, the electronics would still be intact. With some old rod-rigging we made stainless-steel ratlines that reach as far as the upper spreaders, thus giving easy access aloft for ice observation and other work. Strong stainless steel pipe lifelines were added, as was a heavy scuttle over the forepeak hatch. We also gave her a much heavier propeller and a spare.

Forward of the scuttle we mounted a strong hydraulic windlass-and-capstan to carry heavy ground tackle and to keep the chain and anchor line on the spool; this avoids the dampness and odor that often accompanies anchor rode when it is stored below decks. For the main anchor I use a 100-pound CQR (plow-shaped), which is secured with 60 feet of half-inch chain and 180 feet of one-inch line. For back-up anchors *Belvedere* carries a 75-pound CQR and a 100-pound fisherman's (traditional design) anchor. The fisherman's anchor is particularly effective in getting a good hold where dense kelp beds often prevent a plow anchor from setting. We also carry an extra 300 feet of $1^{1}/_{4}$-inch anchor line and a few smaller anchors, as well as another 800 feet of line and chain and coupling equipment to meet the requirements of various anchoring situations.

On deck are two aluminum skiffs, which also serve as storage compartments, and a 14-foot heavy-duty Zodiac inflatable, which is our primary dinghy. We carry two or three outboard motors on a rack aft of the pilothouse. On the foredeck, in the space where the boom-and-traveler staysail was formerly fixed, are two large fiberglass storage boxes and a Givens eight-man emergency survival raft. We now sail primarily with a roller-furling jib and a mainsail with three lines of reef points, but we can add a hanked-on staysail if the conditions favor it.

The navigation and piloting systems were upgraded with a Wagner automatic pilot, a pair of radars, two HF or "single-side-band" radios (one with a vertical whip antenna and one with a back-stay antenna), a pair of hard-wired VHF radios (one antenna is mounted at the masthead and the other is on the mizzen), several VHF hand-sets, an aircraft radio, two hard-wired depth sounders, and a hand-held sounder.

A boat is always a work in progress, and I have continually added new electronics and other tools as they have become available. For weather information we use the radios I have mentioned, as well as a Navtext receiver and a weatherfax receiver. Currently I have three GPS systems (one of them hand-held), a Garmin chart plotter, an INMARSAT (international marine satellite system) mini-M communications system, and a forward-looking sounder, which has proved very useful amid the uncharted rock ledges of Labrador. A few years ago I replaced the old engine with a new Detroit Diesel 6-71. Later, to make her a little "stiffer" when under sail, a few more tons of lead ballast were mounted externally on the bottom. This should also give her some added protection in case of grounding.

Belvedere's hull required insulation because condensation, which creates dampness, can be a big problem for vessels in very cold waters. For heating, we installed a diesel-fired stove and furnace and rigged a parallel hot water heating system with a heat exchanger from the engine coolant. We can also keep the boat warm and dry with electric heaters.

Belvedere has large bins for storing dry goods, and frozen food is carried in a commercial freezer (120 volt). When our fresh water runs low, we fill our tanks by drawing water from streams and large ice floes via a long line of garden hose that is rigged to either an electric pump or a portable auxiliary gasoline-driven pump. Getting freshwater ice isn't a problem when icebergs are nearby. We either find a small bergy bit and chop pieces off with a fire axe or we collect floating shards with a steel basket or dip net.

When we stand watch in the pilothouse we don't need to wear special clothes, and this comfort helps to keep the helmsman and lookout alert and focused on the job. For work outside we carry insulated deck suits, Lirakis safety harnesses fitted with inflatable flotation collars, whistles and lights, and safety tethers with clips to secure to the lifelines that are rigged along the port and starboard sides and along the pilothouse roof.

The power of the Arctic must be respected, and I take its challenges, risks, and rewards very seriously. When we are in the North, we rig Plexiglass storm windows over the portholes and saloon windows, and we carry plywood replacements for all *Belvedere*'s windows.

For emergencies we have the Givens raft, a MOM (man overboard module), a life sling, a "general stations" alarm, a fully rigged "bail-out bag," immersion suits for all, PFDs for all, fire extinguishers in all spaces, an engine-driven high-capacity pump, the portable gasoline-powered auxiliary pump that I described, several Edson hand pumps, a fire suppression system in the engine room, carbon monoxide monitors, and a 405 mhz EPIRB (emergency position-indicating radio beacon).

As I have mentioned, *Belvedere* was designed as a motor sailer. At an efficient throttle setting (about 1,200 rpms) the engine pushes her along at a little more than seven knots while consuming about 3.5 gallons of fuel per hour. When the sails are up and the engine is running we can comfortably exceed eight knots, while simultaneously greatly reducing the fuel consumption. Under sails alone *Belvedere* does better than seven knots when she is on a broad reach. Because she has bilge keels, not a deep central keel, she makes quite a bit of leeway when sailing close-hauled.

To date, *Belvedere* has carried me, happily and safely, nearly 75,000 nautical miles.

Voyages, 1962-2001

1962	Small-boat travel in the Strait of Belle Isle
1965	Small-boat travel near Resolute, Nunavut, Canada
1969	Small-boat travel on St. Lawrence Island, Alaska, and in Bering Strait
1970	Small-boat travel in Norton Sound, Alaska
1971	Small-boat travel in the Bering Strait region
1972	Cape Nome, Alaska, to Cape Bathurst, N.W.T., via umiak
1973	Cape Bathurst, N.W.T., to Barter Island, Alaska, via umiak
1974	North coast of Alaska, via umiak
1975	St. Lawrence Island, Alaska, via umiak
1976	Small-boat travel in the Bering Strait region
1977	Fairbanks, Alaska, to Nome, Alaska (descent of the Tanana and Yukon Rivers), via freighter canoe
1978	Tuktoyaktuk, N.W.T., to Cambridge Bay, Nunavut, via umiak
1979	Cambridge Bay, Nunavut, to Queen Maud Gulf and return, via umiak
1980	Cambridge Bay, Nunavut, to Resolute, Nunavut, via umiak
1981	Small-boat travel in the Mackenzie River delta
1982	San Diego, California, to Victoria, British Columbia, via *Belvedere*

1983	Seattle, Washington, to the Inside Passage, to the Aleutian and Pribilof Islands, to Bering Strait, to Point Barrow, Alaska, to Tuktoyaktuk, N.W.T, via *Belvedere*
1984	The Beaufort Sea and Amundsen Gulf, via *Belvedere*
1985	The Beaufort Sea and Mackenzie River, via *Belvedere*
1986	Banks Island, western Victoria Island, and Amundsen Gulf, via *Belvedere*
1987	Tuktoyaktuk, N.W.T., to Cape Prince Alfred (Banks Island), to James Ross Strait and return, via *Belvedere*
1988	The Northwest Passage: Tuktoyaktuk, N.W.T., to Bellot Strait, to the east coast of Baffin Island, to Sisimiut (formerly Holsteinsborg), Greenland, via *Belvedere*
1989	Sisimiut, Greenland, to New York City, via *Belvedere*
1990	Small-boat travel in the eastern Beaufort Sea
1991	Transatlantic: Massachusetts to the Firth of Clyde, Scotland, via *Belvedere*
1992	The Gareloch, Scotland via Shetland, Orkney, and the coast of Norway to northern Spitsbergen and return, via *Belvedere*
1993	Transatlantic: The Gareloch, Scotland, to the Outer Hebrides, Faroe Islands, Iceland, Newfoundland, and Massachusetts, via *Belvedere*
1994	Northwest Passage: Port Clarence, Alaska, to Sondrestromfiord, Greenland, via *Itasca*
1995	Two voyages: the coast of Chile and Cape Horn, via *Itasca*, and Western Newfoundland and southern Labrador, via *Belvedere*
1996	The central Labrador coast, via *Belvedere*
1997	Circumnavigation of Newfoundland and Gulf of St. Lawrence, via *Belvedere*
1998	Northern Labrador, via *Belvedere*
1999	Northern Labrador, Hudson Strait, and southern Baffin Island, via *Belvedere*
2000	Northern Labrador and Hudson Strait, via *Belvedere*
2001	Sable Island, Nova Scotia, via *Belvedere*

NOTES

Introduction

[1] The umiak is now in the watercraft collection of Mystic Seaport in Mystic, Connecticut.

[2] Those voyages are described in John R. Bockstoce, *Arctic Passages: A Unique Small-Boat Voyage in the Great Northern Waterway* (New York: Hearst Marine Books, 1991 and Quill, 1992).

[3] Bockstoce, *Arctic Passages*, 21.

[4] Ibid., 32–33.

Chapter 2

[1] See, for instance, *New York Times*, May 4, 1992.

[2] Skerry (*sgeir* in Gaelic) is an Old Norse-derived word for an isolated rocky islet.

[3] Carl Emil Petersen, *Rundø runder Svalbard* (Oslo: J.W. Cappelens Forlag, 1975).

[4] Gwyn Jones, *The Norse Atlantic Saga*, 2nd ed. (Oxford: Oxford University Press, 1986), 9, 157.

[5] Olaus Magnus, *Description of the Northern Peoples. Rome 1555*, Peter Foote, ed. (London: Hakluyt Society, 1996), 100.

[6] B. Gjevik, H. Moe, and A. Ommundsen, "Sources of the Maelstrom," *Nature*, 28 August 1997, 837–38; *New York Times*, September 2, 1997.

[7] Susan Barr, "Norwegian Use of the Polar Oceans as Occupational Arenas and Exploration Routes," *Polar Record* 37:201 (April 2001): 99–110.

[8] *New York Times*, May 17, 1998; *International Network for Whaling Research Digest* 16 (November 1998) and 18 (December 1999); Arne Kalland, "The Whalers of Lofoten, Northern Norway," in Milton M.R. Freeman, ed., *Endangered Peoples of the Arctic: Struggles to Survive and Thrive* (Westport, Connecticut: Greenwood Press, 2000), 203–222.

[9] *International Network for Whaling Research Digest* 19 (May 2000): 1.

[10] Valeria Criscione, "Norwegian Whalers Set Out for Killing Grounds," *Financial Times*, May 2, 2001; Walter Gibbs, "Norwegians, Defying Protests, Will Sell Blubber to Japan," *New York Times*, July 23, 2001.

[11] T. Thuen, "Two Epochs of Norwegian-Russian Trade Relations . . . ," *Acta Borealia* 2 (1993): 3–18.

[12] Lawson W. Brigham, personal communication, 6 March 2002.

[13] P.J. Capelotti, ed., *The Svalbard Archipelago* (Jefferson, North Carolina: McFarland & Company, 2000), 53.

[14] Andrew C. Revkin, "Cold Water Flow from Arctic to Atlantic is Falling, Study Finds," *New York Times,* June 21, 2001.

[15] Steven B. Young, *To the Arctic, An Introduction to the Far Northern World* (New York: John Wiley & Sons, 1989), 29–31.

[16] Grethe Authen Blom, "The Participation of the Kings in the Early Norwegian Sailing to Bjarmeland (Kola Peninsula and Russian Waters) . . . ," *Arctic* 37:4 (December 1984): 385–388; Fridtjof Nansen, *In Northern Mists,* vol. 2 (London: Heinemann, 1911), 135–147.

[17] Hein B. Bjerck, "Stone Age Settlement on Svalbard? A Re-evaluation of Previous Finds and the Results of a Recent Field Survey," *Polar Record* 36:197 (April 2000): 97–112.

[18] Tette Hofstra and Kees Samplonius, "Viking Expansion Northwards: Medieval Sources," *Arctic* 48:3 (1995): 235–247.

[19] Richard Vaughan, "The Arctic in the Middle Ages," *Journal of Medieval History* 8 (1982): 319.

[20] Gerrit De Veer, *The Three Voyages of William Barents* . . . 2nd ed., Koolemans Beynen, ed. (London: Hakluyt Society, 1876).

[21] Günter Schilder, "Developments and Achievements of Dutch Northern and Arctic Cartography in the Sixteenth and Seventeenth Centuries," *Arctic* 37:4 (December 1984): 509–510.

[22] G.M. Asher, ed., *Henry Hudson the Navigator* . . . (London: Hakluyt Society, 1860).

[23] M. Conway, *No Man's Land* (Cambridge: Cambridge University Press, 1906).

[24] J. Braat, "Dutch Activities in the North and the Arctic During the Sixteenth and Seventeenth Centuries," *Arctic* 37:4 (December 1984): 476.

[25] J. Braat, "Dutch Activities in the North and the Arctic," 473–480; L. Hacquebord, "There She Blows—A Brief History of Whaling," *North Atlantic Studies* 2:2 (1990); Richard Vaughan, "Bowhead Whaling in Davis Strait and Baffin Bay During the 18th and 19th Centuries," *Polar Record* 23:144 (1986): 289–299.

[26] N.H. Dole, *America in Spitsbergen: The Romance of an Arctic Coal-Mine* (Boston: Marshall Jones, 1922).

[27] T. Mathisen, *Svalbard in International Politics. 1871–1925,* Skrifter 101, (Oslo: Norsk Polarinstitutt, 1954); A.K. Orvin, "Twenty-Five Years of Norwegian Sovereignty in Svalbard, 1925–1950," *Polar Record* 6:42 (July 1951): 179–184; Central Intelligence Agency, *Polar Regions Atlas* (Washington, D.C.: Government Printing Office, 1978), 33; Willy Østreng, *Politics in High Latitudes. The Svalbard Archipelago* (Montreal: McGill-Queens University Press, 1978).

[28] Central Intelligence Agency, *Polar Regions Atlas,* 33.

[29] Capelotti, *The Svalbard Archipelago*, 127–154.

[30] J.D.M. Blyth, "German Meteorological Activities in the Arctic, 1940–1945," *Polar Record* 6:42 (July 1951): 185–226; J. G. Elbo, "The War in Svalbard, 1939–45," *Polar Record* 6:44 (July 1952): 484–495.

[31] W.E. Molett, "Due North? Byrd's Disputed Flight to the Pole," *Mercator's World* 3:2 (1998): 58–63; Roald Amundsen and Lincoln Ellsworth, *First Crossing of the Polar Sea* (Garden City, N.Y.: Doubleday, Doran & Co., 1928); Dennis Rawlins, "Byrd's Heroic 1926 North Pole Failure," *Polar Record* 36:196 (January 2000): 25–50; Keith A. Pickering, review of *To the Pole: The Diary and Notebook of Richard E. Byrd, 1925–1927*, in *Polar Record* 36:197 (April 2000): 158–161.

[32] Beekman Pool, *Polar Extremes. The World of Lincoln Ellsworth* (Fairbanks: University of Alaska Press, 2002), 97–98.

[33] F.W. Beechey, *A Voyage of Discovery Towards the North Pole Performed in His Majesty's Ships Dorothea and Trent . . .* (London: Richard Bentley, 1843), 54.

[34] L. Hacquebord, "A Historical-Archaeological Investigation of a Seventeenth-Century Whaling Settlement . . . ," *Rapportserie*, no. 38 (Oslo: Norsk Polarinstitutt, 1987), 19–34.

[35] P.J. Capelotti, *By Airship to the North Pole: An Archaeology of Human Exploration* (New Brunswick, N.J.: Rutgers University Press, 1999), 19–46; *Skrifter on Svalbard og Ishavet*, no. 80 (Oslo: Norsk Polarinstitutt, 1991); P.O. Sundman, *The Flight of the Eagle* (New York: Pantheon, 1970); Urban Wråkberg, ed., *The Centennial of S.A. Andrée's North Pole Expedition* (Stockholm: Royal Swedish Academy of Sciences, 1999).

[36] Capelotti, *By Airship to the North Pole*, 47–94; Walter Wellman, *The Aerial Age* (New York: A.R. Keller, 1911); P.J. Capelotti, *The Wellman Polar Airship Expeditions at Virgohamna, Danskoya, Svalbard—A Study in Aerospace Archaeology*, Meddelelser No. 145 (Oslo: Norsk Polarinstitutt, 1997).

[37] Conway, *No Man's Land*; G. De Veer, *The Three Voyages of William Barents . . .*, 75–76; G.C.L. Bertram and D. Lack, "Bear Island," *The Geographical Journal* 81:1 (January 1933): 47–53.

[38] Beechey, *Voyage of Discovery*, 36.

[39] *American Neptune* 59:3 (1999): 239.

[40] R. Woodman, *Arctic Convoys* (London: John Murray, 1994); B.B. Schofield, *The Arctic Convoys* (London: Macdonald and Jane's, 1977); D. Pope, *73 North* (London: Weidenfeld and Nicolson, 1958).

[41] *New York Times*, April 8, 1989; *Jane's Fighting Ships* 1988–89, 6.

[42] *Wall Street Journal*, March 14, 1990; *ABC Evening News*, November 23, 1992; *New York Times*, August 1, 1993.

[43] Alan Cowell, "Fish Farms Spawn Trouble for Salmon Anglers," *New York Times*, 17 July 2001.

[44] R.L. Naylor et al., "Nature's Subsidies to Shrimp and Salmon Farming," *Science,* 30 October 1998, 883–884.

[45] Cowell, "Fish Farms."

[46] Magnus Magnusson, *Viking Expansion Westwards* (New York: Henry Z.

Walck, 1973), 42–57; Gerald F. Bigelow, "Issues and Prospects in Shetland Norse Archaeology," in *Norse and Later Settlement and Subsistence in the North Atlantic*, Christopher D. Morris and D. James Rackham, eds. (Glasgow, Scotland: University of Glasgow, Department of Archaeology, 1992), 9–32.

CHAPTER 3

[1] Rev. John Mackinnon, *The Statistical Account of Scotland 1791–1799*, [Kintyre].

[2] Lesley MacDougall, *The Crinan Canal* (Gartocharn, Scotland: Famedram Publishers, n.d.).

[3] Simon Winchester, "In the Eye of the Whirlpool," *Smithsonian* 32:5 (August 2001): 87.

[4] J.M. Boyd and I.L. Boyd, *The Hebrides. A Natural History* (London: Collins, 1990), 64.

[5] Maldwin Drummond, *West Highland Shores* (London: A & C Black, 1990), 134.

[6] Reader's Digest Association, *Illustrated Guide to Britain's Coast* (London: Drive Publications, 1987), 255.

[7] Martin Lawrence, "The Minch and the Sound of Harris," *Yachting Monthly* (December 1990): 52–55; Clyde Cruising Club, *Outer Hebrides Sailing Directions*, part 4 (Glasgow: Clyde Cruising Club Publications, 1988).

[8] Peter Sawyer, ed., *The Oxford Illustrated History of the Vikings* (Oxford: Oxford University Press, 1997), 8.

[9] Boyd and Boyd, *The Hebrides*, 201–208.

[10] John Beatty, "Seabird Hunters of Lewis," *Geographical Magazine* 66:2 (February 1994): 32–39.

[11] Geoffrey Ashe, *Land to the West. St. Brendan's Voyage to America* (New York: Viking Press, 1962): 147.

[12] Vincent H. Cassidy, *The Sea Around Them. The Atlantic Ocean, A.D. 1250* (Baton Rouge: Louisiana State University Press, 1968), 85.

[13] A.G. Macpherson, "Pre-Columbian Discoveries and Exploration of North America," in John Logan Allen, ed., *North American Exploration*, vol. 1, *A New World Disclosed* (Lincoln: University of Nebraska Press, 1997), 16–18; R.H. Fuson, *Legendary Islands of the Ocean Sea* (Sarasota: Pineapple Press, 1995), 28–31.

[14] Gwyn Jones, *A History of the Vikings*, 2nd ed. (Oxford: Oxford University Press, 1984), 270; Anthony Jackson, *The Faroes. The Faraway Islands* (London: Robert Hale, 1991), 22; Magnus Magnusson, *Viking Expansion Westwards* (New York: Henry Z. Walck, 1973), 78–84.

[15] L.K. Schei and G. Moberg, *The Faroe Islands* (London: John Murray, 1991), 16; Magnusson, *Viking Expansion*, 80, 83.

[16] C. Thornhill and W. Ker, *Faroe, Iceland and Greenland* (St. Ives, Huntingdon, Cambridgeshire: Imray, Laurie, Norie & Wilson, Royal Cruising Club Pilotage Foundation, 1998), 11.

[17] Fischer Heinesen, *Streymkort fyri Føroyar, Tidal Current around the Faroe Islands* (Klaksvík, Føroyar: Egið Forlag, 1985).

[18] *Financial Times,* October 30, 1998; "Fish and Ships," *Geographical Magazine* (November 2000): 46–51.

[19] High North Alliance, *Marine Hunters. Whaling and Sealing in the North Atlantic* (Reine, Norway: n.p., 1997), 12–13; H.C. Müller, *Whale-fishing in the Faroe Isles,* (Edinburgh: Blackwood and Sons, 1887).

[20] *Geographical Magazine* (November 2000): 13.

[21] Fred Pearce, "When Killing Things is a Livelihood," *New Scientist,* 28 October 1995; Kate Sanderson, *Grindarap—A Textual History of Whaling Traditions in the Faroes to 1900* (Sydney: University of Sydney, 1992); Jackson, *The Faroes,* 57–62; Schei and Moberg, *The Faroe Islands,* 123–128.

[22] See, for instance, *Mariners Weather Log,* Winter 1994, 72–74, 81.

[23] Richard Woodman, *Arctic Convoys* (London: John Murray, 1994), 382.

[24] Peter Sawyer, personal communication, September 15, 2000.

[25] Kristján Ahronson, personal communication, September 16, 2000.

[26] Vilhjalmur Stefansson, *Ultima Thule* (London: George G. Harrap, 1942), 9–79.

[27] J.A. Williamson, ed., *The Cabot Voyages and Bristol Discovery Under Henry VII,* Hakluyt Society, 2nd series, vol. 120 (Cambridge: Cambridge University Press, 1962), 21.

[28] Stefan Einarsson, "Bjolfur and Grendill in Iceland," *Modern Language Notes* 71:81; Vincent H. Cassidy, *The Sea Around Them. The Atlantic Ocean, A.D. 1250* (Baton Rouge: Louisiana State University Press, 1968), 12; G.J. Marcus, *The Conquest of the Atlantic* (New York: Oxford University Press, 1981), 24.

[29] Magnusson, *Viking Expansion,* 85.

[30] Archibald R. Lewis, *The Northern Seas. Shipping and Commerce in Northern Europe, A.D. 300–1100* (Princeton: Princeton University Press, 1958), 41–42; Arthur E. Noot, "Carausius Carved an Empire from within an Empire," *The Celator* 10:2 (February 1996).

[31] F. Donald Logan, *The Vikings in History,* 2nd ed. (London: Routledge, 1991), 61–62.

[32] Ted Olson, "Implausible Island," *Saturday Review,* September 11, 1965, 54.

[33] John Grattan and Mark Brayshay, "An Amazing and Portentous Summer: Environmental and Social Responses in Britain to the 1783 Eruption of an Iceland Volcano," *The Geographical Journal* 161:2 (July 1995): 125–134.

[34] Lee Dye, "The year that wasn't," *ABCNEWS.com,* March 8, 2000; William A. Oquilluk, with the assistance of Laurel L. Bland, *People of Kauwerak: Legends of the Northern Eskimo* (Anchorage: Alaska Methodist University, 1973), 65.

[35] Glenn Oeland, "Iceland's Trial by Fire," *National Geographic Magazine* 191:5 (May 1997): 58–71; A.T. Gudmundsson, "Waiting at the Flood Gates," *Geographical Magazine* (December 1996): 30–31.

[36] "Iceland Awaits the Big One," *Geographical Magazine* (December 1999): 11; Oddur Sigurdhsson, et al., "Jökulhlaup úr Sólheimajökli 18 júlí 1999," *Jökull* 49 (2000): 75–80.

[37] Sawyer, *The Oxford Illustrated History of the Vikings,* 12.

[38] Debora MacKenzie, "Icelanders Argue Over Their Ancestors," *New Scientist,* 1 June 1996, 10.

[39] Peter Sawyer, personal communication, September 15, 2000.

[40] Lewis, *The Northern Seas,* 267–270.

[41] Gwyn Jones, "The Viking World," *The Norse of the North Atlantic, Acta Archaeologica* 61, (København: Munksgaard, 1990), 8–9; Birgitta Wallace, "The Norse in the North Atlantic," *Cabot and His World Symposium,* Iona Bulgin, ed. (St. John's: Newfoundland Historical Society, 1997), 29–30. Max Vinner, "*Unnasigling*—The Seaworthiness of the Merchant Vessel," *Viking Voyages to North America,* Birthe L. Clausen, ed. (Roskilde, Denmark: Viking Ship Museum, 1993), 95–108.

[42] Cassidy, *The Sea Around Them,* 120–125.

[43] See note 41.

[44] Kirsten Seaver, personal communication, November 13, 2000.

[45] Erik Wahlgren, *The Vikings and America* (London: Thames and Hudson, 1986), 76–77.

[46] Magnus Magnusson and Hermann Pálsson, *The Vinland Sagas. The Norse Discovery of America* (London: Penguin Books, 1965), 17.

[47] Gwyn Jones, *The Norse Atlantic Saga,* 2nd ed. (Oxford: Oxford University Press, 1986), 74.

[48] Jane Smiley and Robert Kellogg, eds., *The Sagas of Icelanders. A Selection* (London: Allen Lane the Penguin Press, 2000), 631, 654–655, 751.

[49] Magnusson, *Viking Expansion,* 111–112.

[50] Jesse L. Byock, *Viking Age Iceland* (London: Penguin Books, 2001), 231–232.

[51] *The Economist,* December 31, 1999.

[52] Knud Frydendahl, "The Summer Climate in the North Atlantic About the Year 1000," in Clausen, *Viking Voyages to North America,* 90–94; A.E.J. Ogilvie, L.K. Barlow, and A.E. Jennings, "North Atlantic Climate c. A.D. 1000: Millennial Reflections on the Viking Discoveries of Iceland, Greenland and North America," in Andrew Wawn and Þórunn Sigurðarðóttir, eds., *Approaches to Vinland* (Reykjavík: Sigurður Nordal Institute, 2001), 173–188.

[53] Marcus, *Conquest of the North Atlantic,* 26; "Hvitserkr," *The Geographical Journal* 89:6 (June 1937): 552–553; Ejnar Mikkelsen, "The Blosseville Coast of East Greenland," *The Geographical Journal* 81:5 (May 1933): 385–403.

[54] Helgi Thorláksson, "The Icelandic Commonwealth Period," in William W. Fitzhugh and Elisabeth I. Ward, eds., *Vikings. The North Atlantic Saga* (Washington, D.C.: Smithsonian Institution Press, 2000), 176–178.

[55] Orri Vésteinsson, "The Archaeology of Landnám," in Fitzhugh and Ward, *Vikings,* 164–167.

[56] Vilhjalmur Stefansson, *Iceland. The First American Republic* (New York: Doubleday, Doran, 1939).

[57] See, for instance, Trausti Einarsson, *Hvalveiðar Við Ísland, 1600-1939* (Reykjavík: Bókaútgáfa Menningarsjóðs, 1987).

[58] *International Network for Whaling Research Digest* 17 (May 1999): 1–2; *The Polar Times* 2:13 (Spring-Summer 1999): 5.

[59] Donald G. McNeil, Jr., "Reykjavik Journal: Whaling Ban, Not NATO, Heats Iceland's Temper," *New York Times,* 15 October 2001.

[60] Olafur Eggertsson, "Origin of the Driftwood on the Coasts of Iceland: A

Dendrochronological Study," *Jokull* 43 (1993): 15–32; Stein Johansen, "The Origin and Age of Driftwood on Jan Mayen," *Polar Research* 17:2 (1998): 113–123.

61 Clive Holland, *Arctic Exploration and Development c. 500 B.C. to 1915. An Encyclopedia* (New York: Garland, 1994), 316–317, 382–383.

62 Jones, *Norse Atlantic Saga*, 189–190.

63 Ibid., 190.

64 Ibid.

65 Ibid.

66 Ibid. 190–191.

67 Ibid., 191–195; Magnusson, *Viking Expansion*, 129–134.

68 E.G.R. Taylor, *The Haven-Finding Art* (New York: Abelard-Schuman, 1957), 70–71.

69 Sivert Fløttum, "The Norse *Vika Sjovar* and the Nautical Mile," *The Mariner's Mirror* 87:4 (November 2001): 390–405.

70 T.J. Oleson, "Thorfinnr karlsefni Thordarson," *Dictionary of Canadian Biography* (Toronto: University of Toronto Press, 1966), 642–643; T.J. Oleson, "Snorri Thorfinnsson," *Dictionary of Canadian Biography*, 612.

71 Birgitta Wallace, "L'Anse aux Meadows Gateway to Vinland," in *The Norse of the North Atlantic*, 166–197; Birgitta Wallace, "L'Anse aux Meadows, the Western Outpost," in *Viking Voyages to North America*, 30–42; Jones, *Norse Atlantic Saga*, 191–194.

CHAPTER 4

1 J.R. Bockstoce, *Arctic Passages. A Unique Small-Boat Journey Through the Great Northern Waterway* (New York: Quill, 1992), 159, 161, 243, 244–245.

2 *Sailing Directions. Arctic Canada (Eastern Part)*, vol. 2, 4th ed. (Ottawa: Department of Fisheries and Oceans, 1985), 49.

3 Richard Vaughan, "The Arctic in the Middle Ages," *Journal of Medieval History* 8 (1982): 317.

4 Else Roesdahl, "L'ivoire de Morse et les Colonies Norroises du Groenland," *Proxima Thule* 3 (Spring 1998).

5 Kirsten A. Seaver, "Land of Wine and Forests. The Norse in North America," *Mercator's World* (January/February 2000): 20.

6 Else Roesdahl, personal communication, September 17, 2000.

7 Birthe Clausen, ed., *Viking Voyages to North America* (Roskilde, Denmark: Viking Ship Museum, 1993), 10; Magnus Magnusson, *Viking Expansion Westwards* (New York: Henry Z. Walck, 1973), 113–114; Helge Ingstad, *The Norse Discovery of America*, vol. 2 (Oslo: Norwegian University Press, 1985), 408–409; Marie Stoklund, "Greenland Runes: Isolation or Cultural Contact?" in C. Batey et al., eds., *The Viking Age in Caithness, Orkney and the North Atlantic. Select Papers from the proceedings of the Eleventh Viking Congress . . . 1989* (Edinburgh: Edinburgh University Press, 1993), 528–544.

8 Peter Schledermann, "Norsemen in the High Arctic?" in Clausen, *Viking Voyages to North America*, 56.

9 The Ven. Mark Hollingsworth, personal communication, February 21, 2000.

10 Ingstad, *The Norse Discovery of America*, 2: 408–409.

[11]   Erik Holtved, "Archaeological Investigations In The Thule District," in *Meddelelser om Gronland* 141:1, 2 (København: C.A. Reitzels Forlag, 1944), 1, plate 44.

[12]   Karen M. McCullough, *The Ruin Islanders. Early Thule Culture Pioneers in the Eastern High Arctic,* Archaeological Survey of Canada, Mercury Series Paper 141 (Ottawa: Canadian Museum of Civilization, 1989); Peter Schledermann, "Ellesmere. Vikings in the Far North," in William W. Fitzhugh and Elisabeth I. Ward, eds. *Vikings. The North Atlantic Saga* (Washington, D.C.: Smithsonian Institution Press, 2000), 251.

[13]   Schledermann, "Ellesmere," 59; Peter Schledermann, "Eskimo and Viking Finds in the High Arctic," *National Geographic Magazine* 159:5 (May 1981): 574–601.

[14]   Peter Schledermann, "Notes on Norse Finds from the East Coast of Ellesmere Island, N.W.T.," *Arctic* 33:3 (September 1980): 454–463; Peter Schledermann, *Voices in Stone* (Calgary: Arctic Institute of North America, 1996), 122–136.

[15]   Inuk is the singular form of Inuit ("people"). For the sake of simplicity, in this book I have used *Inuit* to refer to those native peoples of Canada and Greenland that were formerly called *Eskimo*s.

[16]   Peter Schledermann, "Norse Artifacts on Ellesmere Island, NWT*" Polar Record* 19:122 (1979): 493–494; McCullough, *The Ruin Islanders*; Schledermann, "Ellesmere," 251.

[17]   Heather Pringle, "Hints of Frequent Pre-Columbian Contacts," *Science,* May 5, 2000, 783–785.

[18]   G.S. Nares, *Narrative of a Voyage to the Polar Sea . . . ,* vol. 2 (London: Low, Marston, Searle and Rivington, 1878), 161–162.

[19]   Karen McCullough and Peter Schledermann, "Mystery Cairns on Washington Irving Island," *Polar Record* 35:195 (1999): 289–298.

[20]   Peter Schledermann, personal communication, May 15, 2001.

[21]   Ingstad, *Norse Discovery of America* 2: 461–464.

[22]   Bockstoce, *Arctic Passages,* 246–253.

[23]   Thomas H. McGovern, "Bones, Buildings, and Boundaries: Palaeoeconomic Approaches to Norse Greenland," in Christopher D. Morris and D. James Rackham, eds., *Norse and Later Settlement and Subsistence in the North Atlantic* (Glasgow: University of Glasgow, 1992), 193–230; K.M.B. Christensen, "Aspects of the Norse Economy in the Western Settlement in Greenland," in Gerald F. Bigelow, ed., *The Norse of the North Atlantic, Acta Archaeologica* 61— 1990 (København: Munksgaard, 1991), 158–165.

[24]   Ian Whitaker, "The King's Mirror [Konung's Skuggsjá] and Northern Research," *Polar Record* 22:141 (1985): 615–627.

[25]   Kirsten A. Seaver, *The Frozen Echo. Greenland and the Exploration of North America, ca.* A.D. *1000–1500* (Stanford, California: Stanford University Press, 1996), 104.

[26]   Ibid., 102–109.

[27]   Ibid., 92–99; Finn Gad, *The History of Greenland,* vol. 1 (London: C. Hurst,

1970), 130.

28 Niels Lynnerup, "Life and Death in Norse Greenland," in Fitzhugh and Ward, *Vikings*, 285–294.

29 Thomas H. McGovern, "The Demise of Norse Greenland," in Fitzhugh and Ward, *Vikings*, 334–335.

30 Crispin Tickell, "Climate and History," *Oxford Today*, Hilary Issue (1996): 28.

31 Heather Pringle, "Death in Norse Greenland," *Science,* February 14, 1997, 924–926; Joel Berglund, "The Farm Beneath the Sand," in Fitzhugh and Ward, *Vikings*, 295–303; Seaver, *The Frozen Echo*, 91–138.

32 Kirsten A. Seaver, personal communication, October 16, 2000.

33 Jørgen Fisker and Keld Hansen, eds., *Arsukfjorden* (n.p.: Nordiske Landes Bogforlag, 1982); Christian Berthelsen et al., eds., *Kalaallit Nunaat Greenland Atlas* (n.p.: Greenland Home Rule, 1990), 62–63.

34 Fullerton Waldo, *The Saga of a Supercargo* (Philadelphia: Macrae Smith, 1926), 130–133.

35 Paul Seaman and Chris Jenner, "Frozen Warriors," *Geographical Magazine* (February 1996): 12–14.

36 Henry Rink, *Tales and Traditions of the Eskimo* (Edinburgh: William Blackwood and Sons, 1875), 319.

37 Joel Berglund, *Hvalsø— the Church and the Magnate's Farm*, (n.p.: Qaqortoq Commune, 1982), 36–37; Rink, *Tales and Traditions*, 308–317.

38 Jette Arneborg, "Cultural Borders: Reflections on Norse-Eskimo Interaction," *Ethnographical Studies* 18 (1997): 43.

39 Jette Arneborg, personal communication, September 17, 2000.

40 Seaver, *The Frozen Echo*, 149–150; Gad, *The History of Greenland* 1: 148.

41 Poul Nørlund, "Buried Norsemen at Herjolfsnes," in *Meddelelser om Grønland* 67:1 (Kobenhavn: C.A. Reitzels Forlag, 1924); Seaver, *The Frozen Echo*, 225–253; McGovern, "The Demise of Norse Greenland," 328.

42 William W. Fitzhugh, "Puffins, Ringed Pins, and Runestones," in Fitzhugh and Ward, *Vikings*, 17; Jette Arneborg, "Greenland and Europe," in Fitzhugh and Ward, *Vikings*, 310–317.

43 Kirsten A. Seaver, personal communication, October 16, 2000.

44 McGovern, "The Demise of Norse Greenland," 335; "Hafis vid strendur islands," in *Árferdhi á Íslandi* (Copenhagen: Hidh Íslenska Fraedhafélag, 1916-17), 356–432.

45 Seaver, *The Frozen Echo*, 46.

46 Jesse L. Byock, *Viking Age Iceland* (London: Penguin Books, 2001), 265.

47 Jón Th. Thór, "Why was Greenland 'Lost'? Changes in North Atlantic Fisheries and Maritime Trade in the Fourteenth and Fifteenth Centuries," *Scandinavian Economic History Review* 48 (2000): 28–39.

48 Donna A. Vinson, "The Western Sea: Atlantic History before Columbus," *The Northern Mariner/Le Marin du Nord* 10:3 (July 2000): 3.

49 Byock, *Viking Age Iceland*, 44, 53–54.

50 G.J. Marcus, *The Conquest of the North Atlantic* (New York: Oxford University Press, 1981), 119–122.

[51] Kirsten A. Seaver, "Norse Greenland on the Eve of Renaissance Exploration in the North Atlantic," in Anna Agnarsdóttir, ed., *Voyages and Exploration in the North Atlantic from the Middles Ages to the XVIIth Century* (Reykjavík: University of Iceland Press, 2000), 30–31; Seaver, *The Frozen Echo*, 120–122.

[52] Kirsten A. Seaver, "'A Very Common and Usuall Trade': The Relationship between Cartographic Perceptions and 'Fishing' in the Davis Strait *circa* 1500–1550," in Karen Severud Cook, ed., *Images and Icons of the New World. Essays on American Cartography* (London: The British Library, 1996), 6; Jens E. Olesen, "Iceland in the Politics of the Kalmar Union," in Ingi Sigurðsson and Jón Skaptason, eds., *Aspects of Arctic and Sub-Arctic History. Proceedings of the International Congress on the History of the Arctic and Sub-Arctic Region, Reykjavík, 18-21 June 1998* (Reykjavík: University of Iceland Press, 2000), 91–96.

[53] A.N. Ryan, "Bristol, the Atlantic and North America, 1480–1509," in John B. Hattendorf, ed., *Maritime History, Volume I: The Age of Discovery* (Malabar, Florida: Krieger Publishing Company, 1996), 242–243; Klaus Friedland, "The Hanseatic League and Hanse Towns in the Early Penetration of the North," *Arctic* 37:4 (December 1984): 539–543; Evan Jones, "England's Icelandic fishery in the early modern period," in David J. Starkey, Chris Reid, and Neil Ashcroft, eds., *England's Sea Fisheries: The Commercial Sea Fisheries of England and Wales Since 1300* (London: Chatham Publishing, 2000), 105–110.

[54] Seaver, "Norse Greenland on the Eve of Renaissance Exploration," 38.

[55] Seaver, "Land of Wine and Forests," 18–25; Seaver, "Unanswered Questions," in Fitzhugh and Ward, *Vikings*, 277; E.M. Carus Wilson, "The Iceland Trade," in Eileen Power and M.M. Postan, eds., *Studies in English Trade in the Fifteenth Century* (London: Routledge & Kegan Paul, 1933), 171–182.

[56] Brian Fagan, *The Little Ice Age. How Climate Made History 1300–1850* (New York: Basic Books, 2002), 75–78.

[57] Seaver, *The Frozen Echo*, 159–220; David B. Quinn, *European Approaches to North America, 1450–1640* (Aldershot: Ashgate, 1998), 280.

[58] Niels Lynnerup, *The Greenland Norse: A Biological-Anthropological Study*, (Copenhagen: Danish Polar Center, 1998).

[59] Niels Lynnerup, personal communication, September 17, 2000.

[60] Seaver, "Norse Greenland on the Eve of Renaissance Exploration," 35.

[61] Gad, *The History of Greenland*, 164, 182; Seaver, *The Frozen Echo*, 307–308.

[62] Lynnerup, "Life and Death in Norse Greenland," 294.

CHAPTER 5

[1] Olaf Uwe Janzen, "'Of Consequence to the Service': The Rationale Behind Cartographic Surveys in Early Eighteenth-Century Newfoundland," *The Northern Mariner/LeMarin du Nord* 11:1 (January 2001): 1–3.

[2] Selma Barkham, *The Basque Coast of Newfoundland* (Plum Point, Newfoundland: Great Northern Peninsula Development Corporation, 1989).

[3] Selma Huxley Barkham, "The Basque Whaling Establishments in Labrador 1536–1632— A Summary," in *Unveiling the Arctic* (Calgary: Arctic Institute of North America and University of Alaska Press, 1984), 515–519; Julian

DeZulueta, "The Basque Whalers: The Source of Their Success," *Mariner's Mirror* 86:3 (2000): 261–271.

4 James A. Tuck and Robert Grenier, *Red Bay, Labrador. World Whaling Capital A.D. 1550–1600* (St. John's, Newfoundland: Atlantic Archaeology, Ltd., 1989).

5 Robert M. Bryce, *Cook & Peary: The Polar Controversy Resolved* (Mechanicsburg, Pennsylvania: Stackpole Books, 1997).

6 Christopher Pala, "Unlikely Heroes: The Story of the First Men Who Stood at the North Pole," *Polar Record* 35:195 (1999): 337–342. William M. Leary and Leonard LeSchack, *Project Coldfeet. Secret Mission to a Soviet Ice Station* (Annapolis: Naval Institute Press, 1996), 12–17.

7 *New York Times*, April 20, 1968.

8 Wally Herbert, *Across the Top of the World: The Last Great Journey on Earth* (London: Longmans, 1969).

9 Lawson W. Brigham, personal communication, June 25, 2001.

10 See, for instance, George P. Steele, *Seadragon: Northwest Under the Ice* (New York: E.P. Dutton, 1962).

11 Peter Wadhams, *Ice in the Ocean* (Amsterdam: Gordon and Breach Science Publishers, 2000), 258–261.

12 *Atlas of Pilot Charts. North Atlantic Ocean* (Washington, D.C.: Defense Mapping Agency, n.d.).

13 Derek Schmeling, "The Sinking of the Titanic," *Mariners Weather Log* (April 1998): 26–30; J.J. Murray, "A Titanic Legacy," *Mariners Weather Log* (Winter 1992): 21–23; R. Tuxhorn, "Tracking Iceberg Danger," *Mariners Weather Log* (Fall 1995): 29–32.

14 Michael Dane, "Ice Hunters," *Popular Mechanics,* October 1993, 76–79, 131.

15 *International Ice Patrol* (Washington, D.C.: Government Printing Office, 1993).

16 Alfred T. Ezman, Lt., "Iceberg Warnings," *Mariners Weather Log* (Winter 1993): 56–59.

17 "Deadly Icebergs Will Test Massive Oil Rig," *Ocean Navigator* (July/August 1997): 13.

18 Nathan Vardi, "It's the Tap of the Iceberg," *Forbes*, September 4, 2000, 114–115.

19 Anthony B. Dickinson and C.W. Sanger, "The Origin and Development of North American Modern Shore Station Whaling: Newfoundland and the Norwegians, 1896–1916," in Bjorn L. Basberg et al., eds., *Whaling and History* (Sandefjord, Norway: Kommander Chr. Christens Hvalfangstmuseum, 1993), 92–100; A.B. Dickinson and C.W. Sanger, "Modern Shore-Station Whaling in Newfoundland and Labrador: The Peak Season: 1904," *International Journal of Maritime History* 5:1 (June 1993): 127–154.

CHAPTER 6

1 E.C. Pielou, *A Naturalist's Guide to the Arctic* (Chicago and London: University of Chicago Press, 1994), 22; W.G. Rees, "Polar Mirages," *Polar Record* 25:150 (1988): 193–198.

[2] William H. Hobbs, "A Remarkable Example of Polar Mirage," *Science,* December 1, 1939, 513-514.

[3] Keith C. Heidorn, "The Arctic Mirage. Seeing Beyond the Horizon," *Oceans* (July 1979): 13–15.

[4] H.L. Sawatzky and W.H. Lehn, "The Arctic Mirage and the Early North Atlantic," *Science,* June 1976, 1300–1305.

[5] William Scoresby, Jr., *Journal of a Voyage to the Northern Whale-Fishery . . . ,* (Edinburgh: Archibald Constable, 1823), 189–190.

[6] Magnus Magnusson and Hermann Pálsson, *The Vinland Sagas. The Norse Discovery of America* (London: Penguin Books, 1965), 94–95.

[7] *Grœnlendinga Saga*, Book 5, in Magnusson and Pálsson, *The Vinland Sagas*, 60.

[8] Craig S. Smith, "North Sea Cod Crisis Brings Call for Nations to Act," *New York Times*, 7 November 2002.

[9] John C. Kennedy, "The Impact of the Grenfell Mission on Southeastern Labrador Communities," *Polar Record* 24:150 (July 1988): 199–206.

[10] Evelyn Grondin-Bailey, *Reflections of Times Past by Evelyn Grondin-Bailey 1997*, private printing, 56.

CHAPTER 7

[1] Julian Beltrame, "Two Specks of France off Newfoundland Tout Their Tourist Appeal," *Wall Street Journal*, June 30, 2000.

[2] Fred Anderson, *Crucible of War: The Seven Years' War and the Fate of Empire in British North America, 1754–1766* (New York: Alfred A. Knopf, 2000), 498.

[3] Paul Johnson, *A History of the American People* (New York: HarperCollins, 1998), 126–127.

[4] James A. Williamson, *The Cabot Voyages and Bristol Discovery under Henry VII* (Cambridge: Hakluyt Society, 1962), 54–83; David Beers Quinn, *England and the Discovery of America, 1481–1620* (New York: Alfred A. Knopf, 1974), 93–111.

[5] Williamson, *The Cabot Voyages*; A.N. Ryan, "Bristol, The Atlantic and North America, 1480–1509," in J.B. Hattendorf, ed., *Maritime History Volume I: The Age of Discovery* (Malabar, Florida: Krieger Publishing Company, 1996), 241–256.

[6] Williams, Alan F., *John Cabot and Newfoundland* (St. John's: Newfoundland Historical Society, 1996), 31.

[7] Birgitta Wallace, "The Viking Settlement at L'Anse aux Meadows," in William W. Fitzhugh and Elisabeth I. Ward, *Vikings. The North Atlantic Saga* (Washington, D.C.: Smithsonian Institution Press, 2000), 209.

[8] Birgitta Wallace, "The Norse in the North Atlantic," in Iona Bulgin, ed., *Cabot and His World Symposium* (St. John's: Newfoundland Historical Society, 1999), 39.

[9] Rudyard Kipling, *Captains Courageous. A Story of the Grand Banks* (New York: The Century Co., 1897), 186–187.

[10] Magnus Magnusson and Hermann Pálsson, *The Vinland Sagas. The Norse Discovery of America* (London: Penguin Books, 1965), 57–58.

[11] Páll Bergthórsson, "The Vikings in Brooklyn," *Iceland Review* 2 (2000): 56–61.

[12] Gísli Sigurdsson, "The Quest for Vinland in Saga Scholarship," in Fitzhugh and Ward, eds., *Vikings*, 232–237; Edmund Carpenter, *Norse Penny* (New York: The Rock Foundation, 2003).

[13] Birgitta Wallace, "Norse Expansion into North America," revised manuscript, version of 1996 Internet article published as www.heureka.fi/en/x/nx/wal, February 2001, 11.

[14] Ibid., 39.

[15] Magnusson and Pálsson, *The Vinland Sagas*, 97–98.

[16] Wallace, "The Norse in the North Atlantic," 39.

[17] Bertrand A. Power, "Climatological Analysis of Old Norse Sailing Directions for North Atlantic Routes," *The Journal of Navigation* 55 (2002): 109–116.

[18] Wallace, "Norse Expansion into North America," 14–16.

CHAPTER 8

[1] Alec Douglas, "The Nazi Weather Station in Labrador," *Canadian Geographical Journal* 101:6 (December/January 1981): 42–47; Franz Selinger, "German Automatic Weather Stations in the Arctic, 1942–1945," *Polar Geography and Geology* 10:2 (1986): 89–104; Selinger, *Von "Nanok" bis "Eismitte": Meteorologische Unternehmungen in der Arktis 1940–1945*, Schriften des Deutschen Schiffahrtsmuseum, Band 53 (Hamburg: Deutsches Schiffahrtmuseum, 2001), 181–183.

[2] John T. Rowland, *North To Baffin Land* (New York: Seven Seas Press, 1973), 49.

CHAPTER 9

[1] James McDermott, "'A right Heroicall heart': Sir Martin Frobisher," in Thomas H.B. Symonds, ed., *Meta Incognita: A Discourse of Discovery: Martin Frobisher's Arctic Expeditions*, 1576–1578 (Ottawa: Canadian Museum of Civilization, 1999), xxxvi.

[2] Ann Savours, "A Narrative of Frobisher's Arctic Voyages," in Symonds, *Meta Incognita*, 21.

[3] Vilhjalmur Stefansson and Eloise McCaskill, eds., *The Three Voyages of Martin Frobisher*, vol. 1 (London: Argonaut Press, 1938), 51.

[4] James McDermott, *Martin Frobisher. Elizabethan Privateer* (New Haven: Yale University Press, 2001), 154.

[5] Stefansson and McCaskill, *Three Voyages of Martin Frobisher* 1: cxi, 2: 84. I am grateful to Professor Donald Hogarth for this information.

[6] Donald D. Hogarth, et al., "Martin Frobisher's Mines and Ores," in Stephen Alsford, ed., *The Meta Incognita Project. Contributions to Field Studies*, Mercury Series Directorate paper No. 6 (Ottawa: Canadian Museum of Civilization, 1993), 150.

[7] William W. Fitzhugh, "Exploration After Frobisher," in Fitzhugh and Olin, eds., *Archaeology of the Frobisher Voyages* (Washington, D.C.: Smithsonian Institution Press, 1993), 23.

[8] Stefansson and McCaskill, *Three Voyages of Martin Frobisher* 1:111.

[9] James McDermott, ed., *The Third Voyage of Martin Frobisher to Baffin*

Island, 1578 (London: Hakluyt Society, 2001), 37.

[10] A.H. Markham, *The Voyages and Works of John Davis the Navigator* (London: Hakluyt Society, 1880), xxxvi.

[11] Markham, *Voyages and Works of John Davis*, 47.

[12] Stefansson and McCaskill, Three Voyages of *Martin Frobisher*, 1:92.

[13] Ibid., 1:111–112.

[14] McDermott, *The Third Voyage of Martin Frobisher to Baffin Island*, 228.

[15] Clements R. Markham, ed., *The Voyages of William Baffin, 1612–1622* (London: Hakluyt Society, 1881), 116–117.

[16] Donald D. Hogarth, "Resolution Island, Then and Now," *Terrae Incognitae* 30 (1998): 26–40.

[17] Deborah and George Sabo, "A possible Thule carving of a Viking from Baffin Island, N.W.T.," *Canadian Journal of Archaeology* 2 (1978): 33–42; Guy Mary-Roussèliere, "Exploration and Evangelization of the Great Canadian North: Vikings, Coureurs des Bois, and Missionaries," *Arctic* 37:4 (December 1984): 590–593; T.J. Oleson, "Nicholas of Lynne," *Dictionary of Canadian Biography* 1 (Toronto: University of Toronto Press, 1966), 678–679; Kirsten A. Seaver, "'A Very Common and Usuall Trade': The Relationship Between Cartographic Perceptions and 'Fishing' in the Davis Strait circa 1500–1550," in Karen Severud Cook, ed., *Images and Icons of the New World. Essays on American Cartography* (London: The British Library, 1996), 5.

[18] Kirsten A. Seaver, *The Frozen Echo. Greenland and the Exploration of North America, ca. A.D. 1000–1500* (Stanford, California: Stanford University Press, 1996), 123–124, 136.

[19] Mary-Rousseliére, "Exploration and Evangelization of the Great Canadian North," 591–593; Patricia D. Sutherland, "The Norse and Native Americans," in Fitzhugh and Ward, eds., *Vikings*, 245.

[20] Kirsten A. Seaver, personal communication, October 16, 2000.

[21] Kirsten A. Seaver, personal communication, June 21, 2001.

[22] Robert McGhee, *The Arctic Voyages of Martin Frobisher. An Elizabethan Adventure* (Ottawa: Canadian Museum of Civilization, 2001).

[23] McDermott, *Martin Frobisher*, 176, 220, 226.

[24] Clive Holland, *Arctic Exploration and Development c. 500 B.C. to 1915* (New York: Garland, 1994), 11.

[25] David Beers Quinn, "The Northwest Passage in Theory and Practice," in John Logan Allen, ed., *North American Exploration*, vol. 1, *A New World Disclosed* (Lincoln: University of Nebraska Press, 1997), 295–299.

[26] David B. Quinn, *North America from Earliest Discovery to First Settlements: The Norse Voyages to 1612* (New York: Harper & Row, 1977), 369.

[27] Markham, *Voyages and Works of John Davis*, 46–47.

[28] Thomas Dunrabin, "Waymouth or Weymouth . . . , George," in Brown, *Dictionary of Canadian Biography*, vol. 1, *1000 to 1700* (Toronto: University of Toronto Press, 1966), 667–668.

[29] L.H. Neatby, "Hudson, Henry," *Dictionary of Canadian Biography* 1: 378.

ACKNOWLEDGMENTS

*M*ANY PEOPLE HAVE HELPED to make this book possible, and although I cannot thank all of them, I would like them to know how grateful I am for their kindness and generosity. Nevertheless, a number of persons deserve special mention: Alan Acker, Ron Ackman, Po Adams, Christian Albert, Alex Altschuller, Jim and Susie Andersen, Jimmy and Barb Andersen, Harry Anderson, Ian and Iona Argyll, Sasha Arikaynen, Terence Armstrong, Elizabeth Bailey, Bill Baker, Dudley Baker, Selma Barkham, Christopher and Jackie Barlow, Bill Barr, Charlie Bascom, Jim Beal, Phillipe Beaudoin, Pierre Berton, Harlan Billings, Nigel Blackwell, Johnny Bockstoce, Romayne Bockstoce, Norm Bolotin, Ted Brainerd, Dylan Braund, Steve Braund, Dick Breeden, Lawson Brigham, Warren Brown, Lloyd Bugden, Tiger Burch, Rick Burnes, Robert Burns, Julie Cahill, Randy Cahill, Hamilton Carter, Murdena Charlton, John Church, Ivar and Kay Colquhoun of Luss, Gary Comer, Dennis Conner, Bruce Courson, Joel Cox, Tom Crowley, Sam Crum, Bob Cunningham, Chris Cunningham, Vagn Dahl, Charlie and Posy Dana, Eli Dana, Susan Danforth, Wilson Darwin, Sam Davenport, Herb Davis, Rich von Doenhoff, Dan Donnell, Joseph C. Donnelly, Judy Downey, Hugh Downs, Maldwin and Gilly Drummond, Lori Dyson, Mike Earle, Ruth Edmonds, Kelly Jean Fales, Stuart Farnham, Norman Fiering, Tom and Ingrid Flynn, Trish Fox, Willy Fox, Henry and Judy Fuller, Michael Fuller, Susannah Fuller, Bob Gagosian, Tim Galvin, Craig George, Andy German, Coby Van Der Giessen, Henk Van Der Giessen, Sukie Goodwin, Tom Goodwin, Bill Graves, Elmer Groth, Nick Gumprecht, Bonnie Hahn, Kim Hart, John Hattendorf, Ellen Henderson, Hod Hildreth, Herb Hilgenberg, George Hobson, Don Hogarth, Mark Hollingsworth, Jacquie Hollister, Linda Hopkins, Brooke Howard, Colleen Hurter, Fr. Leonce d'Hurtevent, Dick Jackson, Joe Jackson, Holger Jannasch, David Jenkins, Peter Jenkins,

Carl Jewell, Gary Jobson, Sven Johansson, Oli and Helga Johnsson, Allan Jouning, Susan Kaplan, Rod Kellett, Tug Kellough, Edward M. Kennedy, Willy Ker, John F. Kerry, Robert Glenn Ketchum, Brandon Kimble, Jonathan King, Kristos Kritikos, Christine Laing, Elisha Lee, Molly Lee, Fr. Robert Lemeur, Frank Libby, Steve Lirakis, Chip and Liz Loomis, Bert MacGregor, Brodie MacGregor, Malcolm and Anne MacGregor, Fr. Guy Mary-Rouselliere, Mary Marsh, Lionel Montpetit, Edmund and Doreen Moores, Henry and Iona Mount Charles, Jane Neumann, Scott Oakley, Richard Olsenius, Tony Oppersdorf, Gail Osherenko, Doug Padgett and staff, Tom Padden, Susan Painter, Waring Partridge, Rich Perkins, Carl Emil Petersen, Dick Pittenger, Bob Pittman, Julie Plummer, Ethel Poole, Ed Powers, Tom Pullen, David Beers Quinn, David Ray, Steve Ray, Bob Rice, Henry Roberts, Jurgen Rohwer, Jill Roosevelt, Doug Rose, John Rousmaniere, Andy Rowe, Graham and Diana Rowley, Diana Russell, Trudy Sainsbury, Chesley Sanger, Peter Schledermann, Blayney Scott, Kirsten Seaver, Peter Semotiuk, William E. Simon, Hendrik Skolemose, Dave Smith, E. Newbold Smith, Frederick W. Smith, Nicholas O. Smith, George Solish, the staff of the Southworth Library, Andy Spongberg, Carol Stephenson, Peter Stone, Carl Swanson, Jem and Maur Tetley, Jim Thiel, Steve Thomas, Neil Thompson, Ray Tomsett, Pat Toomey, John Towers, David Tunick, Ross Tuxhorn, Julian Underwood, Terry Vose, Birgitta Wallace, Brian Walsh, Linc and Tahoe Washburn, Steve Waterman, Thomas J. Watson, Jr., Henry Webb, Sarah Webb, Philip Wilson, Jr., Ridge White, Nick Whitman, Toby Winckelhofer, Bertie Winters, Martin Wolman and Geri Zelenick.

INDEX

Page numbers in *italics* refer to photographs and illustrations.

Maps, Chronology, Appendices, Notes, and Acknowledgments are not included in the Index.